CASTING THE NET

CASTING THE NET

From ARPANET to Internet and Beyond

Peter H. Salus

▲▼ Addison-Wesley Publishing Company

Reading, Massachusetts • Menlo Park, California • New York
Don Mills, Ontario • Wokingham, England • Amsterdam • Bonn
Sydney • Singapore • Tokyo • Madrid • San Juan • Milan • Paris

Senior Acquisitions Editor: Thomas E. Stone
Assistant Editor: Kathleen Billus
Production Coordinator: Marybeth Mooney
Cover Designer: Eileen Hoff
Manufacturing Coordinator: Evelyn Beaton
Composition: compuType (Mike Wile)

Inside cover art: Courtesy of John S. Quarterman © 1995 MIDS, Austin, Texas
<mids@tic.com>; reprinted with permission.

Many of the designations used by manufacturers and sellers to distinguish
their products are claimed as trademarks. Where those designations appear
in this book, and Addison-Wesley was aware of a trademark claim, the
designations have been printed in initial caps or all caps.

For more information about Addison-Wesley titles, please visit our gopher
site via the Internet: gopher aw.com to connect to our on-line book information listing.

Library of Congress Cataloging-in-Publication Data

Salus, Peter H.
    Casting the net : from ARPANET to Internet and Beyond / by Peter
H. Salus.
       p.   cm.
    Includes index.
    ISBN 0-201-87674-4 (alk. paper)
    1. Wide area networks (Compter networks)--Standards.
    2. Internetworking.   I. Title.
TK5105.87.S25   1995
004.6'7--dc20   94-46974
                                                            CIP

Series Foreword

Marshall Kirk McKusick
John S. Quarterman

Addison-Wesley is proud to publish the **UNIX and Open Systems Series.** The primary audience for the Series will be system designers, implementors, administrators, and their managers. The core of the series will consist of books detailing operating systems, standards, networking, and programming languages. The titles will interest specialists in these fields, as well as appeal more broadly to computer scientists and engineers who must deal with open-systems environments in their work. The Series comprises professional reference books and instructional texts.

Open systems allow users to move their applications between systems easily; thus, purchasing decisions can be made on the basis of cost-performance ratio and vendor support, rather than on which systems will run a user's application suite. Decreasing computer hardware prices have facilitated the widespread adoption of capable multiprocess, multiuser operating systems, UNIX being a prime example. Newer operating systems, such as Mach and Chorus, support additional services, such as lightweight processes. The Series illuminates the design and implementation of all such open systems. It teaches readers how to write applications programs to run on these systems, and gives advice on administration and use.

The Series treats as a unified whole the previously distinct fields of networking and operating systems. Networks permit open systems to share hardware and software resources, and allow people to communicate efficiently. The exponential growth of networks such as the Internet and the adoption of protocols such as TCP/IP in industry, government, and academia have made network and system administration critically important to many organizations.

This Series will examine many aspects of network protocols, emphasizing the interaction with operating systems. It will focus on the evolution in computer environments and will assist professionals in the development and use of practical networking technologies.

Standards for programming interfaces, protocols, and languages are a key concern as networks of open systems expand within organizations and across the globe. Standards can be useful for system engineering, application programming, marketing, and procurement; but standards that are released too late, cover too little, or are too narrowly defined can be counterproductive. This series will encourage its readers to participate in the standards process by presenting material that details the use of specific standards to write application programs, and to build modern multiprocess, multiuser computing environments.

Newer operating systems are implemented in object-oriented languages, and network protocols use specialized languages to specify data formats and to compile protocol descriptions. As user interfaces become increasingly sophisticated, the level at which they are programmed continues to evolve upward, from system calls to remote procedure call compilers and generic description environments for graphical user interfaces. The effects of new languages on systems, programs, and users are explored in this series.

Foreword

Vinton G. Cerf

On a foggy plain in Salisbury, England, huge stone blocks loom in the mist. Brooding and silent, they await the rising sun with infinite and ancient patience. Who built this mysterious, awe-inspiring place? Why did they build it and how did they use it? Stonehenge: Ancient Temple or Astronomical Observatory?

Today, we believe that Stonehenge was an astronomical observatory and calculator. Built in three phases over the course of 300 years, Stonehenge is a monument to the sophistication and determination of an ancient society. The complexity of its construction seems less daunting, although no less awesome, when examined in detail and the steps better understood. Enormous amounts of information needed to be accumulated, recorded and analyzed to carry out its threefold construction. The logistics, particularly with regard to the sarsen stones weighing up to 50 tons each, are astonishing, and the more so for the time in which they were executed (around 1600 B.C.).

Like Stonehenge, the Internet taken as a whole may seem a daunting and complex thing. It is hard to imagine how something as large and complex could be designed, built and made to work at all. But, also like Stonehenge, the Internet was not built all at once, but in phases. Its size and complexity evolved over time. *Casting the Net* offers an important and valuable historical look at the evolution of packet switching and its application in the ARPANET, its successor, the Internet, and the combination of these networks with computer-mediated applications over a period of about 25 years.

As should be apparent, the ARPA-sponsored pioneering packet networking research program spawned more than an important technological development. The experimental computer science research environment it fostered grew to become a global testbed for new computer application ideas and a vital infrastructure for the research and education communities. As these communities explored computer-enabled, distributed applications, other segments of the research and education world took interest. Moreover, businesses involved in the government-sponsored research efforts found new application ideas with business potential in the *pot pourri* of exploratory applications visible on the "Net." As access to the Internet expanded beyond the research, academic, and educational markets, ideas applicable to consumer and business markets began to emerge as well.

The Internet, together with the software and protocols that determine the operation of applications it supports, is a primitive example of global information infrastructure. "Information infrastructure" is a term coined by Dr. Robert E. Kahn in the course of founding the Corporation for National Research Initiatives (CNRI) in 1986. For nearly a decade, CNRI has conducted a research and development program centered on exploring the technologies needed to enable electronic commerce to manage intellectual property in an on-line environment to harness distributed, heterogeneous processing and information resources, and to understand the social and economic impacts of global, computer-mediated communication.

Early Days

The ARPANET project drew heavily on notions of time-sharing that emerged in other ARPA-sponsored research in the early 1960s. Networking of time-shared systems quickly led to aspirations for remote access, resource sharing, and visions of distributed computing. In actuality, some of these applications have only begun to emerge in a widespread sense. One of the surprises from the early ARPANET was electronic mail. This concept had its roots in the ability of users on a common machine to share files and thus leave messages for one another. The email extension to this idea allowed people to exchange files while located on different machines. This development was important since it permitted the exchange of information without requiring that everyone in the network have login access to everyone else's machine before email would work.

This same public access led to notions for general file sharing, now called anonymous file transfer, by means of a file transfer protocol (FTP) and spawned tools for finding files in the Internet such as archie, Veronica, and Jughead. Public access services are often the mechanism by which possible commercial products are tested in the Internet. This was how the Wide Area Information Service (WAIS) got started, as well as archie, Gopher, and World Wide Web (WWW). Public experiments and publicly downloadable software represent one kind of powerful technology transfer capability that is enabled by global Internet connectivity.

The Legal, Social, and Economic Side Effects of the Internet

As the Internet continues its vigorous expansion and penetration into the everyday fabric of business and social affairs, a variety of legal, social, and economic issues have either already risen or are predicted to do so. As the community of users grew from a fairly homogeneous cohort linked by common research interests to a highly heterogeneous, globally distributed population, concerns about security and privacy emerged.

The Internet is a system for supporting inter-computer communication. Security of the system is dependent on the security of the various switches (routers) comprising the networks of the Internet and also on the security of the host computers using the Internet as the medium for communication. As in most other public service situations, public Internet service is subject to interference by vandals (the usual terms are "hackers" and "crackers"). The Internet community has learned that it must take pains to protect itself against such attacks by careful configuration of the parts of the system under its control.

Such considerations take on increased significance as electronic commerce and transfer of valuables occurs routinely in the Internet. Can a user counterfeit "cybercash"? Is it illegal? Who is liable if someone obtains credit card information by observing a financial transaction on the Internet and then misuses this information?

The same concerns for security also produce concerns for privacy, since breaches of security can lead directly to loss of privacy (and, of course, loss or damage to data, software and information files). What is still in a considerable state of flux is the legal framework in which abuses of the Internet and its services are actionable in civil or even criminal senses. In a widely-publicized event in November 1988, a mobile piece of software called a "worm" was released into the Internet where it proliferated rapidly and interfered with the operation of an estimated 3000–6000 Unix-based systems in the universe of about 60,000 systems then on the Internet. The perpetrator was brought to trial on criminal charges and, successfully prosecuted, fined, and sentenced to a significant number of hours of public service.

Just what is considered tortuous behavior in the Internet is still an open question, and the answers may well differ from one jurisdiction to another. Indeed, the connectivity of the Internet creates genuine dilemmas in law enforcement, since electronic presence can be global in scope. Moreover, thanks to techniques such as multicasting, one can be electronically in many places at once. Multi-destination electronic mail has a similar characteristic. One is confronted by philosophical questions: "Where did the offense occur?" Somewhere in Cyberspace?

Whatever one may think of the legal systems here and elsewhere, it is fair to observe that they all have had varying degrees of success in adapting and accommodating to changed circumstances and new technologies. Copyright law, for example, has accommodated the introduction of recorded sound, movies, television, radio, and now electronic publication without necessarily contemplating fundamental changes. Many of the open questions will be resolved through an accumulation of case law, but also very possibly new legislation will be required or at least adopted in an attempt to cope with some of the unusual characteristics of on-line environments.

For example, what is considered public in the Internet? Is a distribution list public? This is not an idle question. Can libel or slander be perpetrated in a private email exchange? How many people must be exposed to something for a matter to be considered public? Are there any first amendment rights associated with utterances in cyberspace? In whom do these rights reside?

What about information on the Internet that might be considered offensive to some members of the Internet community? Who determines what is offensive? Should censorship be the responsibility of the Internet service providers? In a dramatic ruling recently, a couple who placed sexually explicit information on a bulletin board system in California were successfully prosecuted in another state on the grounds that the material was outside the acceptable norms *in a community somewhere else in the US!*

Should advertising be permitted on the Internet? In its early history, advertising and job announcements were banned on the grounds that the U.S. Government funded system should not be used for commercial purposes. As the system became more self-supporting and its use spread into the private sector, limitations that had made sense under earlier circumstances no longer applied.

In fact, the invention of the World Wide Web launched a whole new industry for creating interesting imagery, multi-font text, and sound in graphical pages found in Web servers on the Internet. Thousands of organizations have put up content on the WWW in the form of so-called home pages, which represent the table of contents of a series of hyperlinked pages. The startling aspect of the Web is the fact that any page can point to any other page *anywhere in the Internet.* These pointers, called Uniform Resource Locators (URLs), make it possible to create a kaleidoscope of reusable content on the Internet. Simply by pointing to a variety of URLs, one can create a virtual database that appears to be uniform but which may be made up, in reality, of many pre-existing pages on many Web-servers.

Companies that are not yet ready to put up their own servers are turning to entrepreneurs to create their presence on the Internet. Over time, the content of these hired servers will change, and eventually, most organizations (and perhaps even individuals) will have their own home pages on the Internet.

Until the advent of information services such as archie, Gopher, Wide Area Information Service and World Wide Web, finding things in the Internet was very difficult and it was also considered inappropriate to send unsolicited advertising messages to arbitrary users by way of email. The WWW and other browsing services allow advertising in a more discreet fashion. It is not necessary to send advertisements into everyone's email system. This and variations which improve indexing and cataloging of content will very likely guide the development of advertising on the Internet.

Many unknowns remain about the way in which the Internet will evolve. One can only speculate about the possibility of regulation to prevent abusive behavior, as has been attempted in the case of the telephone system. In the long run, I am confident that we will understand the system well enough to actively invite all interested parties to work together to establish a kind of Law of the Internet akin, in spirit, to the Law of the Sea.

It seems fair to observe that by the end of the decade, we will very likely have a highly robust and widespread infrastructure in place for purpose of telecommuting, information gathering and exchange, electronic commerce, remote teaching and learning, and general education. We may well find ourselves using the system for voice and video applications as well as group activities ranging from multiparty games to collaborative scientific work. Where this will all end up is anyone's guess. Perhaps Peter Salus will have to write another book to tell us where we went and how we got there!

Vinton G. Cerf
Camelot
February 1995

Preface

At a time when the Internet has occupied the covers of both *Business Week* and *Time* and every daily newspaper speculates on numbers of users and billions of dollars in "opportunities," when the President and Vice President of the United States have their own electronic mail addresses, and when the Supreme Court makes its *dicta* available via anonymous ftp, it is appropriate to look at the origins and development of this wondrous entity.

At the end of 1969, the ARPANET, the first packet-switching computer network, consisted of four sites. At the end of 1994, there were nearly four *million* hosts. While there is much discussion as to just how many users each of these hosts represents, the range is from a (conservative) average of three to a (flamboyantly unrealistic) ten: That is, from 12 to 40 million users worldwide.

Many tens of thousands of networks make up the Internet, which is a network of networks. Many of these networks are not full participants in the Internet, meaning that there are many applications which they cannot employ. In *Neuromancer*, a 1984 science fiction novel, William Gibson used the term "the matrix" for his cyberspace. John S. Quarterman employed the term in his 1990 compendium, and it has since come into common usage. I use the Matrix here to refer to all computers capable of sending and receiving electronic mail. Though not even a part of the original ARPANET, mail is now the prime application for the Matrix user.

Max Beerbohm once criticized Quiller-Couch for writing "a veritable porcupine of quotations." I recognize that the same indictment could be handed down against me. And that some of my "quotations" are not so much quills as battering-rams. However, some of them are feathers (or perhaps down comforters). There is a general feeling that the inventors of technological wonders are deadly dull, that they have no interests outside their work, and that writings about technology are unreadable. And I admit that much of this is (selectively) true. So I have larded this history with lighter works: Len Kleinrock's and Vint Cerf's verse, as well as parodies by a number of others. And the final appendix contains Kleinrock's most recent verse and Cerf's future history in its entirety.

This book could not have been written without the active cooperation of many of the original participants. At the head of the list stand Vint Cerf, Bob Kahn, Alex McKenzie, Mike Padlipsky, Jon Postel, John Quarterman, and Dave Walden. They have tolerated my questions and supplied me with documents with humor and grace. I am beholden to Marlyn Johnson of SRI and to a number of staff members of Bolt Beranek and Newman for locating and giving me access to documents I would never have otherwise read: Ivanna Abruzzese, Jennie Connolly, Lori McCarthy, Bob Menk, Aravinda Pillalamarri, and Terry Tollman.

The assistance of the following is gratefully acknowledged: Rick Adams, Jaap Akkerhuis, Eric Allman, Piet Beertema, Steve Bellovin, Bob Bishop, Roland Bryan, Peter Capek, David Clark, Lyman Chapin, Glyn Collinson, Peter Collinson, Sunil Das, Dan Dern, Harry Forsdick, Donnalyn Frey, Simson Garfinkel, Michel Gien, John Gilmore, Teus Hagen, Mark Horton, Peter Houlder, Peter Kirstein, Len Kleinrock, Kirk McKusick, Bob Metcalfe, Mike Muuss, Mike O'Dell, Craig Partridge, Brian Redman, Brian Reid, Jim Reid, Larry Roberts, Keld Simonsen, Gene Spafford, Henry Spencer, Bob Taylor, Brad Templeton, Ray Tomlinson, Rebecca Wetzel, and Hubert Zimmermann.

Len Tower and Stuart McRobert have saved me from more gaucheries than I care to recall, as have the (anonymous) readers of the manuscript. Tom Stone and Kathleen Billus at Addison-Wesley have once again shepherded me successfully through the reefs from conception to production.

Much of the material in the Time-Lines is derived from that of John Quarterman and Smoot Carl-Mitchell, to whom I am grateful.

As I have neither a dog nor a cat, I can only (as always) thank Dr. Mary W. Salus and almost-Dr. Emily W. Salus for their niggling and carping, which has improved all my work over the past 25 years.

P.H.S.
Boston
January 1995

Contents

Part 1

Chapter 1

Clearing the Ground

This chapter concerns the notion of connecting computers to one another, the establishment of the IPTO, and the invention of packet switching.

Trying to trace the origins of things frequently ends up in infinite regression. Unique inventions are relatively rare. Anyone attempting history, however, has to decide just when or where to begin. In the case of the worldwide network of computers that John Quarterman (after William Gibson) called "the Matrix," both the geographic location and the date are clear.

If the complex Matrix of networks we have today began anywhere, it began at Dartmouth College in September 1940. It was the meeting of the American Mathematical Society (September 10–13), and George Stibitz, of Bell Labs, wanted to demonstrate the Complex Calculator (renamed the Bell Labs MODEL 1). He first planned to take the Calculator from New York City to Hanover, New Hampshire, but Bell then decided that moving the Complex Calculator by truck would be a bad idea. So Stibitz set up a Teletype terminal in the hallway outside the lecture room instead, and made it possible for the attendees to use the calculator in New York remotely, via the telegraph connection (about 230 miles; 370km). It was a great success: Among those who tried out the link were John Mauchly and Norbert Wiener.

World War II intervened, but Stibitz had demonstrated that a calculator could be used from afar. The war brought about the transformation from the calculator to the computer. And, if a computer is a good thing, linking two workers on a computer is better; linking two computers is better still; and connecting many people on many computers is best of all.

Vannevar Bush

Nearly fifty years ago this connection was obvious to Vannevar Bush (1890–1974). Bush had been vice president and dean of engineering at MIT and then president of the Carnegie Institution. He was called thence to become head of Roosevelt's Office of Scientific Research and Development, where he became a leading figure in the development of the atomic bomb. He also did work in power transmission and designed the differential analyzer. He was a visionary of great insight.

In January, 1945 as World War II wound down, Bush published a brief article, "As We May Think," in *The Atlantic Monthly*, in which he "forecast" (among other things) the copier (the "Xerox" machine), the instant ("Polaroid") camera, computer languages like FORTRAN, and "Memex," a writing, reading, filing, communication system that was contained in a desk and comprised of a screen and a keyboard.

Memex was, effectively, the prototype for the personal computer. It was the first attempt at a design that involved a machine in the management of information. Bush also thought that the machine could "help" people think about information. It was a terrific, foresighted article, though it did not predict the kind of network we have nor a machine like the workstation. What it envisaged was a computer more like the Apple Lisa of a decade or so ago but one which used a combination of punch cards and microfilm. But how could Bush have imagined the microchip or the transistor? He was writing at a time when the first real electro-mechanical computers were just being produced, though transistors were but three years away.

Doug Engelbart, the inventor of the "mouse," wrote Bush in 1962 to tell him of how he had come across "As We May Think" in the "Red Cross library on the edge of the jungle on Leyte ... in the Fall of 1945.... I re-discovered your article about three years ago, and was rather startled to realize how much I had aligned my sights along the vector you had described." [letter of May 24, 1962]

Twenty years later, Bush returned to the topic. In 1967 he wrote "Is this all a dream? It certainly was, two decades ago. It is still a dream, but one that is now attainable." In the same essay, Bush wrote of the use of "magnetic tape" for storage in "our future memex" as well as the possibility of "a whole private library [being] reduced to the volume of a matchbox; [and] a library of a million volumes ... compressed into one end of a desk." [*Science is not enough*, New York, 1967] As Engelbart's letter shows, Bush's article had demonstrable influence where hypertext, artificial intelligence and multimedia research are concerned.

The DoD Steps In

Then came the Cold War.

After the Korean War (1950–53) and the launching of the first orbiting satellite, the Sputnik, by the USSR (October 4, 1957), the US Department of Defense began to get increasingly nervous about the problems of communication in the event of an enemy [i.e., Soviet] attack. What would they do if their communications lines between (say) Washington and San Francisco were cut? This was not as weird as it may seem in retrospect.

Sputnik had been followed by Sputnik 2, carrying a live dog (November 3, 1957). Sputnik had weighed over 80kg. And Sputnik 2 had weighed 500kg. But Explorer 1, the first US satellite, which discovered the Van Allen radiation belt (January 31, 1958) weighed in at only 8kg. Then, on September 12, 1958, Luna 2, a Soviet probe, landed on the moon and on April 12, 1961, Yuri Gagarin became the first man to orbit the Earth aboard Vostok 1. The fact that Alan Shepard achieved a suborbital flight three weeks later was little consolation.

But real sabotage occurred. Attack was not mere fantasy. *The New York Times* carried the story on page one on May 29, 1961: "Three microwave relay stations in Utah shattered by mysterious explosions—widespread communications disruption results; national defense circuit shifts automatically to alternate routes; FBI opens probe." On June 19 four arrests of members of the "American Republican Army" were made in Ensenada, Mexico. Two of the felons were given eight-year jail terms (*The New York Times*, November 3).

The DOD sincerely believed that there might be a "heavily manned bomber attack against this country in the next few years."

The Department wanted a survivable national network. Studies were commissioned and, in 1962, Paul Baran and his colleagues at The RAND Corporation produced 13 reports and (for security reasons) published only 11 of them ("On Distributed Communications" 1964), which together constituted the answer: "Distributed Adaptive Message Block Switching." Thanks to Donald Davies we now call that solution "Packet Switching." Baran deserves a great deal of credit for conceptualizing this, but it must be pointed out that none of the papers even considers how a packet network might be set up. Though Baran provided some of the engineering details of the "Distributed Adaptive Message Block Network," the RAND Corporation just wasn't interested in implementation. In this "Block Network," a "multiplexing station" connects up to 1024 heterogeneous terminals. Multiplexing is the use of a single channel for more than one transmission. This is done by "time-sharing" or "frequency-division." Automatic user-to-user cryptography was integrally employed in the switching to ensure efficient implementation of security. Satellite links and microwave relays are suggested as high-rate circuits. Most importantly, Baran introduced the concept of "message block." Vint Cerf told me: "As I recall, this was a digital voice command and control network design."

Just what packet switching means will be examined in the next chapter. In the meantime, let us look at the third individual whose efforts were necessary to the initial setup of the Net: J.C.R. Licklider (1915–1990).

J.C.R. Licklider

"Lick," as everyone who met him was admonished to call him, started his career as a psychologist (Ph.D., University of Rochester, 1942). He was a research associate at Swarthmore and then a researcher in the psycho-acoustic laboratory at Harvard, where he was a lecturer till 1951. He then moved down Massachusetts Avenue to initiate a research program in speech and hearing at MIT. In 1957, Lick switched his interests from analog devices to digital ones and joined Bolt Beranek and Newman

(BBN), where his group purchased the first PDP-1 from Digital Equipment Corporation (DEC) in November 1960. But Lick had already seen publication of his "Man-Computer Symbiosis" in *IRE Transactions on Human Factors in Electronics* [March 1960: 4-11]. In 1961, Command and Control Research (CCR) was assigned to ARPA. In 1962, Lick took a two-year leave from BBN to go to the Advanced Research Projects Agency and run CCR, to be renamed the Information Processing Techniques Office (IPTO) in 1964, as well as a behavioral science funding office.

Lick soon saw that networking was a necessity. On April 25, 1963 he sent a memo to "Members and Affiliates of the Intergalactic Computer Network," in which he said that he wanted to "explore the possibilities for mutual advantage [because to] make progress, each of the active research[ers] needs a software base and a hardware facility more complex than he, himself, can create in reasonable time."

Lick had a strong feeling that the computer was a communications device, not an arithmetic aid. Robert Taylor, who was later director of IPTO, has remarked that "Lick made it easy to think about interconnecting the communities, the interconnection of interactive, on-line communities of people." Most likely this was the direct result of Lick's training in psychology. But, effectively, that was it: once the computer was seen as a communications device, only implementation was left. Dave Clark, Senior Research Scientist at MIT, has said "It is not proper to think of networks as connecting computers. Rather they connect people using computers to mediate. The great success of the Internet is not technical, but in human impact."

Lick returned to MIT only to leave again for ARPA in 1974 to direct the IPTO. In the meantime, Lick was named the director of Project MAC in 1967 and remained an MIT faculty member until his retirement in 1986.

The early directors of IPTO were Licklider (1962–64), Ivan Sutherland (1964–66), Robert Taylor (1966–69), Lawrence Roberts (1969–73), and Lick (again) from 1974–76, when Col. David C. Russell became director (1976–79). It was Lick's successors at IPTO, Larry Roberts and Robert Taylor, who fulfilled Lick's vision in the period that Lick was back in Cambridge, Massachusetts, and Robert Kahn, director from 1979 to 1985, who brought the Internet into being.

Chapter 2

Networks

The concepts of different sorts of networks are explained.

Thirty-five years ago, several different models could be considered when trying to evaluate networks: circuit switching, packet switching, and message switching.

Perhaps the most familiar is the point-to-point circuit, as exemplified by the telephone system. Telephone technology involves the setting up a dedicated electrical circuit from the "dialer" to the destination number for the life of a connection—that connection is broken when one of the instruments hangs up on the other. In circuit switching, if a cable or a node is lost, the connection is broken and must be set up anew. Circuit switches make the end-to-end connection by linking many point-to-point segments through the switches.

In packet switching, the data is divided into small pieces, which are called packets, and these are switched through a variety of different possible routes to reach their destinations. Such packets are sometimes called datagrams, in analogy to telegrams, as each is short and contains a destination address. If one link (wire) or node (switching computer) blew up, data would simply be routed around it. Packet switching thus implies the "interleaving" of packets on lines, multiplexing that is linked to the switching method. This is much the same in the case of message switching (in which whole messages are sent, routed, stored, and received). Time division switching and multiplexing have been integrated, but not in a form that is compatible for

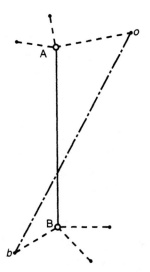

FIGURE 2.1 Circuit Switching between A and B

multi-user computing, though one can have many users hanging from one multiplexor and even a network of multiplexors.

The *Communications Standard Dictionary* defines packet switching as:

> The process of routing and transferring data in the form of packets in a communication system so that a channel is occupied during the transmission of a packet only; upon completion, the channel is made available for the transmission of other packets. A packet may consist of several messages, or an abnormally long message may require several packets. Messages are user units and packets are communication-system units; hence, they can overlap each other or be made up of each other. The process consists of routing, transmitting, and receiving data in the form of addressed packets. Packet mode operation potentially increases the channel traffic capacity. In certain communication networks, the data may be formatted into one or more packets by data terminal equipment (DTE) or by other equipment within the network. The packets are formed for transmission, multiplexing, or other purposes.

Several concepts are important here. First of all, unlike a telephone connection, a packet switching network does not have unique routes between sender and receiver. In a simple packet network of three sites, there are connections between A-B, B-C, and C-A. If A wants to send to B but the A-B line has been disrupted, the connection can be established via A-C and C-B. The Department of Defense wanted the network to be robust. They wanted to be certain that if there were an attack (or, more likely these days, if a backhoe cuts a cable) the network wouldn't go down. While packets are commonly called datagrams, by analogy with telegrams, the packet system is really more like the postal service.

Let us say that you are in Corner Brook, Newfoundland, and want to communicate with a friend in Escondido, California. You write a letter, place it in an envelope, address it, affix postage, and drop it in the letter box. You are quite aware of the fact that there is no direct flight from Corner Brook to Escondido. But it doesn't matter. You have handed your letter to an agent, presumably an intelligent agent. Your letter goes from Corner Brook to St. John's. From St. John's to Montreal (or Boston or New York). From one of those cities to a major West Coast depot: most likely Los Angeles. And from Los Angeles an intelligent agent sends it to Escondido where it will be delivered to your friend's address. The routing is flexible: If there is snow in Montreal, your letter may go to Boston. If there is a storm in Chicago, the letter may go from Montreal to Vancouver to LA; or to New York and then San Diego to Escondido. It doesn't matter. And the same is true of the electronic network. The electronic packet containing your bits is addressed. The addressing follows the rules of a specific protocol, called the Internet Protocol, just as we follow post office rules in addressing a letter. The Internet Protocol tells the routers what to do with the rest of the packet.

Diversion 1

A note on the **Diversions:** As I write this, there are over 1750 RFCs that have been published over a period of nearly 26 years. Though many RFCs are dry, some are silly, a number are funny, and several are witty polemics that are worthy descendents of François Marie Arouet (Voltaire).

Network Working Group   J. Postel (ISI)
Request for Comments: 1121   L. Kleinrock (UCLA)
                                                         V. Cerf (CNRI)
                                                        B. Boehm (UCLA)
                                                         September 1989

                           Act One - The Poems

Status of this Memo

This RFC presents a collection of poems that were presented at "Act One," a symposium held partially in celebration of the 20th anniversary of the ARPANET. Distribution of this memo is unlimited.

Introduction

The Computer Science Department of the University of California, Los Angeles (UCLA) organized a Symposium on Very High Speed Information Networks as the first in a projected series of meetings on Advanced Computer Technologies, thus ACT ONE. The time was chosen to also commemorate the 20th anniversary of the installation of the first Interface Message Processor (IMP) on the ARPANET which took place at UCLA.

The Symposium took on a theatrical theme and a few of the speakers could not resist the temptation to commit poetry. This memo is an attempt to capture the result.

The Poems

WELCOME

by

Leonard Kleinrock

We've gathered here for two days to examine and debate
And reflect on data networks and as well to celebrate.
To recognize the leaders and recount the path we took.
We'll begin with how it happened; for it's time to take a look.

Yes, the history is legend and the pioneers are here.
Listen to the story - it's our job to make it clear.
We'll tell you where we are now and where we'll likely go.
So welcome to ACT ONE, folks. Sit back - enjoy the show!!

ODE TO A QUEUE

by

Leonard Kleinrock

In the 20 years of funding
Many fields has DARPA led.
But the finest thing that they did bring
Was the analytic thread.

By that I mean they nurtured
Quantitative research tools.
And they always felt for all their gelt
They got principles and rules.

Indeed a wealth of knowledge
Was uncovered and was new.
And the common thread with which we led
Was the analytic queue!

Now a queue may have one server.
If there's more, they form a team.
Its dearest wish is just to fish
In a quiet Poisson stream.

If you want to model networks
Or a complex data flow
A queue's the key to help you see
All the things you need to know.

So the next time you feel lonely
And wonder what to do,
You'll soon feel fine if you join the line
Of an analytic queue!

THE PAST IS PROLOGUE
by
Leonard Kleinrock

The past is prologue so they say.
So Scene 1 was played today.
It set the stage to point the way
To high speed nets on Friday.

And old slow IMP, a costly link,
Codes to fix the lines that stink,
Ideas born in tanks that think,
Tomorrow's distance sure to shrink.

But first tonight we'll drink and eat.
We'll take some time good friends to greet.
Hear Bible class from Danny's seat.
Those good old days were bittersweet!

THE BIG BANG!
(or the birth of the ARPANET)
by
Leonard Kleinrock

It was back in '67 that the clan agreed to meet.
The gangsters and the planners were a breed damned hard to beat.
The goal we set was honest and the need was clear to all:
Connect those big old mainframes and the minis, lest they fall.

The spec was set quite rigid: it must work without a hitch.
It should stand a single failure with an unattended switch.
Files at hefty throughput 'cross the ARPANET must zip.
Send the interactive traffic on a quarter second trip.

The spec went out to bidders and 'twas BBN that won.
They worked on soft and hardware and they all got paid for fun.
We decided that the first node would be we who are your hosts
And so today you're gathered here while UCLA boasts.

I suspect you might be asking ``What means FIRST node on the net?''
Well frankly, it meant trouble, 'specially since no specs were set.
For you see the interface between the nascent IMP and HOST
Was a confidential secret from us folks on the West coast.

BBN had promised that the IMP was running late.
We welcomed any slippage in the deadly scheduled date.
But one day after Labor Day, it was plopped down at our gate!
Those dirty rotten scoundrels sent the damned thing out air freight!

As I recall that Tuesday, it makes me want to cry.
Everybody's brother came to blame the other guy!
Folks were there from ARPA, GTE and Honeywell.
UCLA and ATT and all were scared as hell.

We cautiously connected and the bits began to flow.
The pieces really functioned - just why I still don't know.
Messages were moving pretty well by Wednesday morn.
All the rest is history - packet switching had been born!

ROSENCRANTZ AND ETHERNET
by
Vint Cerf

All the world's a net! And all the data in it merely packets
come to store-and-forward in the queues a while and then are
heard no more. 'Tis a network waiting to be switched!

To switch or not to switch? That is the question. Whether
'tis wiser in the net to suffer the store and forward of
stochastic networks or to raise up circuits against a sea
of packets and, by dedication, serve them.

To net, to switch. To switch, perchance to slip!
Aye, there's the rub. For in that choice of switch,
what loops may lurk, when we have shuffled through
this Banyan net? Puzzles the will, initiates symposia,
stirs endless debate and gives rise to uncontrolled
flights of poetry beyond recompense!

UNTITLED

by

Barry Boehm

Paul Baran came out of the wood
With a message first misunderstood
    But despite dangers lurking
    The IMP's were soon working
And ARPA did see it was good.

So in place of our early myopia
We now have a net cornucopia
    With IMP's, TIP's, and LAN's
    Wideband VAN's, MAN's, and WAN's
And prospects of World Net Utopia.

But though we must wind up the clock
With thoughts of downstream feature shock
    We all be can mollified
    For there's no one more qualified
To discuss this than Leonard Kleinrock.

Notes

The Symposium was held August 17 & 18, 1989, a Thursday and Friday.
"Welcome" was presented on Thursday morning during the Overture.
"Ode to a Queue" was presented in the Thursday morning session on
""Giant Steps Forward: Technology Payoffs."
"The Past is Prologue" was presented at the end of the Thursday
afternoon sessions.
"The Big Bang!" was presented during the after dinner events on
Thursday night.

"Rosencrantz and Ethernet" was presented at the morning session on
Friday on "Communication Technologies in the next Millenium" (note that

this version may differ slightly from the actual presentation since it was reconstructed from human memory several weeks later).

The untitled poem by Barry Boehm was presented in the Friday afternoon session on "Impact on Government, Commerce and Citizenry." Barry gave his talk on "The Software Challenge to Our Technical Aspirations" then introduced the next speaker with this poem.

Security Considerations

None.

Part 2

1972   In October, the ARPANET gets its first public demonstration at the First International Conference on Computer Communications in Washington, D.C.

Chapter 3

The Foundations

The beginnings of the IPTO, the early meetings, the design of the IMP, the issuing of the RFQ, and the letting of the contract.

By 1966 the IPTO (Information Processing Techniques Office) was decidedly interested in networking. The Office had funded time-sharing experiments as well as interactive computing. Now the managers of the IPTO came up with the notion of researchers using facilities that were not local. Surely, networking would prove more cost-effective than installing multi-million dollar machinery on each site; the benefits of a given system would accrue without duplication of the computers. (Among the possible systems to be shared were Project MAC at MIT and ILLIAC IV at the University of Illinois.)

But the IPTO was funding 17 sites in 1966 with a variety of hardware and software and a range of incompatibilities. Robert Taylor, then director of the IPTO, needed help. By the end of 1966 he had found it in Larry Roberts.

Roberts came to the IPTO with the specific mission of setting up networking. He had been working at Lincoln Laboratory in Massachusetts since 1963. While there, he and Thomas Marill had conducted a networking experiment connecting the Systems Development Corporation's AN/FSQ-32 in Santa Monica with the TX-2 at Lincoln via a 1200 bps dedicated phone link. This permitted any program on one machine to dial the other computer, log in and run a program from a server, somewhat like a subroutine call. (At the 25th anniversary ARPAfest in Boston, Roberts and Taylor engaged in a mock argument,

Taylor claiming that he had forced the grant on an unwilling Roberts, Roberts claiming that he had applied for the grant. Neither came away bloodied by the fray.) The biggest problem was apparently that dial communication via the telephone network was just too slow to be useful. Marill was with CCA in Cambridge, Massachusetts, and wanted to continue the network by linking in Project MAC's IBM 7094. Roberts and Marill presented their results at the AFIPS Fall Joint Computer Conference in 1966. Ivan Sutherland and Bob Taylor wanted Roberts to come to Washington to work on the network technology. Roberts didn't want to go. So Taylor went to Charlie Hertzfeld (then head of ARPA) and said "Look, you fund 51 percent of Lincoln Lab, why don't you call them up and tell them to send Larry down here?" Hertzfeld called. And the director of Lincoln Lab told Roberts, "I think that you really ought to go to ARPA." So Roberts did within "a week or two." [Editor's Note to Roberts 1988: 145; I confirmed the story with both Hertzfeld and Taylor on October 10, 1994. "It was only mild blackmail," Hertzfeld said.] Roberts then suggested building the IPTO network on the basis of the work he and Marill had already done. Roberts had tremendous enthusiasm when he went to Washington. In 1967, he listed many advantages of computer networks, including shared use of hardware, software, and data. More important, Roberts foresaw that networking would foster "a 'community' use of computers."

Ann Arbor, 1967

Roberts and Taylor took advantage of the April 1967 meeting of the IPTO Principal Investigators at the University of Michigan in Ann Arbor to discuss their hopes for a network. Apparently, some of the researchers were concerned about resource-sharing, but contractors who were present set up a "Communications Group" to work on problems. The problems enumerated included the conventions to be used in exchanging messages between computers and the kinds of communication lines.

It was agreed that work should begin on the conventions to be used for exchanging messages between any pair of computers, which were to be connected via dial-up lines. Frank Westervelt, then of the

University of Michigan, was picked to write a position paper for the *ad hoc* group.

The plan discussed at the Michigan meeting was to connect all the computers by phone lines and data sets, so that every computer could establish contact with any other by means of circuit-switching. During the discussion, one PI, Wesley Clark (then of Washington University; Clark had previously worked on Project Whirlwind and on SAGE at Lincoln Lab) had an idea. The problems inherent in designing a heterogeneous network could be alleviated by adding small computers, each connected to a large computer. He described the notion to Roberts in a shared cab between the University of Michigan and the airport. Roberts described it as an interface message processor in the "Message Switching Network Proposal"—a summary of what had gone on in Ann Arbor for the participants—on April 27, 1967; the IMP had been conceived.

Clark is extremely modest about this. "Someone else would have thought of it in a few days or weeks," he remarked to me. But his notion was tremendously insightful and influential. Putting IMPs into the network design made it easier for the designers to specify most of the network: IMPs would communicate with other IMPs; there was no need to worry about the nature of the various host computers. Moreover, as each host was connected only to its local IMP, each site would merely have to worry about communicating with that IMP—sending and receiving. Moreover, changes to the system—and they all knew there would be such changes— could be made to the IMPs, without regard to the hosts.

> The IMP would perform the functions of dialup, error checking, retransmission, routing, and verifications on behalf of the participants' computers ... Thus the IMPs plus the telephone lines and data sets would constitute a "message-switching network." The protocols which were to be established would define the communications formats between the IMPs. The interface between a host and an IMP would be a digital interface of a much simpler sort requiring no host consideration of error checking, retransmission, and routing. It was clearly

noted that that the major disadvantage of inserting the IMP was the cost of installation of another computer beside each host.   BBN draft *ARPANET Completion Report*, III-27f. [hereafter *Report*]

Westervelt circulated a first draft of the data communications protocols and it was subjected to "intensive review" at a meeting at ARPA in mid-May 1967. Thereafter further work was carried out and a second draft, by Westervelt and Dave Mills (who is now at the University of Delaware), was circulated after the summer. On the physical side, this second "draft specified full duplex binary serial transmission at a minimum rate of 2400 bits per second in each direction. [Furthermore, it] specified that each site should be capable of automatic answering of incoming calls and automatic dialing to originate outgoing calls." [*Report*, III-28]

On the logical side, the draft specified ASCII, 16-bit CRC checksums, use of text or binary format, a syntax, and certain "control conventions." The group met again in early October at ARPA to discuss the protocol paper and specifications for the IMP, which had become accepted over the summer. The meeting announcement also contained a questionnaire to be filled out by each of the 19 potential network locations so that gross estimates of traffic in 1969 could be made. The proposed network began to be called the ARPA Network at this time. Cerf told me: "Later we smiled at our naivete in filling out the traffic forms."

Packet Switching

At the 1967 ACM Symposium on Operating Systems Principles (Gatlinburg, Tennessee, October 1–4), Roger Scantlebury delivered a paper that he, Donald W. Davies, and their colleagues from the National Physical Laboratory in England had written on their "Digital Communication Network." The NPL Data Network, as it was called, bears a resemblance to both what Baran described and to the (future) ARPANET. It was to be a packet-switching network and was to have hierarchical structure. Davies et al. proposed that "local networks" be constructed with "interface computers" which would communicate with a "high

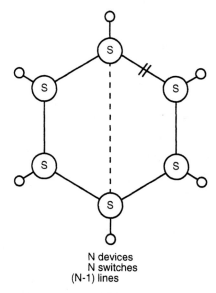

N devices
N switches
(N-1) lines

FIGURE 3.1   Mesh Network

level network" of "switching nodes" connected by megabit rate circuits.

Davies and Larry Roberts had met in 1965 at MIT, where Davies gave a seminar on timesharing. Roberts related:

> Licklider, Davies, and I discussed networking and the inadequacy of data communication facilities for both time-sharing and networking. Davies reports that shortly after this meeting he was struck with the concept that a store and forward system for very short messages (now called packet switching) was the ideal communication system for interactive systems. [Roberts 1988: 144]

Davies wrote two internal papers. In the first he proposed a network using 100Kbps to 1.5Mbps (T1) lines, 128 byte message size, and a switch that could handle 10,000 messages/second (Roberts has noted that it took two decades to accomplish this); in the second, dated June 1966, he coined the word "packet."

In their 1979 book, Davies et al. state that the NPL proposal was

> a store-and-forward system using short message units called 'packets' [that] would be best able to serve interactive computers since they naturally generated and received short messages. The delays which are inherent in store-and-forward methods would be reduced by restricting the length of packets and using high-speed lines between switches. A particular feature of this proposal concerned the interface between the network and the computers and terminals attached to it. The computers would be capable of handling data on a single communication path, interleaving packets from a number of terminals, and in this way the front end computer's functions would be largely eliminated. Terminals presented the more difficult problem which was to be solved by 'interface computers.' [p. 48]

At the same meeting, Larry Roberts gave a paper focused on the reasons for a network, not the details of operation. He mentioned use of the telephone system and concluded:

> It has proven necessary to hold a line which is being used intermittently to obtain the one-tenth to one second response time required for interactive work. This is very wasteful of the line and unless faster dial up times become available, message switching and concentration will be very important to network participants.   *ACM SOSP*, 1967

Scantlebury spoke with Roberts about "packet switching" being the solution to ARPA's problem, but it is unclear how much influence this had on Roberts' thinking. Certainly, Roberts changed some of his ideas. It was the result of the Tennessee meeting that he returned to Washington to read Baran's reports and, subsequently, to meet and talk to Baran. Baran met with the participants of the IPTO network project in late 1967 and attended the March 1968 meeting of the principal investigators. By June 1968, Roberts was describing the ARPA Network as a "demonstration of the distributed network" recommended in the RAND study.

But the Data Network was never built beyond the single node in Middlesex. A decade later, Davies wrote:

> The practical outcome of the NPL work was a local packet-switched communication network which grew, in a number of years, to serve about 200 VDU terminals and give them access to a dozen or so computer services. [p. 49]

But in 1967, to use Cerf's phrase, "it was the first LAN!" As a result, the NPL effort seems to have had only slight influence on the design of the ARPANET. Thus, Baran and Davies had each discussed the principles of packet-switching, but no one had built the sort of entity the IPTO was considering. The NPL group had thought of IMPs, but not of the type of those that would be used in the (future) ARPANET.

Elmer Shapiro

The network working group met first in November 1967. Representatives from RAND, UCSB, SRI, the University of Utah, and UCLA were present. The next month, Roberts awarded a four-month contract to SRI to study the "design and specification of a computer network." [ARPA Order No. 1137] During the winter and the spring of 1968, Elmer Shapiro circulated a series of notes and specification drafts among the group members and the main job was completed by the summer of 1968. (It was published by SRI that December.) This was the first piece of explicitly paid-for ARPANET effort; the previous work had been "extra" on existing ARPA contracts.

Shapiro's "A Study of Computer Network Design Parameters" is still worth reading. Writing nearly a year before the IMP contract was given to BBN, Shapiro noted that there were three kinds of communication involved (IMP-IMP, host-IMP, and host-host) and that

> Ideally, the communication subsystem should represent a "transparent pipe" between hosts, in that a message from host A for host B would arrive at B as an identical copy of the source message.

In early 1968, Shapiro also wrote up notes on the IMP. Len Klein-rock revised these ("I put in the portion on performance specs as well as a full spec on what kind of measurement hooks and software should be implemented," he told me), and "Functional Description of the IMP" was circulated. Glenn Culler apparently wrote a second draft, and Roberts and Wessler at ARPA wrote the final version of the IMP specification.

Program Plan and RFQ

IPTO reported to the Director of ARPA that the specifications were "essentially complete" on March 1, 1968. (The ARPA director at that time was Dr. Eberhardt Rechtin and the IPTO director was Taylor.) Roberts now submitted a "program plan" to the Director of ARPA on June 3. It was approved on June 21, 1968. The ARPA budget for Fiscal 1968 included $500,000 earmarked for the ARPANET. At the end of July the IPTO sent the details of the network to 140 potential bidders in the form of a Request for Quotation (RFQ).

The program plan stated that the program's objectives "were to develop experience in interconnecting computers and to improve and increase computer research productivity through resource sharing. Technical needs in scientific and military environments were cited as justification..." [*Report*, III-34] This justification was not trivial: Congress had passed the Mansfield Amendment, which required all military funding to be devoted to projects directly relevant to the military. Projects could have broader significance, but they had to have military relevance. The Defense Supply Service–Washington (DSS-W) agreed to be the procurement agent for ARPA. There was a bidders' conference which was attended by nearly 100 people from 51 companies. "When BBN received the RFQ," Severo Ornstein said, "Frank [Heart] called me into his office and showed it to me. I couldn't imagine why anyone would want such a thing."

Frank Heart, with both B.S. and M.S. degrees from MIT in Electrical Engineering, had worked at Lincoln Lab for 15 years, participating in both the Whirlwind and SAGE projects. He became the PI on BBN's ARPA contracts and led the team the built the IMPs. He has recently retired from the presidency of BBN's Systems and Technology Division.

Dave Walden told me that he, Ornstein, and Kahn had actually begun earlier, when Frank Heart learned that there would be an RFQ. Walden and Kahn, in different divisions of BBN, met when their respective divisions sent them to Santa Monica, to do a site evaluation of a data base project.

Both of Walden's parents were school teachers. Brought up in Contra Costa County (California), he attended San Francisco State, receiving a degree in mathematics. He worked in the computer center there and then went to MIT for a master's degree. "I was working full time and going to school full time," he remarked to me. "I shared an office with Dave Clark. I did the first draft of my thesis and it came back to be corrected. And I had to get my program to run. But then the whole business with the RFQ came up and I just never went back. I sometimes think that if I had the opportunity, I'd go and ask if there were a way to revive my credits. It's a piece of unfinished work."

Twelve proposals were actually received by DSS-W comprising 6.6 edge-feet of paper and presenting an awesome evaluation task for IPT, which more normally awards contracts on a sole source basis. Attempting to evaluate the proposals "strictly by the book," an ARPA-appointed evaluation committee retired to Monterey, California, to carry out their task.... Four bidders were rated within the zone of contention to receive the IMP contract, and supplementary technical briefings were requested from each of these bidders. Final negotiations were carried out with the two finalists, and one [BBN] was chosen in the week before Christmas, 1968. The contract was awarded and work began on the second day of the New Year in 1969. [*Report*, III-35f]

In parallel to this, ARPA held a competition concerning the supply of lines for the initial network: AT&T was awarded the contract by the Defense Commercial Communications Office (DECCO) in early September 1968.

The Network Working Group

The RFQ had sketched aspects of the network. But there was still a lot to be done. At Elmer Shapiro's suggestion, Roberts now transformed the network group into the Network Working Group, which was made up of representatives from the host sites. Steve Crocker, one of the UCLA graduate students, described this in RFC 1000 (August 1987):

> The precise usage of the ARPANET was not spelled out in advance, and the research community could be counted on to take some initiative. To stimulate this process, a meeting was called during the summer with representatives from the selected sites, chaired by Elmer Shapiro from SRI. If memory serves me correctly, Jeff Rulifson came from SRI, Ron Stoughton from UCSB, Steve Carr from Utah and I came from UCLA. (Apologies to anyone I've left out; records are inaccessible or lost at this point.) At this point we knew only that the network was coming, but the precise details weren't known.
>
> That first meeting was seminal. We had lots of questions—how IMPs and hosts would be connected, what hosts would say to each other, and what applications would be supported. No one had any answers, but the prospects seemed exciting. We found ourselves imagining all kinds of possibilities—interactive graphics, cooperating processes, automatic data base query, electronic mail—but no one knew where to begin. We weren't sure whether there was really room to think hard about these problems; surely someone from the east would be along by and by to bring the word. But we did come to one conclusion: We ought to meet again. Over the next several months, we managed to parlay that idea into a series of exchange meetings at each of our sites, thereby setting the most important precedent in protocol design.
>
> The first few meetings were quite tenuous. We had no official charter. Most of us were graduate students and we expected that a professional crew would show up eventually to take over the problems we were dealing with. Without clear definition of what the host-IMP interface would look like, or even what functions the IMP would provide, we focused on

exotic ideas. We envisioned the possibility of application specific protocols, with code downloaded to user sites, and we took a crack at designing a language to support this. The first version was known as DEL, for "Decode-Encode Language" and a later version was called NIL, for "Network Interchange Language."

Shapiro had stated that "the work of the Group should be fully documented." The first meeting was held in October 1968. It would be a year before any part of the ARPA Network would become available. In fact, the contract to build the IMPs had not yet been let. But the NWG was able to define explicitly the services that would be needed by users—remote interactive login and file transfer, for example. The Group was apparently unaware that Shapiro had written a basic plan for the NWG.

Stephen Crocker was an undergraduate at UCLA who had gone on to the MIT Artificial Intelligence Lab for a year and a half (1967–68). He then returned to UCLA, where he was a graduate student from 1968–71. From 1971–74 Crocker was program manager at the IPTO. He then returned to California to be a researcher at USC's Information Sciences Institute. He was then appointed Director of the Information Sciences Research Office of the Aerospace Corporation (1981–86). From late 1986 till late 1994 he was with Trusted Information Systems. He is now in the post of Vice President at Cybercash. Crocker initiated the NWG (the forerunner of the IETF) and the RFC series.

In an interview with Judy O'Neill, Vint Cerf—another UCLA graduate student at that time—said

> We were just rank amateurs, and we were expecting that some authority would finally come along and say, 'Here's how we are going to do it.' And nobody ever came along, so we were sort of tentatively feeling our way into how we could go about getting the software up and running.

Vinton Cerf received a B.S. in mathematics from Stanford in 1965 and took a job with IBM in Los Angeles. From 1967–1972 he worked at UCLA while earning his master's and doctoral degrees in computer science. He then went back to Stanford to teach (1972–76), while developing the TCP/IP protocols together with Bob Kahn. In 1976 he became program manager at the IPTO, where he remained till 1982, when he became Vice President for Engineering of MCI. He left MCI to join Bob Kahn as Vice President of the Corporation for National Research Initiatives in 1986 and returned to MCI in 1994 as Senior Vice President for data architecture. In 1992, Vint co-founded the Internet Society and served as its first president. He is famed as much for his sartorial splendor and wine expertise as for his technical abilities.

Crocker (in RFC 1000) continues:

In February of 1969 we met for the first time with BBN. I don't think any of us were prepared for that meeting. The BBN folks, led by Frank Heart, Bob Kahn, Severo Ornstein, and Will Crowther, found themselves talking to a crew of graduate students they hadn't anticipated. And we found ourselves talking to people whose first concern was how to get bits to flow quickly and reliably but hadn't—of course—spent any time considering the thirty or forty layers of protocol above the link level. And while BBN didn't take over the protocol design process, we kept expecting that an official protocol design team would announce itself.

A month later, after a particularly delightful meeting in [Alta] Utah, it became clear to us that we had better start writing down our discussions. We had accumulated a few notes on the design of DEL and other matters, and we decided to put them together in a set of notes. I remember having great fear that we would offend whomever the official protocol designers were, and I spent a sleepless night composing humble words for our notes. The basic ground rules were that anyone could say anything and that nothing was official. And to emphasize the point, I labeled the notes "Request for Comments." I never dreamed these notes would be distributed through the very medium we were discussing in these notes. Talk about Sorcerer's Apprentice!

Over the spring and summer of 1969 we grappled with the detailed problems of protocol design. Although we had a vision of the vast potential for intercomputer communication, designing usable protocols was another matter. A custom hardware interface and custom intrusion into the operating system was going to be required for anything we designed, and we anticipated serious difficulty at each of the sites. We looked for existing abstractions to use. It would have been convenient if we could have made the network simply look like a tape drive to each host, but we knew that wouldn't do.

Will Crowther was working at Lincoln Lab and moved to BBN in 1968 because he thought it "would be great to work for Frank.... Frank Heart was prominent in most of the things that I did. I liked to work for Frank." Crowther wasn't the only one. Lots of folks liked to work for Frank: he was a technical manager who wanted to understand what he was managing. He also cared about the people who worked for him. He was known to express his "disappointment" to an employee who had goofed, rather than yell at him or her. Crowther was the inventor of the interactive computer "fantasy" game now known as Adventure. Designed for the PDP-10, it was called ADVENT originally, because the TOPS-10 operating system limited file names to six characters.

Robert E. Kahn attended Queens College (New York) and took his degree in Electrical Engineering from City College of New York. He did his graduate work at Princeton and, on receiving his doctorate, worked on the Technical Staff at Bell Labs and then became an assistant professor of Electrical Engineering at MIT. He took a leave from MIT to join Bolt Beranek and Newman, where he was responsible for the design and development of the ARPANET. Kahn designed the internals of the IMP protocols and spent weeks in 1969 at UCLA testing the net with Vint Cerf.

But in 1972, Kahn moved to DARPA and later became director of the IPTO. Kahn and Cerf designed the first version of TCP/IP. It was Kahn who initiated the billion-dollar Strategic Computing Program, the largest computer research and development program the US government has ever undertaken. (In fact, many of the projects funded by agencies like the Office of Naval Research derived their support from money originally allocated by this program.) After thirteen years at DARPA, Kahn left to found the Corporation for National Research Initiatives, a not-for-profit organization providing leadership where research and development of the "information infrastructure" are concerned.

The RFCs

RFC 1 "Host Software" is dated April 7, 1969. RFC 2, by Bill Duvall, two days later, was on the same subject. In RFC 3, Crocker suggested a set of "Documentation Conventions" (April 9, 1969). This set was "obsoleted" on July 29, 1969, by Crocker's RFC 10. RFC 4 was Elmer Shapiro's "Network Timetable" (March 24, 1969). It contains what must have been the very first net map:

RFC 5 (June 2, 1969) was "Decode Encode Language" by Jeff Rulifson; RFC 6 (April 10, 1969) was Crocker's "Conversation with Bob Kahn"; RFC 7 (May 1), RFC 8 (May 5), and RFC 9 (May 1) were all by Gerard DeLoche. They concerned "Host-IMP Interface," "Functional Specifications for the ARPA Network," and "Host Software." Those readers familiar with contemporary electronic circulation of RFCs may be interested to note that RFCs 7 and 8 were longhand and that most of the early documents were circulated in hardcopy.

Jon Postel became the editor of the RFCs. He still is the czar of paper. Postel received his B.S. in Engineering in 1966, his M.S. in 1968, and his Ph.D. in 1974, all from UCLA. He worked for Mitre, Keydata, and with Doug Engelbart's group at SRI before joining the ISI in March 1976. He is Division Director of the Communications Division there.

But I have run ahead to the spring of 1969. Let us step back to the end of the previous year, when the IMP contract was awarded to BBN.

Wesley Clark has related that Larry Roberts asked him who he thought could handle the construction of the IMPs and that he responded "Frank Heart." Heart and BBN were, indeed, well positioned: They had been involved with earlier IPTO network plans at SDC.

The RFQ that was mailed at the end of July had specified both administrative and technical aspects. Bidders, for example, were asked to quote "cost plus fixed fee." This arrangement is sensible when the government undertakes a risky project in which bids might not be forthcoming if the contractor were forced to bear the risks.

The RFQ specified that the responses would be evaluated with regard to the following criteria:

1. Understanding and depth of analysis of technical problems involved;

2. Availability of qualified, experienced personnel for assignment to software, hardware and installation of the system;

3. Estimated functional performance and choice of hardware;

4. General quality, responsiveness, and corporate commitment to the network concept.

The criteria were to be weighted (in order): 30%, 25%, 25%, and 20%.

Bidders were asked to provide a system design for a 19-IMP network, but to price a four-IMP network. A 13-month performance period was requested to include design and construction of a prototype IMP and implementation and installation of four operational IMPs. The four IMPs were to be installed nine months into the contract, with the contractor supporting them for three months in the field. Sites were responsible for circuits, data sets, and line equipment. The contractor was responsible for the hardware and software necessary to connect the IMPs to each other using telephone circuits and to connect the IMPs to the hosts.

The functional description of the IMP specified message units not longer than 8192 bits which would be broken into packets of not more than 1024 bits. The size limitation was to make the message units manageable for the hosts. (The shorter the packet, the less likely there would be a transmission error.) A routing algorithm was hypothesized that would take connectivity, IMP and line busyness, and message priority into consideration. IMPs would coordinated their activity with other IMPs and with "special hosts."

The host-IMP interface was to be a standard one (rather than different for each host); multiple hosts per IMP had to be provided for, even though only one host interface was required; and there had to be enough program space to perform host-specific character code conversion and binary message repacking.

The type of IMP-telephone interface was also specified, as were a number of network performance characteristics. The most interesting of these were that the "average message delay" for a short message to go from a source IMP to a destination IMP had to be less than half a second for a "fully loaded network"; and that the probability of lost messages and message errors had to be very low. Moreover, capacity was third in importance. IPTO hoped for a 20Kb network. Apparently, Doug Engelbart of the Stanford Research Institute (the inventor, among other things, of the mouse—the "X-Y position indicator for a display system"—and hypertext) was excited about time-sharing: "If this network can't give me a half a second response time, then I can't use it for time-sharing," he is reported to have said at the ARPA meeting in Washington in 1967. So the IPTO made that one of its criteria.

As was related earlier, the contract was awarded to Bolt Beranek and Newman of Cambridge, Massachusetts; Frank Heart was the group leader. (When he heard that an ARPA contract had been awarded to a corporation in his constituency, the junior senator from Massachusetts, Edward Kennedy, sent a telegram to BBN contratulating them, in the spirit of "ecumenism," on winning the contract for the "Interfaith Message Processor.")

Chapter 4

Hardware

The hardware for the original IMP and its successors is described.

The computer hardware for the IMP was motivated by a "defensive design strategy," according to Alex McKenzie and Dave Walden of BBN: It was conservative enough "that the hardware was unlikely to cause problems."

That computer hardware was the Honeywell DDP-516. The 516 wasn't really a Honeywell machine: it had been designed by a company called CCC, which Honeywell bought out. Walden and Kahn had been looking at the specification of a small machine for a different purpose, a data management system, and had selected the 516 because "it offered the widest range of I/O and peripheral equipment from a single vendor. Thus, when a decision had to be made where the future IMP was concerned, they had the data at hand. The 516 had 16-bit words and a 0.96 microsecond cycle. It was configured with 12 Kilowords of memory, 16 multiplexed I/O channels, a 16-level priority interrupt system, a 100 microsecond clock, and a set of programmable status lights. A Teletype and a paper-tape reader were included for maintenance and the loading of software." [*BBN Report No. 1763*, January 6, 1969]

Note that date: the report ("Initial Design for Interface Message Processors for the ARPA Computer Network") was written the first Monday of 1969—right after BBN received the contract from the IPTO. A lot of thinking had gone on over the Christmas-New Year's holidays.

(Derived from the original Proposal, which had been written by Dave Walden and Bob Kahn with a great deal of input from Severo Ornstein and comments by other members of the team, 1763 was written by Kahn. "I actually put pen to paper," Kahn says. He still possesses the "original handwritten copy of the proposal." Vint Cerf told me: "Kahn never throws anything away.") The team that Frank Heart managed in late 1968/early 1969 was filled out by William Crowther; others who subsequently joined the IMP effort included Truett Thach, Bill Bartell, Jim Geisman, Ben Barker, and Marty Thrope.

The IMP's operating system occupied 6K of the words, leaving 6K words for message storage. Later, a protected 512 word block contained programs allowing an IMP that detected internal software corruption to reload a copy of the OS from another IMP.

A few months later, the *Interface Message Processor: Specifications for the Interconnection of a Host and an IMP* appeared. It was *BBN Report No. 1822*, dated "May 1969," and became a vital document of the ARPANET and, later, the Internet. Revised repeatedly, the final full version BBN turned out was dated "May 1978," though the CCITT X.25 standard was appended in "10/80" as Appendix K. For a decade, the 1822 specifications were the Bible of networking. The specifications and the programs will be discussed later, but the first 25 pages of 1822 concern the hardware.

By 1978, when the last revision of 1822 was issued, there were four types of IMPs. The one based on the Honeywell 516 was the original. The Honeywell 316 was a somewhat cheaper and slower version. It was used as the basis for the Terminal IMP (TIP). The 316 TIP was "designed to connect both Hosts and up to 63 terminals to the (316 and 516) network; the terminals are given access to the network directly, without an intervening Host." [1822, p. 1-6] In 1978, neither the Honeywell-based TIP nor IMP was being manufactured any longer; occasionally, however, they were re-deployed within the ARPANET. The Pluribus IMP—the third type—"is based on a flexible multiprocessor design ... A Terminal IMP is also available in Pluribus form, and it can provide access to a much larger number of terminals than the 316 Terminal IMP" [the fourth type]. The Pluribus was the first switch to support T1 lines.

In 1969, BBN provided each host site with four pieces of equipment: "the IMP itself, which is a modified Honeywell H-516R...; an ASR-33 Teletype...; a high-speed paper-tape reader (optional); and a cabinet, approximately the same size as the Model 516R, that contains modems connecting the IMP to the communication lines." [1822, p. 2-1] 1822 notes that "The telephone company will supply modems only for the communications lines actually installed." In 1975, the Pluribus was based on the Lockheed SUE processors.

Originally, the IMP was connected to its Host by a 30-foot cable; the length was "limited by the characteristics of the cable drivers of the IMP. [It connected] a standard Host/IMP interface unit built into the IMP to a *special* interface provided by the Host." Later, the possibility of connecting a "distant host" was provided. A distant host could "be located up to 2000 feet from the IMP, but an addition to the standard Host-IMP interface is required to modify the line-driving scheme.... A distant Host will usually be connected to an IMP which has one or more local Hosts" [1822, p. 2-3]. Yet later, BBN provided for a "very distant Host," which used an "interface designed for use over communication circuits with speeds up to 230.4 kilobits/second and up to tens (perhaps hundreds) of miles long."

Distance was important in 1969, and remained so in 1978. 1822 instructed sites that

> The locations of the IMP, modem cabinet, paper tape reader, and Teletype are to be selected by the Host personnel. These pieces of equipment should be placed within approximately eight feet of one another. A minimum of thirty square feet of floor space is required for the equipment, and additional space must be available for accessing the machine during maintenance and debugging. Access to the Model 516 IMP is via a full-length front door, which is hinged on the left side....

The 516 IMP was 74"x24"x28" and weighed 990 lbs. It required 2100 watts of power. The modem cabinet was about the same size and weighed "up to 750 pounds." The paper-tape reader weighed 25 lbs.; the ASR-33 Teletype, 56 lbs.; and the Infoton Vistar just a bit less. The 316 TIP required 2200 watts and the Pluribus IMP needed about 3000 watts per rack. All in all, "the Honeywell equipment requires six receptacles, and Pluribus machines require one receptacle per rack plus one for the modem cabinet." [1822, p. 2-13]

As the BBN contract (and its successors) required IMP-IMP connectivity via the telephone lines, but not the connections between the various Hosts and their IMPs, 1822 stated:

> *Each participating Host will be responsible for the design and construction of its own special unit to mate to the standard Host/IMP interface unit.* The logical operation of this unit will be the same, regardless of whether a Host is local or distant; however, a different electrical signaling scheme is required to handle a distant Host.

The telephone connections were 50Kbps leased lines. BBN designed special interface boards, which were constructed by Honeywell, to connect to them and to connect IMPs to Hosts.

The IPTO specification had called for one Host and several inter-IMP lines per IMP. But BBN had barely begun work when it became obvious that many sites would have more than a single host computer. The IMP hardware (and the software) initially was redesigned to serve four hosts and then redesigned to support a variety of combinations of Hosts and IMPs to a maximum of seven in all. (Some of these were "GHOSTS," software in the IMP code that looked like hosts to the software.)

Chapter 5

Software

The basic Host-Host software, the NCP, is described.

We now think of internetworking software as TCP/IP-based. Actually, the paper (by Cerf and Kahn) that gave rise to TCP only appeared in 1973. And the first version of the actual protocol, written by Cerf and his graduate students at Stanford, was submitted to ARPA the same year. Cerf told me that there was an unpublished version discussed at the INWG in September 1973. Before this, there were other software programs. And the very word "protocol" wasn't used until the beginning of 1970. There was only IMP software and a Host-Host program (NCP). The first TCP specification was published by IEEE in December 1974. (The ISO subcommittee that eventually published the layered OSI model was established in 1977; the model was first published in 1984, though Zimmermann had published an outline in 1980.)

The IMP software was straightforward. McKenzie and Walden wrote:

> The IMP software was a fairly conventional, real-time interrupt-driven program. It was written in assembly language with the capability of defining macro instructions. Real-time interrupt-handling capacities were calculated based on maximum line speed and message- and packet processing requirements, and the program's interrupt routines were designed and implemented to handle these speeds safely.

The software was implemented as a set of interrupt-driven modules communicating through packet queues and data tables.

Host-Host communication was something else. As 1822 gives full details on operation, I will now quote from it at length, to give the reader the flavor of the early software.

Hosts communicate with each other via *regular messages*. A regular message may vary in length from 96 up to 8159 bits, the first 96 of which are control bits called the *leader*. The leader is also used for sending control messages between the Host and its IMP, in which case only the first 80 bits are used. The remainder of the message is the *data*, or the *text*.

For each regular message, the Host specifies a *destination*, consisting of IMP, Host, and *handling type*. These three parameters uniquely specify a *connection* between source and destination Hosts. The handling type gives the connection specific characteristics, such as priority or non-priority transmission... Additional leader space has been reserved for a fourth parameter, to be used in future inter-network addressing. For each connection, messages are delivered to the destination in the same order that they were transmitted by the source.

For each regular message, the Host also specifies a 12-bit identifier, the *message-id*.[*] The message-id, together with the destination of the message, is used as the "name" of the message. The IMP will use this name to inform the Host of the disposition of the message. Therefore, if the Host refrains from re-using a particular message-id value (to a given destination) until the IMP has responded about that message-id, messages will remain uniquely identified and the Host can retransmit them in the event of a failure within the network.

After receiving a regular message from a Host connected to it, an IMP breaks the message into several packets (currently the maximum data bits/packet is 1008) and passes these through the network in the direction of the destination. Eventually, when all packets arrive at the destination, they are

---

[*]Until mid-1973 the first eight bits of the message-id field were called the "link".

reassembled to form the original message and passed to the destination Host. The destination IMP returns a positive acknowledgment to the source Host. This acknowledgment is called a *Ready for Next Message (RFNM)* and identifies the message being acknowledged by name. In some relatively rare cases, however, the message may be lost in the network due to an IMP failure; in such cases an *Incomplete Transmission* message will be returned to the source Host instead of an RFNM. Again, in this case, the message which was incompletely transmitted is identified by name.

If a response from the destination IMP (either RFNM or *Incomplete Transmission*) is itself lost in the network, this condition will be detected by the source IMP, which will automatically inquire of the destination IMP whether the original message was correctly transmitted or not, and repeat the inquiry until a response is received from the destination IMP. This inquiry mechanism is timeout-driven, and each timeout period may be as little as 30 or as much as 45 seconds in length.

When a message arrives at its destination, the leader is modified to indicate the source Host, but the message-id field is passed through unchanged. Thus, in addition to providing message identification between a Host and its local IMP, the message-id can provide a means for Hosts to identify messages between themselves....

If the *priority* bit of the handling type is set, the message will be expedited through the network by being placed at the front of the various transmission queues it will encounter along the way. This can be useful for transactions requiring minimal delay (e.g. remote echoing or the exchange of control information) but should be used judiciously, since the more it is used the less effect each further use will have. [1822, 3-1–3-3]

Protocols

Recall now Steve Crocker's tale of the origin of the NWG. The graduate students met the pros in the summer of 1969 and discovered that no work of "network geniuses" was in the offing on either side. The first software for the initial sites provided for remote login and for file transfer—effectively Telnet and FTP. Furthermore, the students had decided that only asymmetric (what we might now call "client-server") relationships need be supported. The first installations took place in the autumn of 1969. Roberts was at a meeting in Snowbird, Utah, on December 8, where he told the NWG that this just wasn't good enough: The result was a "host-host" program. This abstract implementation was the first ARPANET interprocess communication software. It was called the "Network Control Program," later renamed the "Network Control Protocol" (NCP). NCP relied on the sequenced message service that was provided by the ARPANET and derived "multiple virtual circuits between pairs of hosts by multiplexing." [Cerf and Kirstein 1978] (I asked Cerf about the origin of "protocol"—he told me that he wasn't certain, but that it had come up during conversation with Crocker and Postel—just which one is lost in the mist of time. They had thought of it in terms of diplomats exchanging handshakes and information. Later they found out the etymology, linking it to the late Greek word for the first page of a papyrus or parchment scroll, bearing the name of the author, the scribe, the contents [*protokollon*]. "It had to do with computers observing conventions," Cerf said.)

The first version of Host-Host procedures had been suggested by Gerard DeLoche in RFC 9 (May 1, 1969) and implemented by him in RFC 11 (August 1, 1969). These involved the GORDO operating system on the Sigma 7. Cerf had criticized them briefly in RFC 13 (August 20). But now Steve Carr (Utah), Crocker (UCLA), and Cerf (UCLA) produced a "New HOST-HOST Protocol" (RFC 33; February 12, 1970). On a cover sheet, Crocker noted that "the attached document does not contain enough information to write a NCP." RFC 36 (March 16) contained Crocker's "Protocol Notes." These led to an extensive discussion over the next sixteen months, which I will relate as an example of the extraordinary workings of the RFCs.

E. Harslem and J. Heafner (RAND) commented on RFC 36 in RFC 39 (March 27); A. Shoshani, R. Long and A. Landsberg added "Comments" in RFC 44 (April 10); Jon Postel and Crocker remarked "New protocol is coming" in RFC 45 (April 14); Bill Crowther added "BBN's

Comments on NWG/RFC #33" (RFC 47, April 20); and the next day Postel and Crocker mentioned a "Possible Protocol Plateau" (RFC 48). J. Newkirk, M. Kraley, Postel, and Crocker then made a "protocol proffering" (RFC 54, June 18), only to supply a "Prototypical implementation of the NCP" (RFC 55) the next day. Kraley and Newkirk "updated" this the same day (RFC 57), and R. Kalin supplied a "Simplified NCP Protocol" four weeks later (RFC 60; July 15). Dave Walden entered the discussion on August 29 (RFC 65), and at the next meeting of the NWG a "glitch cleaning committee" was set up. Crocker reported on the committee in RFC 102 (February 22, 1971), and the "Output of the Host-Host Protocol glitch cleaning committee" by Bressler, Crocker, Crowther, Grossman, and Tomlinson appeared as RFC 107 (March 23). This was then updated by Crocker (RFC 111), J. Melvin (RFC 124), Heafner (RFC 130), and J. White (RFC 132)—bringing us to April 28. Finally, on June 22, 1971, Alex McKenzie brought the entire discussion to a close, updating RFC 107 in RFC 179. The program/protocol was still being called both NCP and Host-Host Protocol.

It was cooperative procedures like these that made the protocols (even the early ones) as good as they were. Here we had two dozen people all over the United States putting in their thoughts in a technical free-for-all that would have been unheard of in other quarters. It is important to keep this mode of operation in mind. Most of the protocols, when they finally appear as RFCs, bear one or two names at the head. In general, however, each protocol was the result of many good minds at work, in meetings, over the phone, and over the (evergrowing) network. As I conducted this research, I came to realize just how many anonymous, unsung "heroes" there were. In fact, a result of the existence ARPANET and the Internet is that these documented discussions-by-memorandum no longer take place: The transactions take place in bars at meetings and in messages to small groups. I can more easily document the early 1970s than the early 1990s.

At the same time, other things were going on among the protocols. In RFC 62, Walden proposed a "message switching host level protocol." It was not accepted. Bob Metcalfe, one of the inventors of Ethernet, in his Ph.D. dissertation (*Packet Communication*, December

1973, though written as a Harvard dissertation, it was published as MIT Project MAC Report TR-114), discusses this interestingly:

> A recurring problem in the development of the ARPANET has been the coordination of remote processes. Any one of a number of existing schemes for interprocess communication might have been expected to offer itself as a ready solution, but, the fact is, the basic organization of ARPANET inter-process communication—a general HOST-HOST protocol—was long in coming and troublesome when it arrived. At the time of the Network Working Group's decision to adopt the current "official" HOST-HOST protocol, two specific proposals were considered: one based on connections (Crocker) and the other on messages (Walden). The earlier proposal, based on connections, was chosen, we believe, because connections, much more than messages, resemble structures in familiar, centralized computer operating systems.
>
> We believe, in retrospect, that Walden's proposal would have been the better choice—that the underlying structures of ARPANET interprocess communication should be modeled, not after the centralized computing systems they join, but after the distributed packet-switching system they use. [p. v]

Walden's proposal was an interesting one. It is dated August 1, 1970— less than a year after the ARPANET began to function. Unlike most of the material in previous RFCs, which were centered about planning for the future network, implementing the network, or announcements or minutes of meetings, RFC 62 attempted to

> construct an intellectual position of how things should be done in an ideal network...and then present this position for the designers of future networks to study....
>
> The actual act of resource sharing can be performed in two ways: in an *ad hoc* manner between all pairs of computer systems in the network; or according to a systematic network-wide standard.

Walden viewed "the fundamental problem of resource sharing to be the problem of interprocess communication." Like Carr, Crocker, and Cerf, in their 1970 *AFIPS* paper, he viewed "interprocess communication over a network" as a "subcase of general interprocess communication in a multi-programmed environment."

Having looked at interprocess communication in the PDP-1, the Multics system, and the SDS 940, Walden's insights might have changed a great many things later in operating system history; moreover, as noted by Metcalfe, basing inter-machine interprocess communication on the messages, not on the connections, might have resulted in a very different network from that which grew over the ensuing decades. Walden's suggestion was a more elegant solution. But it was a "road not taken." Cerf pointed out to me that "UDP/IP packets are messages like those Walden contemplated! Maybe we took that road after all."

By the end of 1969, BBN had found that their implementation of the network software had a major problem: The whole network would crash if too much traffic was directed to any one of the initial nodes. With only four nodes, there was a quick fix at hand. The ARPANET users simply agreed not to swamp any single node. Even a few years later, when there were 20 sites, such a simple fix would have been impossible. And in the meantime, people went to work on the programs.

Handshaking

"Handshaking" is a familiar phenomenon. In computing it has long referred to the operation of signals across an interface in which each signal on one side is followed by a response on the other. The operation is thus shared by both sides. In 1822, there was a control logic for a bit-by-bit handshaking procedure between each IMP. As bit transfer was asynchronous, the transmission of each bit was controlled by a *Ready-For-Next-Bit, There's-Your-Bit* handshake. Each bit was transferred only when both sender and receiver had indicated preparedness.

Both a two-way and a four-way handshake were provided for.

In the four-way handshake, the receiver awaits the dropping of There's-Your-Bit before raising Ready-For-Next-Bit. A full cycle of the four-way handshake works as follows: The sender readies the next data bit and the There's-Your-Bit signal is sent to the receiver (1st cable transit). The receiver takes in the bit and notifies the sender by dropping Ready-For-Next-Bit (2nd cable transit). The sender responds by dropping the There's-Your-Bit signal (3rd cable transit) and after the receiver has noted this, the Ready-For-Next-Bit signal can be turned back on (4th cable transit), registering preparedness for a new bit.

The two-way handshake involved only two cable transits, but had a brief delay before the receiver's sending Ready-For-Next-Bit. All together, there were twelve signals on the Host cable: IMP Master Ready, IMP Ready Test, Host Master Ready, Host Ready Test, Host-to-IMP Data Lines, There's-Your-Host-Bit, Ready-For-Next-Host-Bit, Last-Host-Bit, IMP-to-Host Data Line, There's-Your-IMP-Bit, Ready-For-Next-IMP-Bit, and Last-IMP-Bit. This was a truly parsimonious bit of programming on the part of the BBN crew. There were also a group of IMP "background" programs: TTY, DEBUG, PARAMETER-CHANGE, DISCARD, TRACE, and STATISTICS. [1822, 4-1 – 4-26, 5-1]

It is instructive to compare this with Crocker's notes in RFC 1 (April 7, 1969), where the "Summary of Primitives" listed:

    a. Initiate TTY-like connection with HOST x;

    b. Terminate connection;

    c. Send/Receive character(s) over TTY-like connection;

    d. Initiate file-like connection parallel to TTY-like connection;

    e. Terminate file-like connection;

    f. Send/Receive over file-like connection.

Crocker also stated that the NWG proposed to create "a language for console control. This language, currently named DEL, would be used by subsystem designers to specify what components are needed in a terminal and how the terminal is to respond to inputs from its keyboard, Lincoln Wand, etc." To say this was optimistic is mild: Rob Pike at AT&T Bell Labs is now trying to do this.

The work on DEL had begun at a meeting of Andrews, Baray, Steve Carr (Utah), Crocker, Jeff Rulifson, and Ron Stoughton (UCSB) at

SRI, October 25–26, 1968. Crocker then met with Rulifson at SRI on November 18 and Stoughton met with Rulifson at SRI on December 12. The NWG then met in Utah in January, and the NET group met at BBN in Cambridge on February 18, 1969. Rulifson's sketch of the DEL was first made available at the BBN meeting. DEL was subsequently reworked and then "published" as RFC 5 (June 2). In RFC 5, Rulifson noted:

> The Decode-Encode Language (DEL) is a machine independent language tailored to two specific computer network tasks:
>
>> accepting input codes from interactive consoles, giving immediate feedback, and packing the resulting information into message packets for network transmission.
>>
>> and accepting message packets from another computer, unpacking them, building trees of display information, and sending other information to the user at his interactive station.

From this explanation and my details of the give and take on the Host-Host Protocol discussed earlier, the reader can see how the protocols developed. Moreover, as they became more elaborate over the first two years (1969–1971), they were hierarchized. The protocol hierarchy was made explicit by Davies and Barber:

1. The Initial Control Protocol (ICP), providing a standard method for processes in different HOSTs to establish a connection.

2. The Telecommunication Network (TELNET) protocol, used to provide communication between a keyboard terminal and a terminal-serving HOST. This uses the Network Virtual Terminal to overcome terminal hardware differences.

3. The Data Transfer Protocol (DTP), specifying standard methods of formatting data for passage through the network, allowing it to be used to implement higher level protocols.

4. The File Transfer Protocol (FTP) defines standard methods for reading, writing and updating files stored at a remote

HOST in an endeavour to shield users from the differences between filing systems at various sites.

5. The Data Reconfiguration Service (DRS) attempts to deal with the problem of reconciling the different input-output data formats that are used by various applications programs. It uses an interactive procedure between user processes and an interpreter called the Form Machine (analogous to filling out a form by hand).

6. The Mail Box Protocol (MBP) provides a service for passing messages between people, and is widely used to facilitate the work of protocol development by members of study groups.

7. The Graphics Protocol (GP) is being considered by a group thinking about the difficult area of specifying standard ways of handling graphical information. [1973, p. 308]

There are many more protocols today. The *ARPANET Protocol Handbook* issued by the Defense Communications Agency on April 1, 1976, was a slim volume of 300 pages. It was under an inch thick. The 1978 edition was double that size. The 1985 version came in three volumes, each of which was far larger than the original.

I have spent so much time on protocols and will return to the subject again later because of Cerf's remark that "The history of the net is the history of the protocols." I believe that this was true for (at least) the first decade of the net. As will be seen, it is no longer true.

Diversion 2

Network Working Group   V. Cerf
Request for Comments: 968   MCI
                                                       December 1985

'Twas the Night Before Start-up'

STATUS OF THIS MEMO

This memo discusses problems that arise and debugging techniques used
in bringing a new network into operation. Distribution of this memo is
unlimited.
DISCUSSION

Twas the night before start-up and all through the net,
 not a packet was moving; no bit nor octet.
The engineers rattled their cards in despair,
 hoping a bad chip would blow with a flare.
The salesmen were nestled all snug in their beds,
 while visions of data nets danced in their heads.
And I with my datascope tracings and dumps
 prepared for some pretty bad bruises and lumps.
When out in the hall there arose such a clatter,
 I sprang from my desk to see what was the matter.
There stood at the threshold with PC in tow,
 An ARPANET hacker, all ready to go.
I could see from the creases that covered his brow,
 he'd conquer the crisis confronting him now.
More rapid than eagles, he checked each alarm
 and scrutinized each for its potential harm.

On LAPB, on OSI, X.25!
TCP, SNA, V.35!

His eyes were afire with the strength of his gaze;
 no bug could hide long; not for hours or days.
A wink of his eye and a twitch of his head,
 soon gave me to know I had little to dread.
He spoke not a word, but went straight to his work,
 fixing a net that had gone plumb berserk;
And laying a finger on one suspect line,
 he entered a patch and the net came up fine!

The packets flowed neatly and protocols matched;
 the hosts interfaced and shift-registers latched.

He tested the system from Gateway to PAD;
 not one bit was dropped; no checksum was bad.
At last he was finished and wearily sighed
 and turned to explain why the system had died.
I twisted my fingers and counted to ten;
 an off-by-one index had done it again...

Chapter 6

Startup

The beginnings of the ARPA Network.

All through July and August of 1969 the students at UCLA heard rumors that BBN was having trouble with the IMP and that delivery of the IMP would be late. It wasn't.

Truett Thach was working at BBN's Santa Monica office. He was waiting for the crate when it arrived in Los Angeles. Ben Barker told me: "I wrote 'Do it, Truett!,' on the outside of the crate." He then flew to LA, as he had designed several of the hardware interfaces and was responsible for the installation. On Saturday, August 30, IMP #1 was delivered by Thach to Professor Leonard Kleinrock's lab.

Kleinrock received a bachelor's in Electrical Engineering at City College and went on to graduate work at MIT, where he received both a master's and a Ph.D. in Electrical Engineering. Larry Roberts and Ivan Sutherland were among his classmates. Wes Clark was in charge of the group at Lincoln Lab within which he worked (on the TX-2 machine). Ken Olsen, soon to found Digital Equipment Corporation (DEC), was his first supervisor—the circuits in the box that Digital sold when it was founded had been designed by Kleinrock. Kleinrock's thesis was done while he was at MIT's Research Lab in Electronics, working with Ed Arthur (subsequently at Bell Labs). The proposal was presented in 1959 and the degree awarded in 1962. Kleinrock, Roberts, and Sutherland all did their final defenses together at Lincoln Lab: Claude Shannon and Marvin Minsky were among the examiners. Kleinrock's work was an analytical model of computer communication networks, well

51

before its time. (Roberts' work was on machine perception of three-dimensional objects; Sutherland did Sketchpad, the first drawing program.)

Kleinrock's thesis appeared as *Communication Nets* (1964). Interestingly, Baran's work on packet switching was cited by Kleinrock in his book, but not in the dissertation: it wasn't interesting because Kleinrock's research was driven by the notion of a message-switching network. I asked Kleinrock about the work of Davies and Baran. "Neither one had been published," he said. "My dissertation was handed in and filed in 1962. It was published as a McGraw-Hill book in 1964. The closest thing was some work published by R. Prosser, but it was limited in scope. I was the first to discuss the performance gains to be had by packet switching."

In reference to the DEC circuits, Kleinrock remarked: "I had just come to MIT on a special 'staff associateship' from Lincoln Laboratory. This was basically a terrific scholarship to pursue graduate work at MIT and be paid by the Lab. I had come from CCNY in New York City, attended evening session to get my bachelor's degree in EE, and had graduated first in my class (day and evening). As part of this very generous scholarship, I was to spend my summers at Lincoln Lab. The first summer I spent there, summer 1957, I worked for Ken Olsen and designed a 'variable delay pulse amplifier' for him. This was a digital circuit that allowed you to specify when a pulse of a given width would fire (the delay and width could be set by the user). Later that summer, Ken told me he was leaving Lincoln Lab to set up a company and asked me to join him. I pointed out that I could not since I wanted to pursue my graduate work—a decision I have never regretted. He then formed DEC, and the first products DEC produced was a set of digital circuits, each in their own modular boxes. My variable delay pulse amplifier was one of them!"

Kleinrock was offered a post at UCLA in August 1963. He's still there. He became interested in queueing theory and, in 1967, when Roberts was interested in putting together a network, he was among those summoned to Washington and subsequently became one of the designers. Because of his interest in performance evaluation, design and measurement, his lab at UCLA became site number one. He is frequently referred to as "the Poet Laureate of the ARPANET."

Among the graduate students who worked in Kleinrock's lab were Steve Crocker, Vint Cerf, and Jon Postel, though Crocker and Cerf did their dissertations with Jerry Estrin and Postel did his with Dave Farber at UC Irvine. I asked Kleinrock what it had been like.

> I had a team of about 40 people driving to get the first node up. Crocker was head of the software effort, and Postel and Cerf worked under Crocker. We had a number of segments, including analytic, design, implementation, measurement, etc. Those three (along with some other software aces) were interesting to supervise, since, as with all hackers, they were very independent, and always pressing me for more resources (e.g., equipment, staff, travel money, software, etc.). They were a delight to work with—full of ideas (some brilliant, some flawed)—and the experience was exciting for all of us.

What began at the 1967 IPTO meeting was the creation of a community which cooperated more-or-less harmoniously for over 15 years. The ARPANET community was vital to the successes of the Net, just as the tightly-knit group of Unix users and developers made for the success of that operating system.

Let me go back to Crocker's remarks in RFC 1000:

> Over the spring and summer of 1969 we grappled with the detailed problems of protocol design. Although we had a vision of the vast potential for intercomputer communication, designing usable protocols was another matter. A custom hardware interface and custom intrusion into the operating system was going to be required for anything we designed, and we anticipated serious difficulty at each of the sites. We looked for existing abstractions to use. It would have been convenient if we could have made the network simply look like a tape drive to each host, but we knew that wouldn't do.
>
> It was clear we needed to support remote login for interactive use—later known as Telnet—and we needed to move files from machine to machine. We also knew that we needed a more fundamental point of view for building a larger array of protocols. Unfortunately, operating systems of

that era tended to view themselves as the center of the universe; symmetric cooperation did not fit into the concepts currently available within these operating systems. And time was pressing: The first IMP was due to be delivered to UCLA September 1, 1969, and the rest were scheduled at monthly intervals.

At UCLA we scrambled to build a host-IMP interface. SDS, the builder of the Sigma 7, wanted many months and many dollars to do the job. Mike Wingfield, another grad student at UCLA, stepped in and offered to get interface built in six weeks for a few thousand dollars. He had a gorgeous, fully instrumented interface working in five and one half weeks. I was in charge of the software, and we were naturally running a bit late. September 1 was Labor Day, so I knew I had a couple of extra days to debug the software. Moreover, I had heard BBN was having some timing troubles with the software, so I had some hope they'd miss the ship date. And I figured that first some Honeywell people would install the hardware— IMPs were built out of Honeywell 516s in those days—and then BBN people would come in a few days later to shake down the software. An easy couple of weeks of grace.

BBN fixed their timing trouble, air shipped the IMP, and it arrived on our loading dock on Saturday, August 30. They arrived with the IMP, wheeled it into our computer room, plugged it in and the software restarted from where it had been when the plug was pulled in Cambridge. Still Saturday, August 30. Panic time at UCLA.

Beginning the Net

Apparently, everyone in Cambridge had done their part. Dave Walden also flew to LA for the installation. (BBN later flew Walden to Norway to work with LFK/Siemens on the second packet-switching network, a NATO effort: he was thus present at both the first and the second installations.) With the 516 operating correctly, the next job was the connec-

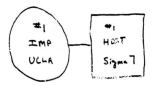

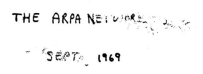

THE ARPA NEIWORE

SEPT. 1969

I NODE

FIGURE 6.1   Drawing of September 1969
(Courtesy of Alex McKenzie)

tion of the Host (the Sigma 7) to the IMP by means of Wingfield's interface. On Tuesday, September 2, the Sigma 7 (running SEX—the Sigma Experimental Operating System) exchanged test messages with the IMP. The first Host-IMP interface worked, too.

The group at UCLA was delighted. Their opposite numbers at the Stanford Research Institute in Menlo Park really had to buckle down. BBN was responsible for the IMP-IMP program. But each site was responsible for the Host-IMP interface. SRI's SDS 940 was sufficiently different from the Sigma 7, that nontrivial work was necessary. But when IMP #2 was delivered in October, Shapiro, Engelbart, and the students were prepared. Stanford's IMP and Host duly communicated with each other and the big moment arrived. Test messages were exchanged between Menlo Park and Los Angeles. In November this original link appeared stable and Larry Roberts and Barry Wessler flew to California. On November 21, 1969, they gathered in Kleinrock's lab and connected to Engelbart's 500 miles away. The first Telnet session.

No one seems to recall what the actual first message was. It wasn't either "Come here, Watson..." or "What hath God wrought?" But it was amazing.

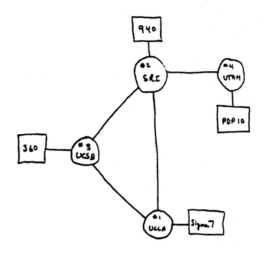

THE ARPA NETWORK

DEC 1969

4 NODES

FIGURE 6.2   Drawing of 4 Node Network
(Courtesy of Alex McKenzie)

Also in November, the third IMP was delivered to the University of California at Santa Barbara, where it was connected to UCSB's IBM 360/75 in Roland Bryan's lab. Bryan, who is now CEO of ACC, has the distinction of running the first installation to exchange data rather than mere test messages. (Bob Braden wrote the first Network Control Program for the 360/75 [later a 360/91] in assembly language.) In December, the fourth IMP went into service at the University of Utah, its Host was a PDP-10 running TENEX. Crocker (in RFC 1000) wrote:

> The contract called for four IMPs to be delivered to UCLA, SRI, UCSB and The University of Utah. These sites were running a Sigma 7 with the SEX operating system, an SDS 940 with the Genie operating system, an IBM 360/75 with OS/MVT (or perhaps OS/MFT), and a DEC PDP-10 with the Tenex operating system. Options existed for additional nodes if the first experiments were successful.

The experiment was successful. BBN had fulfilled its contract: there were four sites and the first delivery of an IMP had, as required, been made within nine months. Frank Heart's group received a contract extension. The network looked like Fig. 6.2; Map 1.

It was not yet the packet-switching network originally envisioned, as IMP #4 was connected only to IMP #2, but it was a network and it worked.

The first four ARPANET sites didn't remain alone long. At the beginning of 1970, Honeywell delivered IMPs 5, 6, and 7 to BBN, each with a 516 as its processor. BBN meanwhile developed a "distant Host interface," so that host computers could be "up to 2000 feet from an IMP." More important, a phone line test program was developed and BBN found only 1 error per 20,000 bits transmitted on a 50-Kbps line.

By October 1970 there were 11 sites and by December two more were added: Stanford connected to both SRI and UCLA on the West Coast; Lincoln Lab joined the Massachusetts contingent; and Case Western Reserve University in Ohio and Carnegie Mellon University in Pennsylvania became the first sites between Greater Boston and Utah. (On January 11, 1971, Alex McKenzie wrote to Nico Haberman at Carnegie Mellon, estimating that there would be a "network user community of 2000 people, distributed over 14 sites.")

The connectivity was also growing. MIT was connected to Lincoln, Utah, and BBN; Lincoln to MIT and Case; Case to Lincoln and CMU; CMU to Case and Harvard; Harvard to CMU and BBN; and BBN to Harvard, MIT, and RAND. In the West, Utah re-established the line to SRI and connected to both MIT and SDC; SDC connected to Utah and RAND; SRI to Utah, Stanford, UCLA, and UCSB; and RAND to UCLA, SDC, and BBN.

By the time the "experiment" was 16 months old, it was a genuine packet-switching network, with at least two routes between any two points. It was also a real success.

The BBN *Quarterly Reports*

As part of its contract from ARPA, BBN Computer Systems Division issued "Quarterly Technical Reports." I have already cited Report 1763, which preceded these. BBN's view of what was going on can be seen from the ensuing reports.

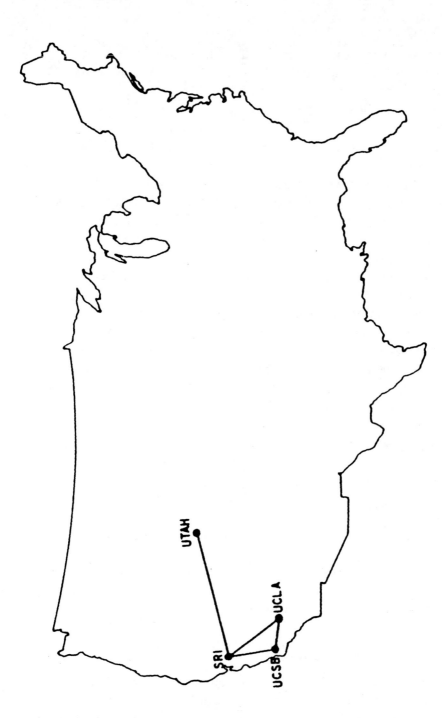

MAP 1   December 1969
(MAPS 1–4 Courtesy of Alex McKenzie)

BBN Report No. 1783; April 1969

The initial design plans had appeared in Report 1763. Modifications were now introduced: "hardware modifications to the 516 IMP; the development of a debugging package for use with the IMP; the expansion of the IMP program to handle four Hosts rather than a single Host...; and the design of a minimum delay routing algorithm."

BBN Report No. 1837; July 1969

"Software design has been substantially completed; the structure of the IMP program is described here by considering each of the interrupt levels and data structures in turn. Preliminary plans for the IMP's network measurement facilities are presented." On the hardware side, this report noted that "The IMP cabinet has space for an additional 4000 words of core"—a great deal of memory in 1969.

BBN Report No. 1890; October 1969

"The first IMP was delivered to UCLA during this period." It was on schedule and had an operational program. "The IMP successfully communicated with the UCLA Host computer (Sigma 7)....

"Within a few days of its delivery to UCLA on Saturday, August 30, the IMP was connected to and operating with both the Sigma 7 and the phone company equipment." The "tests were conducted with the UCLA-SRI phone line looped at the SRI end, and messages were successfully sent around this loop."

Comically, "We found the phone company installations at UCLA and SRI to be inconsistent with regard to physical configurations of the voice circuits cabinetry, original design, etc. These difficulties were reported to the telephone company."

It would not be the last phone problem.

BBN Report No. 1928; January 1970

"The network expanded to 4 sites... A distant Host interface was developed for Hosts up to 2000 feet from an IMP. A phone line test program was developed and found 1 error per 20,000 transmissions on a 50-kilobit-per-second network line." It was also noted that ARPA had ex-

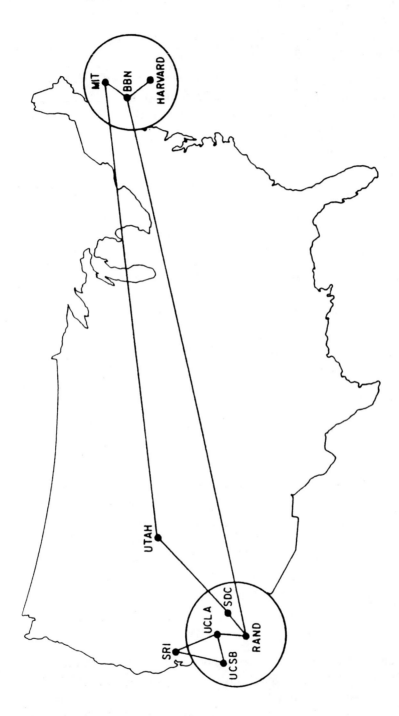

MAP 2   June 1970

tended BBN's contract till December 31, 1970. The original bid had been for just over $500,000. When the actual contract arrived in December 1968, it was for about double that amount for 1969. The 1970 contract was for $2,013,492 and provided for at least eight more IMPs.

BBN Report No. 1966; April 1970

IMPs 5, 6, and 7 were delivered by Honeywell. BBN streamlined the assembly process by using a cross-assembler. "Some testing of the four node network under heavy load found only minor software problems."

All was not sweetness and light, however. BBN had constructed a "test cell." IMPs 5, 6, and 7 were installed and tested. "Testing revealed a number of minor problems" and a good deal of work was required on the parts of both BBN and Honeywell to rectify them. Furthermore, "The original four IMPs were delivered with certain known deficiencies, which will be remedied by field retrofits during the next quarter..." The first IMP to receive full treatment was #5, the first "ruggedized" IMP.

However, another landmark was achieved: "In late March, AT&T succeeded in providing a 50-kilobit circuit across the country. IMP No. 5 (BBN) was then connected into the network via a temporary tie to the IMP at UCLA. The standard IMPTST program was run between these two machines and shortly afterwards the operational IMP programs were in communication over this line" (3100 miles). And: "there is no delay noticeable to a person at a teletype in echoing single character messages back and forth across the country" (p. 4).

BBN Report No. 2003; July 1970

The second quarter of 1970 saw the ARPANET double in size. After #5 was installed at BBN, #6 went to MIT, #7 to RAND, #8 to SDC, and #9 to Harvard. Unfortunately, AT&T had "not yet provided circuits to Harvard, but the eight-node subnet is operational." Yet another phone problem.

AT&T did, however, supply a dedicated circuit between BBN and RAND, so the "temporary tie" to UCLA was taken down.

BBN now set up the Network Control Center. "Each IMP in the net reports to the Network Control Center every fifteen minutes or

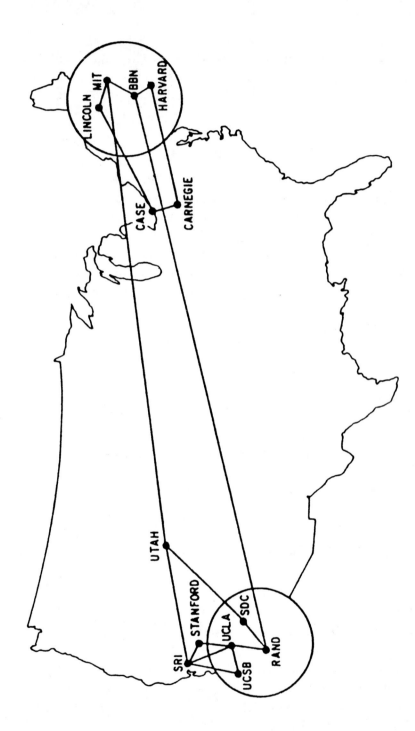

MAP 3   December 1970

whenever important status changes occur" (p. 2). BBN also issued "a fourth revision" of the IMP system, recalling the March 1 system. Revised versions of the Host Specification (Report No. 1822) and of the IMP Operating Manual (Report No. 1877) were issued.

The configuration of the lines connecting the nine sites was interesting. There was a long, thin trapezoid with Utah, RAND, MIT, and BBN at the vertices and SDC between Utah and RAND. Harvard connected to BBN. SRI, UCSB, and UCLA were the vertices of a triangle, and UCLA connected to RAND. The line between Utah and SRI, which was the December 1969 connection, was dropped for nearly a year.

BBN Report No. 2059; October 1970

During the third quarter of 1970, one year into the "experiment," IMP #10 was installed at Lincoln Laboratory and IMP #11 at Stanford University. At BBN, experimental testing of 230.4 kilobit/sec circuits was begun in the test cell. Yet another version of the "operational IMP program" was completed (it was distributed in November) and extensive discussions of the Host protocol were underway. BBN also completed the initial design for the terminal IMP (the TIP) and for a multi-line controller that would be able to "handle up to 64 asynchronous or synchronous terminal devices."

BBN Report No. 2103; January 1971

Two years after BBN received the contract for the IMP, things were going well. IMP #13 had been installed at Case-Western Reserve University and IMP #14 at Carnegie-Mellon University. IMP #15, destined for Burroughs (the first truly commercial site) in Paoli, Pennsylvania, had been delivered to BBN. Moreover "the telephone company has installed three additional circuits, connecting BBN/Harvard, MIT/Lincoln, and Case/Carnegie." This was not insignificant: Recall that when Harvard received its IMP six months earlier, AT&T had not yet connected the appropriate circuits. BBN also progressed on its work towards a terminal IMP and issued revised versions of both 1822 and 1877.

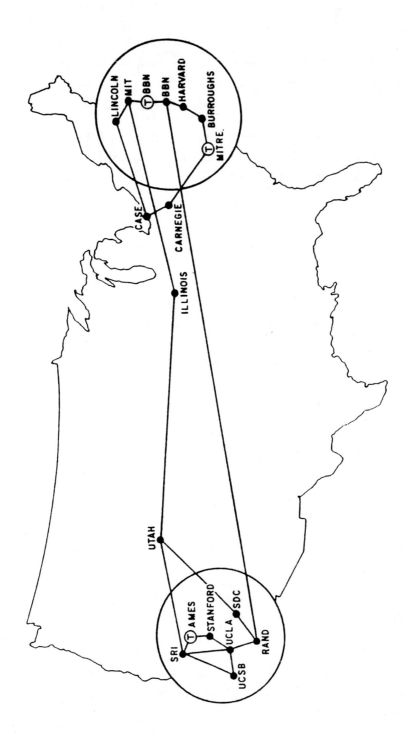

MAP 4   September 1971

BBN Report No. 2123; April 1971

IMP #12 was installed at the University of Illinois and #15 at the Burroughs Corporation. BBN "also received delivery from Honeywell of a prototype 316 IMP, a prototype Terminal IMP, and the first deliverable Terminal IMP...The telephone company installed six additional circuits during this quarter, connecting Utah/Illinois, Illinois/MIT, Lincoln/Case, Case/Carnegie, Carnegie/Paoli, and Paoli/Harvard. The temporary MIT/Utah circuit, which was installed in June 1970, has been discontinued. The total number of wideband circuits in the net is now 19."

BBN also completed design "of the Multi-Line Controller" and continued work on the TIP.

BBN Report No. 2175; July 1971

BBN's efforts "during this period were devoted primarily, though not exclusively, to the Terminal IMP....our participation in the Network Working Group increased substantially..."

On the hardware front, Honeywell delivered three more 316s to BBN, two Multi-Line Controllers were in "final construction," and three more "under construction." A terminal "connected to the prototype Terminal IMP had successfully logged into the BBN TENEX system."

BBN Report No. 2270; October 1971

"The first two TIPs were delivered to NASA/AMES and MITRE. The first of these was installed on schedule early in August. The second installation was delayed due to severe damage to the Terminal IMP during shipping from BBN to MITRE. Damaged components were replaced in the field and the machine was in use about one week behind schedule."

Once the TIPs were in place, bugs were discovered and the programs were rewritten, as was the TIP's terminal-handling program.

BBN Report No. 2309; January 1972

"The first Model 316 IMP was installed...at ETAC (Environmental Technical Applications Center, Washington, D.C.)." It was to be replaced by a TIP early in 1972. A third TIP was installed at the National Bureau of Standards. 1822 was revised yet again; Report No. 2183 (*User's Guide to the Terminal IMP*) was revised; and a paper describing the TIP ("The Terminal IMP for the ARPA Computer Network, " by Ornstein, Heart, Crowther, Russell, Rising, and Michel) was circulated prior to delivery at the 1972 Spring Joint Computer Conference. Frank, Kahn, and Kleinrock delivered their paper on "Computer Communications Network Design" at the same conference. Kleinrock told me "That paper was lots of fun to write. The three of us interacted beautifully and did lots of creative work and thinking to write it. We spent some very long nights working on that paper. But it was a landmark paper and was part of a famous session at the 1972 SJCC."

There had been complaints concerning the 2000-foot cable length limitation inherent in the Host interface; now BBN introduced a "very distant Host" interface, incorporating error detection and recovery procedures. Furthermore, BBN arrived at a tentative solution to the problem of connecting remote batch terminals and continued work on the problems inherent in connecting tape drives to TIPs.

ARPA was interested in a heterogeneous network, so it is worth looking at the host machines in April 1971, prior to the installation of the first TIP. The ARPANET had 15 nodes with 23 host computers. These were:

UCLA	Sigma 7 and 360/91
SRI	PDP-10 and PDP-15
UCSB	IBM 360/75
Stanford	PDP-10
RAND	IBM 1800 and IBM 360/65
SDC	IBM 360/67
Utah	PDP-10
Illinois	PDP-11
MIT	PDP-10 and GE-645
Lincoln	TX-2 and IBM 360/67
Case	PDP-10
Carnegie	PDP-10

Burroughs	B6500 and Illiac IV
Harvard	PDP-1 and PDP-10
BBN	two PDP-10s

BBN and SDC also had DDP-516s connected.

Alex McKenzie

Alex McKenzie joined BBN in February 1967. At the beginning of 1970 he took a six-month leave of absence and went camping in Europe with his wife. He returned to BBN in November and was asked by Frank Heart to become the liaison with the many questioners—as McKenzie put it, "I became BBN's first generalist in the ARPANET." A graduate in mathematics of Stevens Institute of Technology in Hoboken, New Jersey, McKenzie had gone on to Stanford, where he did a master's thesis on the Burroughs 5000 compiler (the Burroughs supported only ALGOL). When he received his degree (April 1964), he took a job with Honeywell Information Systems because he wanted to live in New England. He worked there till he moved to BBN.

In 1971, McKenzie assumed responsibility for the Network Control Center, a position he held until mid-1976, after the ARPANET was formally handed off to the Defense Communications Agency for operation. "In the first years of my association with the ARPANET, beginning late in 1970 and going through most of 1972, most of the world seemed to believe that packet switching couldn't work," McKenzie has said. While UCLA, with Kleinrock, Cerf, Postel, Crocker, and others, was enthusiastic, "there wasn't much enthusiasm anywhere else." Apparently, it was a "not-invented-here" feeling that McKenzie sensed. But there was certainly an acceptance barrier to overcome; a feeling that with the government involved it would be five years late and nothing would work. It took a demonstration to turn things around. A big, public demonstration.

ICCC '72

On July 12, 1972, Robert Kahn of BBN issued RFC 371, "Demonstration at International Computer Communications Conference." It read:

The International Computer Communications Conference, scheduled for 24-26 October 1972 at the Washington, D.C. Hilton Hotel, is a newly organized conference intended to address a broad set of issues in the Computer Communications field. Approximately 17 sessions are currently planned for the conference. The social implications of this field are a matter of widespread interest that reaches society in almost all walks of life; education, medicine, research, business and government. All these areas will be affected as the field develops.

I am organizing a computer communications network demonstration to run in parallel with the sessions. This demonstration will provide attendees with the opportunity to gain first hand experience in the use of a computer network. The theme of the demonstration will be on the value of computer communication networks such as data base retrieval, combined use of several machines, real-time data access, interactive cooperation, simulation systems, simplified hard copy techniques, and so forth. I am hoping to present a broad sampling of computer based resources that will provide attendees with some perspective on the utility of computer communication networks.

Terminal equipment has already been offered by many different manufacturers and we are beginning to home in on the application areas. The plan is to deliver a TIP to the Hilton and to connect it into the ARPANET. All terminals at the Hilton will then be connected directly to the TIP. Software resources on the ARPANET as well as resources in other nets that can be temporarily connected to the ARPANET and made available for the purpose of demonstration will be available. In most cases it is possible to arrange for terminal access via the ARPANET to non ARPANET sites without hardware or software development on their part.

A significant amount of preparation by ourselves, the NIC [Network Information Center], and others is being devoted to making it convenient for naive users to sit down at a terminal and effectively use "selected" resources without assistance. This involves the generation of "explicit" documentation in easy to understand terms—a non-trivial task. However, we hope this effort will also be useful for other applications in the long run.

We need the help of sites in the network community to pitch in and lend a hand. This is a large undertaking and much too big to be pulled off without a large commitment in time and energy between now and October....

Later that same day, Richard W. Watson of SRI issued RFC 372, reporting on "a good chat" with Bob Kahn on the ICCC. He revealed that:

- UCLA Kleinrock will have some network measurement stuff to demonstrate.
- Stanford AI has indicated they will have some programs to demo.
- Utah Tony Hearn will have his REDUCE program to demo, Barry Wessler plans to demo something, Harvey Greenfield has some sort of medical program.
- RAND before recent shakeup indicated interest, status now not known.
- SDC will have some natural language programs and their data management systems.
- MIT Vezza and Kahn are looking into having some hardcopy device such as Photon attached to a GE TS system. AI has some other things to demo.
- Bob has contacted a number of non net sources such as the NY Times (data base), Eastern Airlines, etc., but has no definite commitments yet.
- We at ARC will of course have a number of things to demonstrate.

This ARPANET demo is the only show at the conference. Larry Roberts has invited the ASIS people over for Thurs afternoon.

The TIP has at this time never been tested with 64 terminals, but they are going to be putting as many terminals on as possible during July and testing the terminals to be supplied for the conference....

ARPA except for Bob does not seem to have set up any budget for this show... [I have cleaned up Watson's typos.]

Many thought the whole thing would be a bust. It wasn't. The objective evidence was in RFC 413 (November 13, 1972): "Traffic Statistics (October 1972)." The internode traffic for the month was 40,711,450 packets; the daily average was 1,357,048 packets; and the average per node-day was 43,449. For the three days of "ICCC Tryout" (October 20–23), the daily average was 2,163,637 packets; the average per node-day was 67,614. For the ICCC itself (October 24–26) the daily average was 2,812,443 packets; the average per node-day was 87,889. No only had the ARPANET demo not been a bust, it was the hit of the conference. And the net had sustained a load over double its average. To give some idea of just how high the peak usage was, the December 1973 numbers (RFC 612, January 16, 1974) were a daily average of 2,382,313 packets, and an average of 52,940 packets per node-day; in June 1988, the average was 77,448,692 packets per day.

In 1986, Larry Roberts stated:

> The technical and operational success of the ARPANET quickly demonstrated to a generally skeptical world that packet switching could be organized to provide an efficient and highly responsive interactive data communications facility....
>   The ARPANET was first demonstrated publically at the first International Conference on Computer Communications (ICCC) in Washington, D.C., in October 1972. Robert Kahn of BBN organized the demonstration installing a complete ARPANET node at the conference hotel with about 40 active terminals permitting access to dozens of computers all over the United States. This public demonstration was, for many (if not most) of the ICCC attendees, proof that packet switching really worked.... The network provided highly reliable service to thousands of attendees during the entire duration of the conference. [Roberts 1988, p. 150]

McKenzie told me:

> I think ICCC 72 was a seminal event in two ways:
>   First, it convinced a lot of people that packet networking was real. They came to scoff and they went away believers. I remember overhearing a hallway conversation the first evening in which Phil Enslow, who I think was a Colonel at

the time, telling someone that ARPA was going to fall on its face. By the end of the conference I believe Phil was a packet network booster, or became one soon after.

Second, the organizational meeting of the International Network Working Group (INWG) took place at ICCC 72. It was the first time representatives of the ARPANET, the British National Physical Laboratory (NPL) networking group, and the French CYCLADES project had been together in one room. By the end of ICCC 72 there was INWG (later to become IFIP Working Group 6.1), and Vint Cerf was elected/appointed Chairperson.

I DO NOT think that ICCC 72 was very important from a technical point of view. I don't think it forced the development of any new capabilities, protocols, or applications. It gave the members of the ARPANET community a chance to show off and be proud of themselves, but I don't think it forged any NEW bonds—I think the bonds had already developed.

Finally, Kahn told me: "The ARPANET demonstration at the ICCC conference was a major milestone in the development of packet switching. It convincingly demonstrated the concept in a realistic network environment and was the driving force in getting the research community to connect their machines to the network and use it."

Documents

Kahn had mentioned the need for documents to enable the naive user to take part in the public demonstration at ICCC. Net hosts had, of course, documents of their own. For example, on April 30, 1971, Harvard had produced a "Preliminary User's Guide to the ARPA Network." It was four pages long and began:

1   Overview
The socket connection is viewed as a device and setting up a connection is analogous to mounting a disk pack or, in

the 10/50 system, to assigning a logical name to a device. The user establishes a connection (via the UUO given below) and performs normal I/O, including file manipulations (initially not implemented). The connection is permanent for the life of the user's job (unless it is explicitly closed). The user interface to the network is a pseudo-device labelled an "IMP." Each IMP is capable of a transmit and/or a receive socket connection. The IMP has been constructed to resemble as much as possible the device types on the PDP-10 timesharing system. Thus existing programs can be expected to work over the network.

2   Implementation

2A   NCP Interface

2A1 The user interfaces with the NCP via a single UUO....

For the ICCC 72, a real handbook was put together for the "naive" users to employ in running the demos. It was 62 pages, called "Scenarios for using the ARPANET at the International Conference on Computer Communication, Washington, D.C., October 24–26, 1972." The introduction was by Bob Metcalfe. There were 20 different scenarios.

Nearly two decades later, books dedicated to "users" and "new users" of the Internet began appearing. By late 1994, there were over 150 of them. The need foreseen by Kahn in 1972 was finally being filled.

NIC 11863

SCENARIOS

for using the

ARPANET

at the

INTERNATIONAL CONFERENCE ON COMPUTER COMMUNICATION

Washington, D.C.
October 24–26, 1972

ARPA Network Information Center
Stanford Research Institute
Menlo Park, California 94025

FIGURE 6.3   Title Page of ICCC '72 *Scenarios*

Diversion 3

Arpa Network Working Group   Bob Metcalfe (PARC-MAXC)
Request for Comments: 602   Dec 1973
NIC #21021

"The Stockings Were Hung by the Chimney with Care"

The ARPA Computer Network is susceptible to security violations for at
least the three following reasons:

(1) Individual sites, used to physical limitations on machine access,
have not yet taken sufficient precautions toward securing their systems
against unauthorized remote use. For example, many people still use
passwords which are easy to guess: their first names, their initials,
their host name spelled backwards, a string of characters which are
easy to type in sequence (e.g. ZXCVBNM).

(2) The TIP allows access to the ARPANET to a much wider audience than
is thought or intended. TIP phone numbers are posted, like those
scribbled hastily on the walls of phone booths and men's rooms. The TIP
required no user identification before giving service. Thus, many
people, including those who used to spend their time ripping off Ma
Bell, get access to our stockings in a most anonymous way.

(3) There is lingering affection for the challenge of breaking
someone's system. This affection lingers despite the fact that everyone
knows that it's easy to break systems, even easier to crash them.

All of this would be quite humorous and cause for raucous eye winking
and elbow nudging, if it weren't for the fact that in recent weeks at
least two major serving hosts were crashed under suspicious
circumstances by people who knew what they were risking; on yet a third
system, the system wheel password was compromised — by two high school
students in Los Angeles no less.

We suspect that the number of dangerous security violations is larger
than any of us know is growing. You are advised not to sit "in hope
that Saint Nicholas would soon be there."

Chapter 7

Packet Radio, Packet Satellite, and Ethernet

Important early developments in the nature of packet switching and networking.

There were a number of other interesting projects going on in the early 1970s, two of them sponsored by ARPA in the early 1970s: packet radio and satellite transmission.

ALOHA and Packet Radio

In 1970 Norman Abramson of the University of Hawaii delivered a paper at the AFIPS conference on "The ALOHA System." ALOHA was a packet *radio* system, connecting the seven campuses of the University of Hawaii (on four islands) at 9600 bps. It was a broadcast system which allowed simple dynamic allocation of the channel with checksums and positive acknowledgements. It was based on the principle of every site broadcasting whenever it wanted to. At those times when one and only one site wanted to broadcast, this was fine, with the packets transmitted being received correctly. But whenever there was a conflict, no packet would get through with a valid checksum and all packets would be ignored. This (obviously) reduced the bandwidth tremendously. Basically, this was a Star network.

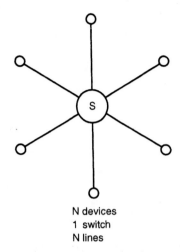

N devices
1 switch
N lines

FIGURE 7.1   Star Network

A far more mobile version was described by Larry Roberts in a paper at AFIPS 1972, "Extension of Packet Communication Technology to a Hand Held Personal Terminal." The system that Roberts described was to have a high-powered central station communicating to small (personal) radios. When a similar system was actually built several years later, it was more slanted to the needs of the US Army— survivability and rapid deployment. The packet radio research was focussed on a hierarchical store-and-forward system, with radios also capable of acting as repeaters.

At the National Computer Conference in 1975 Bob Kahn, who had moved from BBN to ARPA, summed up the possible uses of packet radio:

- personal radio terminals
- cable TV [two-way cable systems]
- computer architecture [wireless connection of devices]
- rapid deployment [to a work site]
- frequency management

Again, an ARPAnaut was way ahead of his time.

Ethernet

Robert M. Metcalfe had been a brilliant student at Harvard. His dissertation, as noted earlier, can still be read for its content, though it was not accepted initially by the Harvard committee as lacking in "analytic content." Metcalfe was "rescued" by Steve Crocker (then at ARPA), who took him off to Hawaii where he made valuable contributions to ALOHA. It was during his time in Hawaii that he took the idea of the multi-access channel of ALOHANET and applied it to coaxial cable at vastly higher speeds. The thesis was accepted after he added some equations. But it was the notion of doing packet switching at high speed on a coaxial cable that was developed by him and by David Boggs at Xerox: Ethernet was the result. It was a three megabit/second experiment that worked by using shared communication channels: The various sources of traffic contended with one another for access to these channels in such a way that packet loss was more than a mere possibility. It was a "best-effort" system.

In 1978 this system was standardized by Xerox, Intel and DEC. Ethernet consists of a coaxial cable with a maximum length of 500m. It can be extended by using repeaters as long as there are no more than two repeaters between machines. The original 3Mbps was been upgraded to a 10Mbps broadcast bus. All stations share one channel; all stations receive every transmission. Transceivers don't filter what goes where (as routers do), but the host interface between the computer bus and the transceiver does. It is called a best-effort system because no information on delivery status is supplied to the sender.

At the same time, David J. Farber at the University of California, Irvine, was working on the token ring, called DCS. The token ring requires hosts to be connected in a one-way ring topology, employing an accessing method called "token passing." The token ring achieves "fair" access by having machines take turns in using the ring. At a given moment, only one machine holds a "token" which permits it to send a packet. After a machine sends a packet, it passes the token to the next machine, which is thus enabled to send a packet. If a machine has no packet to send, it passes the token. The Cambridge—*Orange Book*—protocols for token rings only appeared in 1982. (Though it is possible to use token-passing on an Ethernet, it is simpler to use it on a system where the topology of the physical connections determines the sequence.)

SATNET

ALOHA was interesting, however, to the BBN group and to Bob Metcalfe, Larry Roberts, Len Kleinrock, and others. If the ARPANET were to reach US (Military) installations in Europe and in the Pacific region as well as naval vessels at sea, satellite communications would have to be used. A series of privately circulated "ARPA Satellite System Notes" (known as "ASS Notes") spoke of partitioning the ALOHA channel into "'slots' and adding the constraint that packet transmission must start at the beginning of a slot." This "Slotted ALOHA" doubled the capacity of the system. However, all attempts at raising capacity to over 0.36 of the bandwidth increased the delay.

Employing satellites yielded the benefits of serving a wide geographic area—including air- and seaborne users and rapid deployment. It also meant "shared-channel" networking. "However, satellite channel capacity is a relatively scarce resource, and this method of use is quite inefficient. Point-to-point satellite link technology allocates the entire bandwidth of a satellite channel to what appears to end-user applications as a long-delay, full-duplex circuit." [McKenzie and Walden 1991, p. 363]

A group at BBN (Crowther, Rettberg, Walden, Ornstein, and Heart) also studied systems in which slots in the channel "are dynamically allocated on the basis of requests by the nodes." It was called CPODA, or contention, priority-oriented dynamic assignment of capacity, in jargon; they ended up with a satellite system called "Reservation-ALOHA," or R-ALOHA.

Packets arrive for transmission to the satellite and are placed in a queue. A slot arriving from the satellite is marked one of **Empty** (transmit a packet with a probability which is proportional to the length of the queue but less than would cause excessive collisions), **Mine** (transmit a packet in this slot if there is a packet to transmit) or **Other** (do not transmit a packet in this slot). This produces a "cyclic utilization of the channel in which the period of the cycle is equal to the round trip delay to the satellite." The paper was delivered at the Sixth Hawaii International Conference on System Sciences in January 1973. Cerf and Sunshine delivered a paper on gateways at the next Hawaii conference. By May a satellite link to Hawaii had been established from an IMP at Ames in Mountain View, California, to a TIP at the University of Hawaii. By September 1973, the TIP at SDAC was linked to NORSAR in Kjeller, Norway, and through it to a TIP in London via a dedicated line. [RFC 588 (October 29, 1973, by Adrian V. Stokes, UKICS) begins: "The London node of the ARPANET has been on the Net (Address 42) since early September. It consists of a TIP (Address 170) and, at present, a local HOST (0), a PDP-9 which front-ends the Rutherford High Energy Laboratory 360/195 located 60 miles from London and connected to it by a 2.4Kbps line."]

The London TIP was in Peter Kirstein's lab at University College London. He told me that Larry Roberts had told Davies that the UK should link up with ARPA. But at that time the general political tenor was that with the advent of the Common Market, connection with Europe was good, but with the US it was bad. "Donald couldn't get tough," Kirstein said. "So I did. It wasn't much money. Two of the five directors of BT agreed to supply the line between London and Norway, but the SRC [Science Research Council] nearly torpedoed it: the SRC sent a cable to the director of ARPA who responded that he'd never heard of it. The SRC gave me no funding. Davies gave me as much as he could: £5000. But the UK had established the VAT in 1971, and when the TIP arrived in 1973, the government had slapped a £6000 VAT on it. We couldn't afford to pay, so I fought. Finally, in 1976 there was ministerial intervention. The Treasury then decided that the machine was held for the US, not imported to the UK, and thus free of VAT." Kirstein laughed.

"From 1973 till 1985 I got a small sum from the Ministry of Defence to maintain the line to the DoD. But BT kept control."

In 1977, Sunil Das, who had been teaching mathematics at City University, London, was hired as a researcher by Kirstein. He went to Trinity College Dublin in September 1977 to a European Community networking workshop. "I met Michel Gien and Hubert Zimmermann," he told me. "Morris Sloman was there, too. We talked about CYCLADES and the EPSS as well as PDP-9s and TENEX." (See Chapter 8.) The next year (1978), Das went to the ISI in Marina del Rey for a workshop ("My first trip to the USA and the only thing I saw was meeting rooms and the inside of a Japanese restaurant," he complained to me.)

Das then travelled to the Bay Area, where he visited SRI in Menlo Park and spoke to Ray Tomlinson, who was visiting from BBN at that time. UCL had been having trouble implementing the MOS. "Ray helped me with the implementation," he said. "We were sitting in a bar and he diagrammed how I could get the LSI-11 to talk to itself—as though there was someone at the other end." Tomlinson had heard that the first topless bar was still operating in San Francisco and wanted to tell people at BBN that he had been there. So he took Das in tow. "He drew on a cocktail napkin. It had to do with reverse byte ordering 0-7 and 8-15 rather than 15-8 and 7-0. He also told me how to get the hardware to work. 'Just do this wiring diagram,' he told me."

At least he saw more than he had in Los Angeles. I never asked about the topless bar.

For Department of Defense reasons, the maps from 1975 through 1983 carry the legend: "This map does not show ARPA's experimental satellite connections." (I have it on good authority that this was really because DCA didn't operate the packet satellite links.) However, SATNET was used from 1975 to 1989 to interconnect research institutions in the US, the UK, Norway, Italy, and Germany. Originally, this was a single 64Kbps channel, but it was expanded to two parallel (but independently-scheduled) 64Kbps channels. Finally, from 1980 to 1989, the ARPA Wideband Net served 10 continental US sites using a 3Mbps channel. It supported experiments in videoconferencing, which required greater bandwidth than the ARPANET could supply.

The original program plan had stated that once the "experiment" was complete, a common carrier would be asked to take over the network. Larry Roberts still wanted to do this in 1972, when the Office of Telecommunications Policy of the White House wrote a letter to ARPA urging them to divest the network to private industry. The IPTO contracted Paul Baran and his colleagues at Cabledata Associates for help in figuring out the transfer (Cerf was consulting at Cabledata at that time). Between April 1973 and January 1974, the study took place and a final report was issued (January 14, 1974), but the appeal had gone from the idea and (after a lot of matchmaking) there was a memorandum of agreement finally signed in March 1975, calling for a transfer beginning on July 1 (with a six-month phaseover). In January 1976, DCA actually was doing the day-to-day management of the network.

Part 3

1978   UUCP invented at AT&T Bell Laboratories by Mike Lesk.

1979   USENET invented by Truscott, Ellis and Bellovin, mimicking
            the ARPANET mailing lists.

1980   The ISO-OSI Reference Model is published.

1981   BITNET created by Ira Fuchs, starts to connect IBM com-
            puter centers worldwide, using mostly 9600 bps leased lines,
            and delivering mail and other services.

            CSNET established to provide ARPANET-like services to
            computer science departments without ARPANET access.

            Teletel, commonly known as Minitel after the terminals it
            uses, established by France Telecom throughout France.

Chapter 8

Europe and Japan in the '70s

The beginnings of networking elsewhere in the world.

Though I mentioned Davies, Scantlebury and the work at the NPL, as well as that of Pouzin and his colleagues in France, earlier, it is important to recognize that the US was not the only place that networking efforts were proceeding in the late 1960s and the early 1970s. This chapter will be devoted to a brief attempt at describing those efforts.

France

The French government's Delegation a l'Informatique initiated a prototype network project in 1972, handing coordination off to IRIA, the predecessor of INRIA (l'Institut National de Recherche en Informatique et Automatique). Called CYCLADES, after the group of Southern Aegean islands, the system had a subnet (called CIGALE, or grasshopper). CYCLADES had its first public demonstration in November 1973, at which time there were three hosts and a packet switch. File transfer, remote job entry and inter-user communication were demonstrated. The following February, CIGALE had four hosts and three packet switches, and there were seven packet switches in June 1974. The next month, four terminal concentrators were installed. Louis Pouzin [1982] gives the date of last quarter of 1974 for the initial operation of

CYCLADES. Prior to then, at the 1st European Workshop on Computer Networks in Arles (April–May 1973), Pouzin gave a paper on architectures and components, which clearly gives full credit to both Davies and to the ARPANET. The paper appeared as International Network Working Group (INWG) Note #49 [this was one of several series totally separate from the RFCs].

Pouzin had visited Project MAC at MIT in the mid-1960s. In fact, he is the originator of the term "shell" for the command interpreter used in CTSS, Multics, and Unix. He (and Roger Scantlebury) had spent a good deal of time at BBN, too. The protocol layering later used in OSI clearly originates from these visits—and Walden's and Padlipsky's ideas.

As has been remarked, CYCLADES took a very different path from that of the ARPANET. The early ARPANET attempted to provide as many services as possible for its hosts and failed (or fell short) in several cases; CYCLADES went in the direction of making things as simple as possible for CIGALE, putting the burden on its hosts. Where

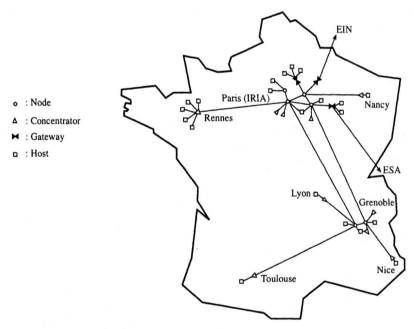

o : Node
Δ : Concentrator
⋈ : Gateway
◻ : Host

MAP 5   CYCLADES (Adapted from Pouzin 1982, p. 258)

the ARPANET worked on the "virtual circuit" approach (internally), CIGALE used the "datagram" approach so that the communications subnetwork didn't provide flow control. The ARPANET Host/IMP interface was datagram. In some ways, CYCLADES was a high-speed electronic postal system, rather than a switched circuit system. (Dave Walden told me he had asked Pouzin why CYCLADES hadn't just adopted the ARPA system. "Pouzin said that if they did, it would be adopted worldwide and we [ARPANET and BBN] would get the credit; but if they did something different, [Walden gave a very French shrug] who knew who might get the credit.")

The project had a rocky financial road: Funding difficulties caused all but three of the packet switches to be lost in February 1975, though several of the concentrators were converted to host machines (both were based on MITRA-15 computers). As Quarterman points out [1990, p. 149], "The most notable *missing* service was electronic mail. The communications subnet, *CIGALE*, was actually operational only intermittently until early 1976... The network grew to 20 hosts... *CIGALE* was arranged as a closely connected graph..."

In August 1974 a connection was established to the NPL. In October 1975, one with the European Space Agency in Rome was added; and in June 1976, one to the new European Informatics Network (EIN), about which more below.

Perhaps the most important contribution of CYCLADES was its host-level protocols, which became the basis for the flawed ISO-OSI (Open Systems Interconnection) model. The CIGALE datagrams were swept away by the virtual circuits of RCP and X.25.

At about the same time, the French PTT began RCP (Reseau Communication par Paquet). In INWG Note #67, a paper by Remy Despres and P. Guinaudeau for ICCC 1974 outlined this "data transmission service." At that time it comprised "three switching computers and three time-division multiplexors in six different towns spread over the country." The six sites were Bordeaux, Rennes, Paris, Lille, Lyon, and Marseille. Paris, Rennes, and Lyon were connected in a triangle, with each of the other sites connected to one of them. The sides of the triangle were connected by two 9600 bps lines each; the other sites were connected at 4800 bps as were customers' computers. Transmissions were based on the establishment of virtual circuits. Despres was later involved in the X.25 network-interface specification and RCP became Transpac, the French X.25 service.

Germany

The earliest networking experiments in Germany appear to have taken place at the Hahn-Meitner Institute in Berlin. Instituted in 1974, the first version of HMI-NET lasted till 1976, when it was superseded by HMI-NET2 (1976–1979). Professor Karl Zander was one of HMI-NET's original proponents. He was later a motive force for COSINE ("Cooperation for Open Systems Interconnection in Europe," 1987), created to form a market for OSI, and TUBKOM, a European fiber-optic network to run at 100Mbps or faster.

HMI-NET1 was also succeeded in 1976 by BERNET—connecting the Technical University of Berlin, the Free University of Berlin, the Konrad-Zuse-Zentrum fuer Informationstechnik Berlin, and the Bundesanstalt fuer Materialpruefung—two CDC Cyber 180s, a Cray X-MP/24 and several VAXes. This was succeeded by BERNET2 (1979–1982) and several other versions.

Japan

At the 7th Hawaii International Conference on System Sciences (January 8–10, 1974), Juro Oizumi gave a paper on "Plans for a Japanese University Computer Network." It appeared as INWG Note #66, January 1974. In this all-too-brief paper, Oizumi discussed TECNET, the experimental internal network at Tokyo University, and KUIPNET, the Kyoto University inhouse network. He also mentioned Tohoku University's participation in ALOHA and the remote time-sharing terminals connected to Tohoku's computer center. The immediate plan was to internetwork four university centers: Tohoku (north of Tokyo), Tokyo, and Kyoto and Osaka (both west and south of Tokyo).

United Kingdom

In addition to the work of Davies and Barber at the NPL, the British post office (GPO) did extensive work on a packet switching network. Work on the Experimental Packet-Switching Service (EPSS) began in the early 1970s, and the network was open for use in mid 1975. Several papers were published (in the *Post Office Electrical Engineering Journal* in 1974–1977) and a customer brochure was published. Vint Cerf circulated the final specification (which he had received from Roy Bright, the Post Office's Head of Market Studies) as INWG Protocol Note #1 (October 28, 1974). But the EPSS preceded the first version of X.25 and its protocols were incompatible. The EPSS was closed in 1980.

In the first paper on EPSS, Belton and Smith (1974) state that "the original concept is based on work carried out by a research organization in the U.S.A." They cite Baran's RAND reports. Initially, the EPSS was set up for three exchanges: London, Manchester, and Glasgow. The post office decided that rather than have equipment on the various customers' premises, the customer would have a virtual terminal and an acoustic modem, and all the switching equipment would reside in the post office. As many of the initial customers were university computer centers, this proved to be an unsatisfactory decision.

It did, however, lead to a network set up by the Science Research Council (later the Science and Engineering Research Council, hence SERCnet). SERCnet was initially based on EPSS, but moved over to X.25 in 1977. The switching centers for SERCnet were in Rutherford Appleton Laboratory, Daresbury Laboratory, the University of London, Edinburgh University, and Cambridge University. At the same time, the Computer Board for Universities and Research Councils set up a Network Unit (1976). SERC and the Computer Board merged everything on April 1, 1979 into the Joint Network Team: JANET—the Joint Academic Network was born.

EIN

In 1968 the scientific research committee of the European Economic Community (EEC) listed "Informatics" as an important "international project." The following year, COST (the cooperative scientific and technical body) set up study groups, of which number eleven was "a pilot informatics Network." On November 23, 1971, an agreement to set up a multi-government project was signed.

By 1973 technical objectives and specifications were defined. The next year tenders were invited, and a contract was awarded to build a

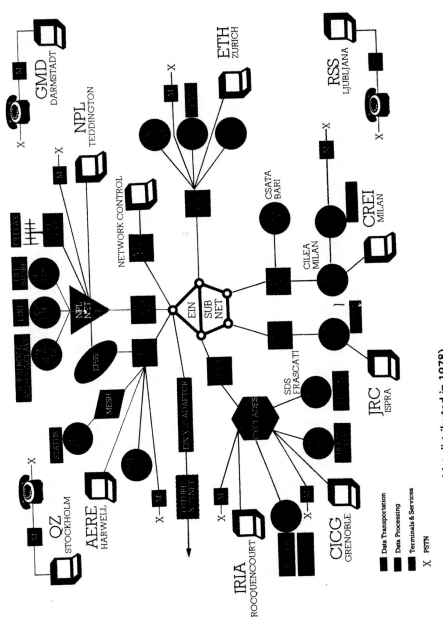

MAP 6   EIN (From pamphlet distributed in 1978)

packet switching subnetwork of five centers. Development and testing went on through 1975, with a great deal of discussion of interconnection problems. In 1976 the computers were connected. During 1977 extensive work was done on high level protocols and on Wednesday, April 5, 1978, there was a public presentation concurrently in the various centers. The European Informatics Network (EIN) never went further. The primary centers in Teddington (NPL), Paris (IRIA), Zurich (ETH, the Technical University), Ispra (JRC), and Milan (CREI) were both the beginning and the end. On a software level, the UK "Coloured Books" protocols grew out of this.

Diversion 4

Network Working Group   B. Miller
Request for Comments: 1097   CMU-NetDev
                                                      1 April 1989

TELNET SUBLIMINAL-MESSAGE Option

Status of this Memo

This RFC specifies a standard for the Internet community. Hosts on the
Internet that display subliminal messages within the Telnet protocol
are expected to adopt and implement this standard. Distribution of this
memo is unlimited.

1. Command name and code.

   SUBLIMINAL-MESSAGE 257

2. Command meanings.

   IAC WILL SUBLIMINAL-MESSAGE

The sender of this command REQUESTS permission to, or confirms that it
will, display subliminal messages.

   IAC WONT SUBLIMINAL-MESSAGE

The sender of this command REFUSES to display subliminal messages.

   IAC DO SUBLIMINAL-MESSAGE

The sender of this command REQUESTS that the receiver, or grants the
receiver permission to, display subliminal messages.

   IAC DONT SUBLIMINAL-MESSAGE

The sender of this command DEMANDS that the receiver not display
subliminal messages.

   IAC SB SUBLIMINAL-MESSAGE <16-bit value> <16-bit value> <string> IAC
   SE

The sender specifies a message to be subliminally displayed by the
remote host. If the client has agreed (via the standard WILL WONT DO
DONT mechanism) to display subliminal messages, it must accept this
subnegotiation and attempt to display the message string on the users

console for the specified duration and continue to do so at fixed
intervals until another SUBLIMINAL-MESSAGE subnegotiation is received.
The position and rendering of the message of implementation dependent.

The first 16-bit value specifies the duration of the message in
milliseconds. It is sent MSB first. The second 16-bit value specifies
the frequency with which the message is displayed. It represents the
number of seconds between displays and is also sent MSB first. The
final parameter is the message itself.

The syntax for this subnegotiation is:

```
IAC SB SUBLIMINAL-MESSAGE
   DURATION[1] DURATION[0]
   FREQUENCY[1] FREQUENCY[0]
   MESSAGE_STRING
   IAC SE
```

As required by the Telnet protocol, any occurence of 255 in the
subnegotiation must be doubled to distinguish it from the IAC character
(which has a value of 255).

3. Default.

   WONT SUBLIMINAL-MESSAGE

   DONT SUBLIMINAL-MESSAGE

i.e., subliminal messages will not be displayed.

4. Motivation for the option

Frequently the use of "Message of the day" banners and newsletters is
insufficient to convince stubborn users to upgrade to the latest
version of Telnet. Some users will use the same outdated version for
years. I ran across this problem trying to convince people to use the
REMOTE-FLOW-CONTROL Telnet option. These users need to be gently
"persuaded."

5. Description and implementation notes.

The quality of the client implementation will depend on its ability to
display and erase text strings in a small amount of time. The current
implementation at CMU takes into acount terminal line speed, advanced
video capabilities, and screen phospher persistence when calculating
how long to wait before erasing a message.

While it is permitted for the client to display the message text "in-line," best ·results at obtained by printing the message at the top or side of console screen where it will just catch the corner of the user's visual field.

A version is currently under development at CMU to display the message using morse-code over the keyboard caps-lock LED.

6. Examples

In the following example all numbers are in decimal notation.

1. Server suggests and client agrees to use SUBLIMINAL-MESSAGE.

   (Server sends) IAC DO SUBLIMINAL-MESSAGE
   (Client sends) IAC WILL SUBLIMINAL-MESSAGE
   (Server sends) IAC SB SUBLIMINAL-MESSAGE 0 5 0 20 "Use VMS" IAC SE

   [The server is "suggesting" that the user employ a stable operating system, not an unreasonable request...]

The client should immediately begin displaying the message and should continue to do so at regular intervals.

2. Server preempts previous subliminal message.

   (Server sends) IAC SB SUBLIMINAL-MESSAGE 0 5 0 20 "Go home" IAC SE

The client should now no longer display the previous message and should immediately begin displaying the new one.

3. Server has messed with user enough for one day.
   (Server sends) IAC SB SUBLIMINAL-MESSAGE 0 0 0 0 "" IAC SE

The client must cease display of any subliminal messages.

7. Acknowledgements.

We do things just a little sneakier here at CMU.

Chapter 9

Mail

The application that hadn't been thought of.

On every system that followed CTSS (Fernando Corbato's Compatible Time Sharing System) over 30 years ago, users were able to communicate with other users on the same machine. In fact there were a fair number of mail systems on various pieces of hardware.

Ray Tomlinson was working in BBN's computer center when the SDS-940 was traded in for a PDP-10. The result of the work that he and others did (under the leadership of Ted Strollo) was the TENEX operating system, the rights to which DEC purchased from BBN. However, when BBN acquired first a second PDP-10 and then IMP #5, the notion of sending messages arose. By July 17, 1970, internal mail was possible. Within a few months, Tomlinson had written a Network Control Program that would open connections and send them over the local net (machine A to IMP to machine B). But this meant sending from one machine and running over to the other. So a daemon-like program was written to govern the push-pull. Within a "week or two" it was possible to copy files from A to B and B to A. "I then made that file be a mailfile," Tomlinson said. "It was possible to open and append and put things into other people's mailboxes." It was the first electronic mail between two machines.

Tomlinson and others at BBN gave the program to sites on the net that had PDP-10s running TENEX (like Utah); soon it was adapted to the IBM 360, the SDS, and the Sigma machines. It was inserted into TENEX as the command MAIL and rode as an extension of FTP.

Thus, with the advent of distant connectivity, the notion of computer-mediated communication with someone on another computer (or a broadcast message to a number of others) was a popular one. However, it was not among the first problems. The Network Working Group, for example, met from May 16 through May 19, 1971. The minutes (by Heafner of RAND; RFC 164) show that there were 66 attendees from 34 sites (many of which were not yet connected to the ARPANET). Mail was not among the topics minuted.

But mail was important, as was demonstrated by the flurry of discussion the protocol went through, once the application had spread. Only two months after the May meeting, Watson at SRI issued "Mail Box Protocol" (RFC 196; July 20, 1971). This was obsoleted by his "Version 2" (RFC 221; August 27, 1971), which was commented upon by Alex McKenzie (RFC 224; September 14, 1971), and then made obsolete by a group of authors (including both Watson and McKenzie) in RFC 278 (November 17, 1971). And there the issue rested until Michael Kudlick of SRI called a meeting "to discuss a network mail system" (RFC 453; February 7, 1973). The meeting summary appeared as RFC 469 (March 8, 1973); Abhay Bhushan's comprehensive summary of the issues was RFC 475 (March 6) and RFC 479 (March 8) contained "what the NIC would like to see included in the File Transfer Protocol for Network Mail purposes." There were 15 people at the February meeting: Bob Kahn (ARPA); Nancy Mimno and Ray Tomlinson (BBN); Alan Bomberger and Wayne Hathaway (Ames); Charles Irby, Dave Hopper, Jim White, and Kudlick (SRI); Abhay Bhushan and Rajendra Kanodia (MIT); Crocker and Postel (UCLA); Mark Krilanovich (UCSB); and L. Peter Deutsch (Xerox PARC). Among other things, the group decided upon a new mail command and the subcommands:

TO	user@host
FROM	a return address for notification as well as a clearcut id
AUTHOR	providing for multiple authors
TITLE	the 'subject' of the mail
TEXT	The text of the mail message.

other "commands" were ACKNOWLEDGEMENT, RECORDED, and TYPE.

Both Kahn and Bhushan raised questions and problems. The most important thing was that the mail system was to be based on FTP—the File Transfer Protocol with which the users were familiar. As Eric Allman pointed out to me, "originally, mail was sent as a file transfer.... This was the protocol that was used before SMTP." Mike Padlipsky, (the author of "What is 'Free'?" [RFC 491], and many other RFCs), told me: "Originally, netmail (later known as 'e-mail') was sent via an FTP command called MAIL. In order to let this happen on systems that needed to create a process (rather than have the Network Daemon 'receive' the mail, say), an agreed-on USER NETMAIL, PASS NETMAIL command pair would conventionally be offered... "

It should be pointed out that the "ftpmail" of Paul Vixie that is distributed by DEC is unrelated to the original FTP mail. Vixie, who admits to knowing of the original FTP mail when he wrote his, told me:

> I wrote ftpmail as a simple hack back when my non-connected friends were driving me crazy with endless requests to ftp, uuencode, split, and mail things. It evolved a lot and ultimately so many friends were using it that I had to move it from my home machine (56K) to decwrl (my work machine) to barrnet. Each friend told two friends. Now it does about 1GB a day and has a machine dedicated to it.

Quarterman has pointed out to me that Vixie's was the inverse of the original FTP mail, which was "bag-on-the-side mail through **ftp**...Vixie's thing calls **ftp** through mail." There was a parallel system done on a BITNET machine at Princeton. Over the next few years, mail was a frequent topic of discussion. If we look at the RFCs alone, we can comprehend what the discussions must have been like. RFC 458 (R. Bressler and R. Thomas, February 20, 1973) was "Mail Retrieval via FTP"; it proposed two new FTP commands called ReaDMailFile and ReaDMail.

RFC 475 (Bhushan; March 6, 1973) was "FTP and the Network Mail System" and described Bhushan's understanding of the results of the Network Mail System meeting and its implications for FTP.

RFC 524 (J. White; June 13, 1973) was "A Proposed Mail Protocol," which actually proposed a specification for handling mail in the ARPA network.

Dave Crocker and Jon Postel then wrote RFC 539 (July 7, 1973), which was in response to RFC 524. Crocker and Postel felt that while the protocol is extremely rich, there were some minor and some major problems.

White responded in RFC 555 and in RFC 577 (October 18), Dave Crocker suggested interpretations for urgency values, based on arguments presented in RFC 555. Bhushan, Ken Pogran (MIT), Tomlinson, and White had issued RFC 561 (September 5, 1973) to standardize "Network Mail Headers." Rather than go to lengths to explain their suggestion, I will merely give their example:

> From: White at SRI-ARC
>
> Date: 24 JUL 1973 1527-PDT
>
> Subject: Multi-Site Journal Meeting Announcement
>
> NIC: 17996
>
> At 10 AM Wednesday 25-JULY there will be a meeting to discuss a Multi-Site Journal in the context of the Utility. Y'all be here.

The Network Information Center issued a "Mail Protocol" document; in RFC 630 (April 10, 1974) J. Sussman made a suggestion concerning mail reliability, in August 1976, D. Crocker wrote RFC 720 concerning "Address specification syntax," and, in November 1977, Crocker et al. issued their "Format for ARPA network text messages" (RFC 733), which remained the standard until RFC 822 was issued in August 1982.

Let's retreat five years to look at the protocols and their development again.

Chapter 10

Protocol Problems

The limitations of the early protocols are recognized.

The Network Control Program that became the Network Control Protocol just wasn't good enough. In January 1973, Cerf gave a paper on the Protocols in Honolulu. Seven months after the ICCC demonstration and while the ARPANET was under 25 sites, the INWG met in New York. Present were Eric Aupperle (Merit), Vint Cerf (Stanford), Bob Kahn (BBN), Peter T. Kirstein (University College London), Bob Metcalfe (Xerox PARC), Roger Scantlebury (NPL), Dave Walden (BBN), and Hubert Zimmermann (CYCLADES). Following the meeting, Gary R. Grossman (University of Illinois) and Gerard LeLann (CYCLADES) added their thoughts. The international nature of the group—with participation of both the NPL and CYCLADES teams—made this an important meeting.

The result was a document by Cerf and Kahn, "Towards Protocols for Internetwork Communication" [INWG Note #39; September 13, 1973]. One of the problems that had arisen in the ARPANET concerned the very heterogeneity of the machinery that had been the driving force in 1968–1969. Cerf and Kahn, after an extensive discussion, introduce the *Transmission Control Program*—a TCP different from the one we now think of—within each HOST, "which handles the transmission and acceptance of messages on behalf of the processes it serves. The TCP is in turn served by one or more packet switches connected to the HOST in which the TCP resides. Processes which want to communicate present messages to the TCP for transmission, and TCPs

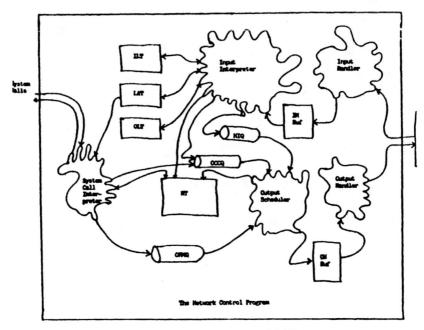

FIGURE 10.1 Network Control Protocol (From RFC 048)

deliver incoming messages to the appropriate destination processes."
They go on to describe "a simple but very powerful and flexible protocol" and then implementation issues. The document concludes with:
"The next important step is to produce a detailed specification of the
protocol so that some initial experiments with it can be performed."

Before going further, I think it important to point out that the
protocols in use in the 1970s had two things in common: (1) They established path conventions, and (2) they defined path control procedures. These last "establish a virtual communications medium
between the communicating entities; this medium has certain desir-
able characteristics which may not be possessed by the physical
medium." [Walden and McKenzie 1979: p. 29] Moreover, the
ARPANET was built upon a foundation of cooperation: I mentioned
this earlier with regard to the evolution of protocols to *de facto* standards; accompanying this was a very important, though unenunciated
rule of thumb: Two working implementations before a "standard" was
accepted. Had the International Standards Organization considered
this, the OSI exercise would never have occurred.

Before the ARPANET, in point-to-point connections and in "star" networks, the "network" was a simple data pipe. With the advent of a variety of apparatus (terminals, front-end processors, cluster controllers, data concentrators, remote front ends), a change in both the architectural model and in the protocols was needed. Specifically, with "common user" communication networks, a new level of protocol was required. The facility was no longer a virtual data pipeline that might be tapped at two points in order to fulfill the needs of a given application. The user now had to supply addressing, for example. This, however, meant that terminals and hosts had to follow standard protocols, otherwise they wouldn't make any sense of the messages conveyed from one to another.

The following paraphrases Walden and McKenzie's excellent tutorial. In the ARPANET, a layered approach was employed: Higher-level protocols use the services of lower-level protocols. The lowest host level was the IMP-to-host protocol (specifying the electrical interface, link control, and message format). The next layer, the host/host layer, specifies methods for establishing communications paths between hosts. The Initial Connection Protocol (ICP) specifies the way a remote user "attracts the attention" of a network host. The Telecommunications Network (telnet) protocol was designed to provide terminal access remotely. The next layer consists of function-oriented protocols: the File Transfer Protocol (FTP) and Remote Job Entry (RJE). (There are other function-oriented protocols: graphics, digital speech, etc., were provided for. As early as RFC 759 [August 1980] there was a multimedia mail protocol.) And, of course, there are *ad hoc* protocols.

Among the flaws of the host/host protocol were: only one message could be traversing a connection at any one time, severely limiting bandwidth; the allocation mechanism was incremental, without a provision for resynchronization; no provision for end-to-end error control; and the connections were simplex, where full duplex connections were preferred.

It was the "desire to have a host-to-host protocol which is suitable for use in a multi-network environment, and which does not have the problems of the Arpanet host/host protocol, led to the specification of TCP" [Walden and McKenzie, p. 32].

Cerf has said that TCP was "literally a back-of-the envelope thing. I was at some conference and had time and wrote down things on the

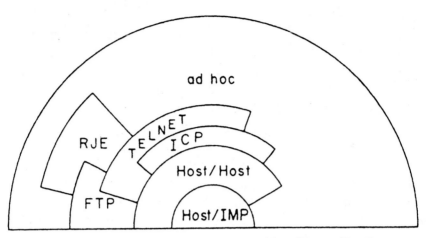

FIGURE 10.2 Layered Relationship (From D. C. Walden, "Host to Host Protocols," in *International Computer State of the Art Report No. 24* (Maidenhead, UK, 1975); with permission of the author)

back of an envelope." He said that the need to write new protocols was spurred by the fact that "we had three packet-switched networks—ARPA, packet radio, SATNET—which didn't use the same format. We had a need to encapsulate packets so that they could be put into other formats." The first result of the "desire" mentioned by Walden and McKenzie was the Cerf and Kahn draft mentioned above; the next was their paper of May 1974: "A Protocol for Packet Network Communication." In November 1974, Mike Padlipsky proposed a common command language (RFC 666, "Specification of the Unified User-Level Protocol"). This was part of the protocol revision that was to replace NCP (host-to-host) with TCP. It was a good idea, but like many others wasn't picked up. The next month, Cerf issued RFC 675, "Specification of Internet Transmission Control Program," the first detailed description of TCP. It is also the first use of "Internet" in the RFCs. Cerf told me that "Yogen Dalal, then a grad student at Stanford, was a key aide in completing this document."

The ARPANET was a network. So were CYCLADES, NPL, EIN, etc. But the real goal of all this was to enable connectivity among all of these, to begin the packet-switching network that would connect all the

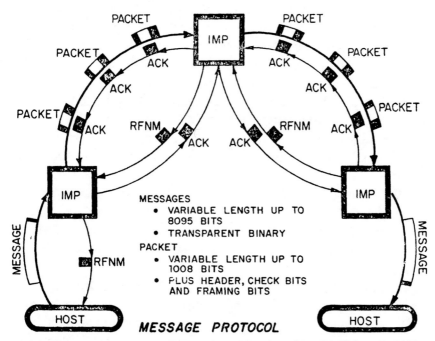

FIGURE 10.3 Message Protocol (From a presentation of D. C. Walden at AFCET (May 25, 1972); with permission of the author)

subnetworks. And the network to enable this was the Internet: the network of networks. Vint Cerf and Bob Kahn get the credit for this, with major bouquets to McKenzie, Scantlebury, Walden, and Zimmermann. (Padlipsky mentioned to me the visits of Scantlebury and Peter Kirstein to Project MAC as further instances of trans-Atlantic cross-fertilization.)

The INWG was transferred to the International Federation for Information Processing (IFIP) in 1974. Alex Curran, then chair of IFIP Technical Committee 6, and Cerf set it up as a working group (WG6.1) to consider a "universal" host-to-host protocol as well as other problems relating to the interconnection of packet networks. IFIP WG6.1 developed a proposal which was a crossing of American (TCP) and European (CYCLADES) ideas. Barely a year after they began, the "Proposal for an International End to End Protocol" by Cerf, McKenzie, Scantlebury, and Zimmermann was published in *Computer Communi-*

cation Review [January 1976, pp. 63–89]. Cerf told me that this was a "compromise protocol, which I concluded couldn't be sold to the community that had already gone through two iterations of TCP."

This proposal was based on the "concept of established, used, and cleared virtual circuits. An end-to-end 'window' mechanism handles flow and error control. The protocol also defines the concept of a logical data unit (called 'letter') which may consist of many packets. ... The IFIP proposal assumes no more than a simple datagram service from any of the interconnected networks." [Walden and McKenzie, pp. 32f.]

But even as the WG6.1 protocol was designed, it was being bypassed. The Department of Defense adopted TCP and the Consultative Committee for International Telegraphy and Telephony (CCITT) adopted yet another standard. (These developments will be discussed in later chapters.)

In April 1976, the *ARPANET PROTOCOL HANDBOOK* made its appearance. A paperbound volume of just over 300 pages, it was written for the Defense Communications Agency by Elizabeth ("Jake") Feinler and Jon Postel. It contained everything except 1822, which was too massive and, as pointed out at the beginning of its introduction, "distributed to the Liaison of each new host on the ARPANET." Postel (at that time) was at SRI, as was Jake, who told me that Engelbart had hired her to "do user guides."

The *Handbook* was divided into IMP-HOST Protocols (from 1822); Network Control Protocols (Alex McKenzie's January 1972 revision of the Host-Host Protocol); Initial Connection Protocols (Postel's version of June 1971; the Wolfe-Postel RFC 202 on deadlocks); Telnet Protocols (22 protocols and options, plus an early version of ASCII; the actual Telnet specification was dated August 1973); File Transfer Protocols (RFC 542, edited by Nancy Neigus, July 1973); Mail Protocol (NIC document 24664); Remote Job Entry Protocols; Network Graphics Protocols; and Data Configuration Protocols.

The July 1976 ARPANET map shows over 50 hosts, running IMPs, TIPs, and Pluribus IMPs, well as satellite connections to Norsar-London and to Hawaii. The first of these was connected to SDAC and the second to Ames. (The Pluribus was a BBN multiprocessor.) The network was growing fast; the protocols were increasingly inadequate. The time was ripe for rethinking.

Over the next few years, the suggestions of Kahn and Cerf were adopted by the ARPANET community. The protocols were rewritten. The notion of compromise lingered for over a decade.

Diversion 5

Network Working Group   R. Merryman (UCSD-CC)
Request for Comments: 527   6/22/73

ARPAWOCKY

Twas brillig, and the Protocols
    Did USER-SERVER in the wabe.
All mimsey was the FTP,
    And the RJE outgrabe,

Beware the ARPANET, my son;
    The bits that byte, the heads that scratch;
Beware the NCP, and shun
        the frumious system patch,

He took his coding pad in hand;
    Long time the Echo-plex he sought.
When his HOST-to-IMP began to limp
    he stood a while in thought,

And while he stood, in uffish thought,
    The ARPANET, with IMPish bent,
Sent packets through conditioned lines,
    And checked them as they went,

One-two, one-two, and through and through
    The IMP-to-IMP went ACK and NACK,
When the RFNM came, he said "I'm game,"
    And sent the answer back,

Then hast thou joined the ARPANET?
    Oh come to me, my bankrupt boy!
Quick, call the NIC! Send RFCs!
    He chortled in his joy.
Twas brillig, and the Protocols
    Did USER-SERVER in the wabe.
All mimsey was the FTP,
    And the RJE outgrabe.

                                                        D.L. COVILL
                                                        May 1973

Chapter 11

Commercialization

The first attempts at the commercialization of networking are detailed.

In 1972, Larry Roberts said that he intended to sell the U.S. government's interest in the ARPANET to commercial firms by 1974. The major corporations were skeptical as to whether computer networks could be turned "into viable economic entities" [*Datamation* 18 (April 1972) p. 43]. The divestiture didn't occur, though the ARPANET was transferred into the jurisdiction of the Defense Communications Agency in 1975. But it didn't take much for the notion that money could be made from offering networking services to get around at BBN. After trying to get the company to form a commercial network, a group of disaffected BBN employees (Lee Talbert, Ralph Alter, and Stephen Russell) left in July 1972 and formed Packet Communications Incorporated (PCI). In 1986, Ralph Alter told Simson Garfinkel:

> They [BBN] made the claim that we were all being much too impatient. That the concept was good and that BBN was planning to proceed with it... [They said] that we were not willing to wait and participate inside BBN. I don't believe that.

BBN formally incorporated Telenet Communications Incorporated in Washington, D.C., on December 16, 1974. But they had filed a number of briefs with the FCC prior to that date, including an application to establish a public packet switched network. Alter went on:

> I believe that BBN never would have formed Telenet, or at least would not have formed it anywhere near the time that

they did. It would have been years later, if ever, if we had stayed there...

On January 23, 1973, PCI petitioned the FCC for a certificate to establish a national packet switched communications network [FCC 73-1168, paragraph 1]. In reply to comments that PCI filed on April 6, 1973, it said that it believed in the concept of "open entry" for other carriers wishing to offer a value-added service [FCC 73-1168, paragraph 13]. PCI had hoped to get approval in the summer of 1973 and be transmitting data by March 1974. They received FCC approval on November 14, 1973. They were hoping for $30 million in capital. They never got it. PCI was unable to attract investors and ceased to exist in August 1975.

Telenet had petitioned the FCC on March 9, 1973 for permission to establish a packet switching network; their petition was granted on April 16, 1974. Telenet had estimated $6 million to achieve break even, but that by 1980 their revenues would be over $1 billion. Telenet managed to obtain funding from BBN, the Palmer Organization, Lehman Brothers, and Time, Inc. BBN put in $471,300 for a 42% interest. By 1977, Telenet had consumed $15 million in equity and debt capital; by 1978, it was up to $21 million. During the five years from 1973 through 1978, BBN lost money on Telenet every year. On June 13, 1979, Telenet was purchased by a wholly-owned subsidiary of GTE for 503,729 shares of GTE ($13,915,500). After BBN paid off its $3 million in debt, it retained a $10 million gain. [*BBN Annual Reports*]

Telenet's application of March 9, 1973, asked for permission to serve 18 cities, expanding to 44 cities within four years, from the FCC. They proposed using 50Kbps, 100Kbps and 1.544 Mbps links. Western Union filed a petition to deny. Telenet's petition was accepted; Western Union's was denied. In 1985, the Telenet network was locally dialable from nearly 400 US metropolitan areas and 67 countries. Western Union's opposition to Telenet was part of an ongoing scenario on the part of all the major telecommunications companies: Confronted by something new, oppose it. I will not go into the details, but only mention a few of these retrograde interventions here.

However, part of the FCC process resulted in AT&T requesting a waiver of FCC policy so that its long line service could be resold by these private networks. Telenet supported AT&T; MCI and Datran opposed it. The FCC approved the request. Early in 1976, Telenet and Graphnet (another start-up) petitioned the FCC to extend their networks from the US to the UK and beyond, as Western Union International and RCA Global Communications had done. Graphnet's petition was opposed by RCA, WUI, and ITT. Telenet's petition was opposed by RCA, WUI, and ITT. RCA's request was opposed by ITT; WUI's by ITT, AT&T, Graphnet, and Telenet. The FCC denied all the objections and granted all four petitions.

RCA then filed a petition for "Partial Reconsideration" on the grounds that the FCC had given "significant competitive advantage over RCA" to Telenet and Graphnet. The Commission rejected that, but limited the certificates: Graphnet was restricted to facsimile transmissions and Telenet to packet switched data. Next, ITT claimed that Telenet's extension to Hawaii (via the Hawaii Telephone Company) was inconsistent with the FCC's gateway policies, as applied to "international telegraph operations." The application for review was denied.

This takes us to November 30, 1978. One of the reasons for Telenet's unprofitability was the many millions in legal expenses they had as a result of the petitions by RCA, ITT, AT&T, and Western Union. On December 28, 1978, GTE and Telenet filed a joint letter with the FCC outlining GTE's proposed purchase and why FCC authorization was not required (an obvious attempt at an end run). The Commission rejected the letter. Telenet and GTE successfully went through the authorization process and six months later (June 1979) the sale was completed. [I am indebted to Simson Garfinkel for permitting me to use material from his unpublished paper and interview, posted to the com-priv (commercialization-privatization) newsgroup.]

Chapter 12

The New Protocols

TCP/IP hits stage center.

Before getting into the new protocols, it is important for readers, who have heard TCP, IP and TCP/IP bandied about to gather a bit more tutorial information.

The NWG had adopted a "layered" approach to the protocols: Higher layers use the services of lower layers. The lowest layer was the IMP-to-host protocol; the next was the host-to-host protocol. The initial connection protocol (ICP) specified the way that a user (or process) got the attention of a host; the next layer contained TELNET; and the topmost layer contained FTP and RJE (the "function-oriented" protocols). The very first use of the term "layer" that I know of is in a paper delivered by Dave Walden at an on-line conference in 1975, published that year [*International Computer State-of-the-Art Report #24* (Infotech)] and later reprinted in several anthologies [McQuillan and Cerf, *A Practical View of Computer Communication Protocols* (IEEE, 1978), for example].

Recall that the original IMPs or packet switching nodes (PSNs), could connect to up to 22 computers (hosts or terminals) by means of protocols outlined in 1822. Unfortunately, because it was a BBN *Report*, 1822 never became an industry standard. With the burst of new machines in the 1970s, it became increasingly difficult to connect new hardware to the IMPs. When, in 1976, CCITT issued the first version of X.25 (network interface specification; revised in 1980, 1984, and 1986; now also ISO 8208), ARPA adopted it (at that time there were 58 nodes in the ARPANET). X.25 is organized in a three-layer architecture: physical, frame, and packet levels [intended, post hoc, to parallel the physical, data link, and network layers of OSI]. The first version of the X.25 PSN implementation involved only the data transfer level. A number of nodes use X.25, mostly public data networks and some military and research sites, but it is not universally supported. The format of X.25 address space is given in CCITT X.121.

There was a good deal of criticism of X.25 (including Pouzin's excellent paper "Virtual circuits vs. datagrams" [*NCC 1976* Proceedings]), but my favorite criticism remains that of Padlipsky, the obstinately proud curmudgeon of the Net. (After leaving MIT, Padlipsky worked for the MITRE Corporation in Bedford, Massachusetts. He wrote a number of protocols; a large number of RFCs; and several pungent critiques. These last were collected in a slim volume *The Art of Networking Style* [1985], which remains my favorite book on the topic.) In RFC 874 ("A Critique of X.25," September 1982), Padlipsky concluded, with no apology to Seller or Yeatman: "X.25 is not a good thing."

A portion of his polemic runs:

> X.25 is not (and should not be) an "end-to-end" protocol in the sense of a Transport or Host-to-Host protocol. Yet it has several end-to-end features. These add to the space-time expense of implementation (i.e., consume "core" and CPU cycles) and reflect badly on the skill of its designers if one believes in the design principles of Layering and Least Mechanism.... X.25 is at least meant to specify an interface between a Host (or "DTE") and a comm subnet processor (or "DCE"), regardless of the ambiguity of the conceptual model about whether it constrains the CSNP [Communications Subnet Processor] "on the network side." ... Examples of mechanisms superfluous to the interface role:
>
> 1. The presence of a DTE-DTE Flow Control mechanism.
>
> 2. The presence of an "interrupt procedure" involving the remote DTE.
>
> 3. The presence of "Call user data" as an end-to-end item (i.e., as "more" than IP's Protocol field).

4. The "D bit" (unless construed strictly as a "RFNM" from the remote DCE).

5. The "Q bit" (which we find nearly incomprehensible, but which is stated to have meaning of some sort to X.29—i.e., to at least violate Layering by having a higher-level protocol depend on a lower level mechanism—and hence can't be strictly a network interface mechanism).

The final "personality problem" of X.25 is that some of its advocates claim it can and should be used as if it were a Host-Front End protocol.... Granted that with sufficient ingenuity—or even by the simple expedient of conveying the entire H-FP as data (i.e., using X.25 only to get channels to demultiplex on, and DTE-DCE flow control, with the "DCE" actually being an Outboard Processing Environment that gets its commands in the data fields of X.25 data packets)—X.25 might be used to "get at" outboard protocol interpreters, but its failure to address the issue explicitly again reflects badly on its designers' grasp of intercomputer networking issues....

X.25, then, is rather schizophrenic: It exceeds its brief as an interface protocol by pretending to be end-to-end (Host-Host) in some respects; it is by no means a full end-to-end protocol (its spec very properly insists on that point on several occasions); it's at once too full and too shallow to be a good interface; and it's poorly structured to be treated as if it were "just" an H-FP.

Many of Padlipsky's criticisms arise from the dislike he (and many others) had for the makeup of the CCITT and its committees—nearly totally representatives of national PTTs and therefore carriers of telephone circuit experience, and thus outmoded point-to-point and star networks. The problems begun here grew with the entry of the International Standards Organization into the fray.

Before getting to ISO, let me cite the (draft) Table of Contents of the 1980 *Protocol Handbook*, for it illustrates just how the US networking community forged ahead, despite the Europeans.

Network Working Group   J. Postel
Request for Comments: 774   ISI
                                                     October 1980

Obsoletes: RFC 766
Obsoletes: IEN 118

Internet Protocol Handbook
Table of Contents

The internet family of protocols is replacing the old ARPANET
protocols. To this end an Internet Protocol Handbook will be prepared
by the Network Information Center. This Handbook is tentatively planned
to be available at the end of 1980. This Internet Protocol Handbook
will closely parallel the old ARPANET Protocol Handbook, and will
primarily be a collection of existing RFCs and IENs.

Attached is the current draft table of contents for the Internet
Protocol Handbook. Any suggestions for additions should be sent to Jon
Postel (Postel@ISIF).

RFCs and IENs are public access document files and may be copied from
the Network Information Center online Library at SRI-KL via FTP using
the FTP user name ANONYMOUS and password GUEST. The IENs have pathnames
of the form "<NETINFO>IEN-nnn.TXT", and the RFCs have pathnames of the
form "<NETINFO>RFCnnn.TXT", where "nnn" is replaced by the document
number. [Note the inconsistency: IENs have a hyphen in the pathname,
RFCs don't.]

Table of Contents

Overview

```
Host Level

    User Datagram Protocol                              RFC768

    Transmission Control Protocol            IEN-129 RFC761

    Multiplexing Protocol                              IEN-90

Application Level

    Time Server Protocol                               IEN-142

    Name Server Protocol                               IEN-116

    Trivial File Transfer Protocol                     IEN-133

    Telnet Protocol                          IEN-148 RFC764

    File Transfer Protocol                   IEN-149 RFC765

    Mail Transfer Protocol                             RFC772

    Internet Message Protocol                IEN-113 RFC759

Appendices

    Assigned Numbers                                   RFC770

    Address Mappings                                   IEN-115

    Document File Format Standards                     RFC678

    Mail Header Format Standards                       RFC733
```

The Internet had succeeded the ARPANET.

Diversion 6

Network Working Group   D. Waitzman
Request for Comments: 1149   BBN STC
                                                        1 April 1990

     A Standard for the Transmission of IP Datagrams on Avian Carriers

Status of this Memo

This memo describes an experimental method for the encapsulation of IP
datagrams in avian carriers. This specification is primarily useful in
Metropolitan Area Networks. This is an experimental, not recommended
standard. Distribution of this memo is unlimited.

Overview and Rational

Avian carriers can provide high delay, low throughput, and low altitude
service. The connection topology is limited to a single point-to-point
path for each carrier, used with standard carriers, but many carriers
can be used without significant interference with each other, outside
of early spring. This is because of the 3D ether space available to the
carriers, in contrast to the 1D ether used by IEEE802.3. The carriers
have an intrinsic collision avoidance system, which increases
availability. Unlike some network technologies, such as packet radio,
communication is not limited to line-of-sight distance. Connection
oriented service is available in some cities, usually based upon a
central hub topology.

Frame Format

The IP datagram is printed, on a small scroll of paper, in hexadecimal,
with each octet separated by whitestuff and blackstuff. The scroll of
paper is wrapped around one leg of the avian carrier. A band of duct
tape is used to secure the datagram's edges. The bandwidth is limited
to the leg length. The MTU is variable, and paradoxically, generally
increases with increased carrier age. A typical MTU is 256 milligrams.
Some datagram padding may be needed.

Upon receipt, the duct tape is removed and the paper copy of the
datagram is optically scanned into a electronically transmittable form.

Discussion

Multiple types of service can be provided with a prioritized pecking
order. An additional property is built-in worm detection and

eradication. Because IP only guarantees best effort delivery, loss of a carrier can be tolerated. With time, the carriers are self-regenerating. While broadcasting is not specified, storms can cause data loss. There is persistent delivery retry, until the carrier drops. Audit trails are automatically generated, and can often be found on logs and cable trays.

Security Considerations

Security is not generally a problem in normal operation, but special measures must be taken (such as data encryption) when avian carriers are used in a tactical environment.

Chapter 13

TCP vs. OSI

Protocol wars and their result.

In 1977, the British Standards Institute proposed to ISO that a standard architecture was needed to define the communications infrastructure. (This, as with IFIP, CCITT, and other efforts, shows how the road to hell is paved with good intentions. Because X.25 was unsatisfactory, the IFIP Working Group was set up in the hope that the technological community could forestall the political arena of ISO. It didn't.) ISO set up a subcommittee of a technical committee to study this [ISO/TC 97/SC 16]. The next year (1978), ISO published its "Provisional Model of Open Systems Architecture" [ISO/TC 97/SC 16 N 34]. This was labelled a "Reference Model," and referred to as OSIRM (ISORM—pronounced "eye-sorm"—by Padlipsky). In general, it was based on work done by Mike Canepa's group at Honeywell Information Systems, which came up with a seven-layered architecture, which itself owed much to IBM's proprietary Systems Network Architecture (SNA). SNA had been announced in 1974 and its seven layers do not correspond exactly to OSI/ISORM's. TC 97/SC 16 turned over proposal development to the American National Standards Institute (ANSI), to which Canepa and his technical lead, Charlie Bachman, presented their layered model. This, in turn, was the *only proposal* presented to the ISO subcommittee at a meeting in Washington in March 1978. It was accepted and published immediately. Hubert Zimmermann has told me that it was not as monolithic as it appears:

The first version of the OSIRM...was developed at the first meeting of SC16 based on contributions received from a number of countries including the U.S., France, the U.K. and Japan.

However, Zimmermann conceded that:

Although SNA had been a source of inspiration for all people involved in networking at that time, the main influence was...the work done internationally within IFIP (with major contributions from CYCLADES, ARPANET, and EIN). An essential difference (at that time) from SNA was the decentralized peer-to-peer architecture promoted by IFIP which was retained in the OSIRM and which later influenced SNA.

A "refined" version of the ANSI submission to ISO appeared in June 1979. This published version is nearly identical to Honeywell's version of 1977. After an elaborate set of meetings, four International Standards were legislated:

- ISO 4335-1979: "Data Communication—High Level Data Link Control Procedures"
- ISO 7498-1983: "Basic Reference Model"
- ISO 8072-1984: "Transport Service Definition"
- ISO 8073-1984: "Transport Protocol Specification"

These have since multiplied (like the heads of the Hydra) to well over twenty standards and service definitions. (Table 13.1 is from Stallings 1993, p. 33.)

As Walden and McKenzie pointed out in 1979, both virtual circuit and datagram services are valuable. "An international standard would do well to support both." The 1977–1979 models were such that the extant host-host protocols did not fit ISORM. ISO was trying to construct a nice set of geometric figures that would be a "tidy model." As was mentioned earlier, the ARPANET workers were interested in getting things to actually work—to push bits around a system.

The OSI model has been described by the irascible Padlipsky as two high rises with parking garages. The basic model is a pair of seven-story buildings (Figure 13.1).

Reality unfortunately necessitated a more complicated representation (Figure 13.2).

CCITT Recommendation	ISO/IEC Standard
X.211 Physical Service Definition	ISO 10022 Physical Service Definition
X.212 Data Link Service Definition	DIS 8886 Data Link Service Definition
X.213 Network Service Definition	ISO 8348 Network Service Definition
	ISO 8348 AD 1 Connectionless-Mode Transmission
	ISO 8348 AD 2 Network Layer Addressing
	ISO 8348 AD 3 Additional Features of the Network Service
	ISO 8348 DAM 4 Removal of the Preferred Decimal Encoding of the NSAP Address
X.214 Transport Service Definition	ISO 8072 Transport Service Definition
	ISO 8072 AD 1 Connectionless-Mode Transmission
X.215 Session Service Definition	ISO 8326 Basic Connection Oriented Session Service Definition
	ISO 8326 DAD 1 Session Symmetric Synchronization for the Session Service
	ISO 8326 DAD 2 Incorporation of Unlimited User Data
	ISO 8326 DAD 3 Connectionless-Mode Session Service
	ISO 8326 PDAM 4 Additional Synchronization Functionality
X.216 Presentation Service Definition	ISO 8822 Connection Oriented Presentation Service Definition
	ISO 8822 DAD 1 Connectionless-Mode Presentation Service
	ISO 8822 PDAD 2 Support of Session Symmetric Synchronization Service
	ISO 8822 PDAM 3 Registration of Abstract Syntaxes
	ISO 8822 PDAM 5 Additional Session Synchronization Functionality for the Presentation User
X.217 Association Control Service Definition	ISO 8649 Service Definition for the Association Control Service Element
	ISO 8649 DAD 2 Connectionless-Mode ACSE Service
X.218 Reliable Transfer: Model and Service Definition	ISO 9066–1 Reliable Transfer—Part 1: Model and Service Definition
X.219 Remote Operations: Model, Notation and Service Definition	ISO 9072–1 Remote Operations—Part 1: Model, Notation and Service Definition

TABLE 13.1   OSI Service Definitions (From Stallings, *Networking Standards: A Guide to OSI, ISDN, and MAN Standards* (p. 33), © 1993 Addison-Wesley Publishing Company, Inc.; reprinted with permission of the publisher)

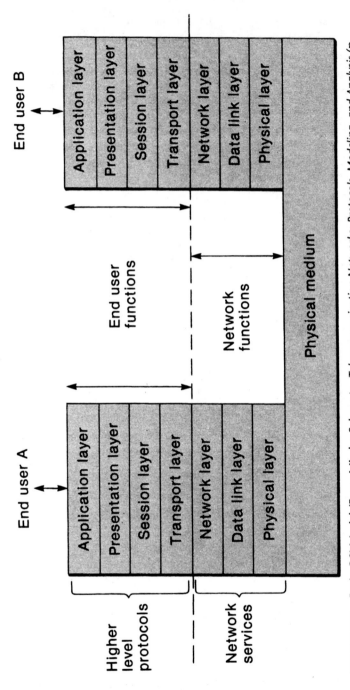

FIGURE 13.1   Basic OSI Model (From Mischa Schwartz, *Telecommunication Networks: Protocols, Modeling, and Analysis* (p. 15), © 1987 by Addison-Wesley Publishing Company, Inc.; reprinted with permission of the publisher)

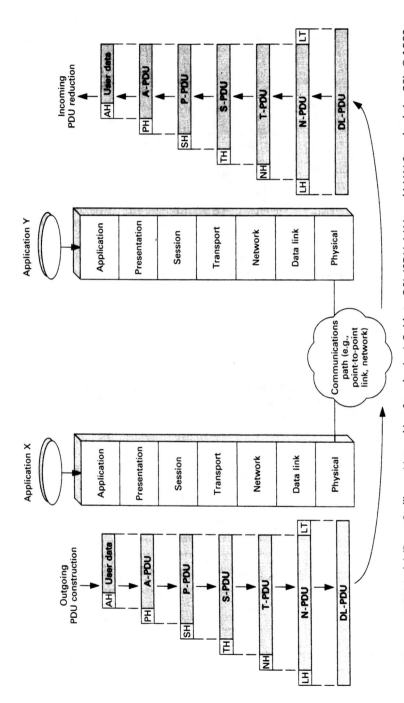

FIGURE 13.2 OSI Model (From Stallings, *Networking Standards: A Guide to OSI, ISDN, LAN, and MAN Standards* (p. 28), © 1993 Addison-Wesley Publishing Company, Inc.; reprinted with permission of the publisher)

The seven-layer shape of the model led to many parodies. The t-shirt sold by the students at the University of Colorado exemplifies the sentiment:

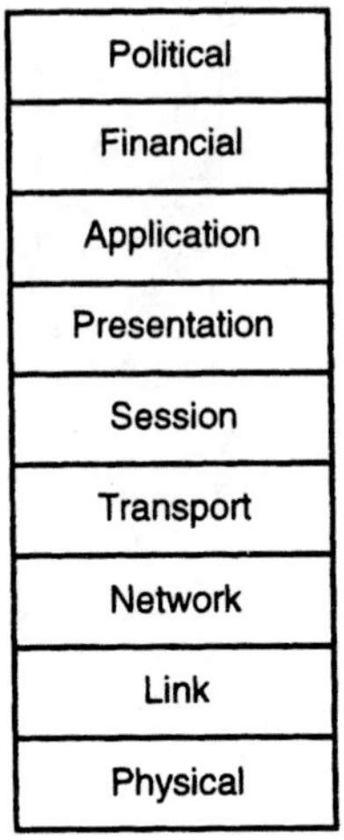

Political
Financial
Application
Presentation
Session
Transport
Network
Link
Physical

UNIVERSITY OF COLORADO STACK

FIGURE 13.3   9-Layer Stack (From a t-shirt sold by the graduate CS students at the University of Colorado)

The UKUUG produced:

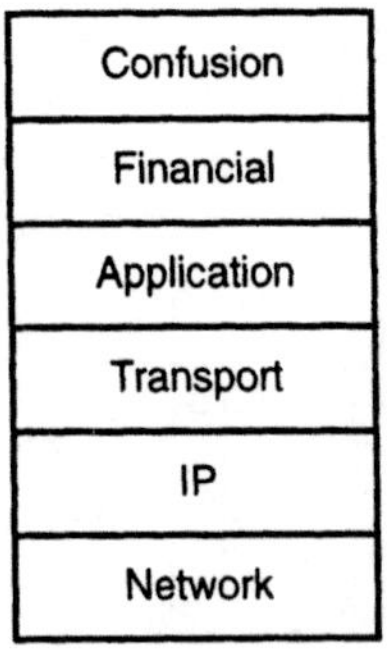

Confusion
Financial
Application
Transport
IP
Network

UKUUG STACK

FIGURE 13.4   6-Layer Stack (From a t-shirt given away at the UKUUG IP Workshop 1994)

I spoke to several people about the failure of OSI. John Quarterman remarked:

> First, note how many of the early participants no longer have anything to do with it. Then try to count implementations (there are a few, but only a few). Then try asking how many hosts there are on OSI networks. You'll get either an inflated count claiming whole networks that are actually IP networks with a few OSI test hosts or no real answer.
>
> OSI specified before implementation. So specification took forever and implementation never really happened, except for bits and pieces. In addition, heavy government backing (by the EC—now the EU—and various national governments) led some OSI participants to attempt to substitute official authority for technical capability. OSI and IP started at about the same time (1977). OSI wandered off into the weeds and IP won the race. Those governments that backed OSI bet on the wrong horse.

In my opinion, this last is the answer: Specification before implementation doesn't work. Recall that ARPA had specified the original IMP in 1968. A few weeks into the contract, BBN had altered the specs. The necessity of delivering functioning hardware and software was what motivated both the IMP team and the NWG. This sort of group was not involved, beyond the very beginnings, in the bureaucracy of ISO and the creation of OSI.

The other problem was that TCP/IP was a suite with a real installed base. The implementations had evolved between 1974 and 1978 and were widely accepted within the technical community. By supporting a theoretical specification with no implementation, the PTTs of Europe and Japan were both sticking to the "old" telephony and telegraphy way of thinking at the same time they appeared to be mired in the "Not Invented Here" morass. The U.S. government had funded the ARPANET and it was (despite the NPL and CYCLADES) a largely American creation. (The presence of Scantlebury's and Zimmermann's names on the IFIP proposal cut no ice.) A final reason that has been adduced is that the Japanese and European governmental representatives (all the PTTs were governmental) didn't want U.S. manufacturers to have an unfair advantage selling their extant TCP/IP products. Real money was involved; future profits were at stake.

The actual result was that many companies wasted a decade trying to produce OSI products while the networking community increasingly used TCP/IP. As early as 1986, Jack Haverty and Gary Tauss wrote that the market had "the choice between a well understood, widely implemented protocol set, namely the Internet Suite, and an evolving, incomplete, not widely available set, representing the OSI model" [*Government Data Systems* 15.3 (April/May 1986)]. While Mischa Schwartz (in 1987) could still believe that "TCP and ISO TP class 4 will coexist for some time, but...as more manufacturers and users begin to adopt the ISO suite of transport protocols, use of TCP will begin to decrease" [p. 387]; Fred Halsall, a staunch OSI supporter, has pointed out "In practice...there are two major open system (vendor-independent) standards: the TCP/IP protocol suite and those based on the evolving ISO standards." [1992, p. 19] Halsall's full diagram of ISO and CCITT standards is indicative of the complexity and the fallacy of issuing standards counter to practice and implementation (Figure 13.5).

The fact that local area networks and desktop workstations supported TCP/IP meant that there was an ever-increasing infrastructure built upon TCP/IP in Europe. The changing political situation in Eastern Europe and in the erstwhile USSR also meant increasing TCP/IP support (as all the specifications were in the public domain and thus no fees were payable). So far as I can tell, while OSI networking still exists in many places, it is not waxing; TCP/IP networks are Store-and-forward networks (like BITNET) are shrinking while others (like FidoNet and UUCP) are still growing.

The US Department of Defense also contributed to this. Originally, the DOD had a communications network called AUTODIN (Automatic Defense Integrated Network). In the mid-1970s there was a move to replace this with AUTODIN II. The Department let contracts and the result was a mare's nest involving Western Union, Ford Aerospace, CSC, and Mitre. The various companies couldn't come to grips with the government specifications. (A major issue was that the packet switches were supposed to be multilevel secure.) Padlipsky told me: "They were also screwing up the protocols. Finally, some sort of 'Murder Board' was convened, and DIN II was given the much overdue ax."

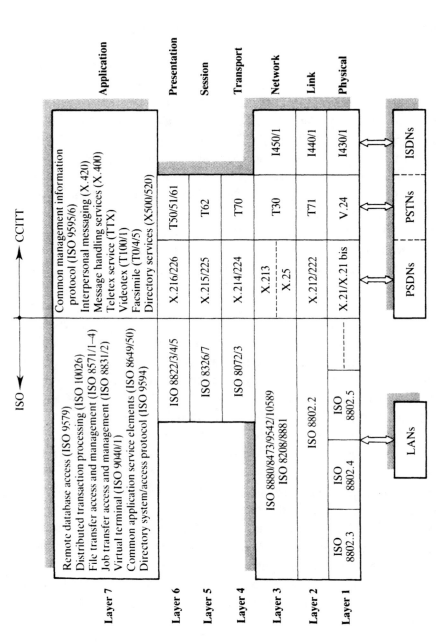

FIGURE 13.5   Standards Summary (From Halsall, *Data Communications, Computer Networks and Open Systems* (p. 20), © 1992 Addison-Wesley Publishing Company, Inc.; reprinted with permission of the publisher)

(Padlipsky, it must be admitted, is not exactly an impartial source. I have heard a tale that he walked into one meeting with the vendors, pulled an airline "barfbag" from his case, put it on the table and said "OK, you guys, I'm ready for you.")

I spoke with Dave Walden about the debacle. "The Defense Department procurement folks had divided everything up into bits and pieces. BBN won everything. We had all the pieces right, but we didn't know how to talk to the military. Western Union did. They wanted security, for example. And we said 'This part's easy, this part's hard, this part's impossible.' Western Union just said, 'Of course we can do that.' We had a decade's experience with the ARPANET. You would have thought that AT&T or Western Union or DEC would just pick up our stuff and run with it. They didn't. But Defense just invented a new way of evaluating, rescored, and Western Union won the scoring." It was a forerunner of IBM winning the NSFNET contract.

It turned out that Western Union couldn't do the job. It cost many millions of dollars but finally Cerf, Kahn, and a number of others prevailed and persuaded the military brass that the ARPANET protocols were reliable, available, and survivable. I was told that it was Frank Carlucci who finally signed off on abrogating the Western Union agreement. Heidi Heiden was at the DoD at that time, he recalled that "in 1981...I was told to develop a potential alternative to the then-current AUTODIN II plan.... ARPANET technology won..." The result was MILNET, an ARPANET clone, which lasted until 1983, when it split from ARPANET and DDN (the Defense Data Network) was formed. For a while, DDN was a TCP/IP network, made up of ARPANET clones, and run for the military by BBN. Walden had been the BBN manager who coordinated the ARPA to DCA transfer. Winning DDN for BBN came at a time when he became Executive Vice President and CEO of BBN Communications Corporation, leading its change into BBN Systems and Technologies in 1983. DDN is now made up of IP-based router nets, rather than X.25-based BBN nets.

While all but a few would regard the war as won by TCP/IP, I can only be aghast at the energy and time that went into the protocol wars, which have only ended late in 1994, with the US govenment's recognition of the *de facto* victory by TCP/IP.

Chapter 14

UNIX on the Net

UNIX is introduced to the ARPANET community.

At the same time that the protocols were being hewn into TCP/IP, a new operating system had been gaining in popularity among the research and university community: UNIX. Invented in 1969 at AT&T Bell Labs in New Jersey, the UNIX operating system was internal to AT&T/Western Electric until 1973. In October of that year, Ken Thompson and Dennis Ritchie delivered a paper at the Symposium on Operating Systems Principles. "Outsiders" immediately began requesting the system and, when their paper was published in July 1974, a flood of inquiries ensued. By early 1975, UNIX had made it to Laxenburg, Austria; Queen Mary College, London; the University of New South Wales in Australia; Heriott-Watt in Scotland; Louvain in Belgium; five Canadian universities; and a large number of U.S. sites. Sixth Edition appeared in May 1975. But UNIX had a significant drawback: Until 1979, it only ran on the PDP-11.

In May 1973, only UCSB, the National Bureau of Standards, Harvard, and the University of Illinois had PDP-11s connected to their IMPs or (NBS) their TIP. But the popularity of UNIX and the economical price of the PDP-11 meant that more and more institutions would be using both of them. (For a more detailed history of UNIX, see my *A Quarter Century of UNIX*, 1994.)

On May 14, 1975, Steve Holmgren, a graduate student at the University of Illinois posted RFC 681 ("Network UNIX"). It began:

```
                        NETWORK UNIX

                     RFC 681 NIC 32157

INTRODUCTION

THE UNIX TIME-SHARING SYSTEM PRESENTS SEVERAL INTERESTING CAPABILITIES
AS AN ARPA NETWORK MINI-HOST. IT OFFERS POWERFUL LOCAL PROCESSING
FACILITIES IN TERMS OF USER PROGRAMS, SEVERAL COMPILERS, AN EDITOR
BASED ON QED, A VERSATILE DOCUMENT PREPARATION SYSTEM, AND AN EFFICIENT
FILE SYSTEM FEATURING SOPHISTICATED ACCESS CONTROL, MOUNTABLE AND DE-
MOUNTABLE VOLUMES, AND A UNIFIED TREATMENT OF PERIPHERALS AS SPECIAL
FILES.

THE NETWORK CONTROL PROGRAM (NCP), IS INTEGRATED WITHIN THE UNIX FILE
SYSTEM. NETWORK CONNECTIONS ARE TREATED AS SPECIAL FILES WHICH CAN BE
ACCESSED THROUGH STANDARD UNIX I/O CALLS; VIZ. READ, WRITE, OPEN,
CLOSE. SPECIAL FILES HAVE DIRECTORY ENTRIES SIMILAR TO NORMAL FILES
EXCEPT THAT CERTAIN FLAG BITS ARE SET. THESE FLAG BITS CAUSE SYSTEM I/O
ROUTINES TO TAKE SPECIAL ACTION. IN UNIX, SPECIAL FILES SIGNIFY
PERIPHERAL DEVICES. FOR EXAMPLE, I/O TRANSACTION WITH MAGTAPE ZERO
WOULD BE ACCOMPLISHED BY ACCESSING THE SPECIAL FILE, "/DEV/MT0". FOR
THE UNIX NETWORK SYSTEM, ADDITIONAL SPECIAL FILES WERE CREATED EACH OF
WHICH SPECIFIES A HOST ON THE ARPA NETWORK. FOR EXAMPLE "/DEV/NET/HARV"
REPRESENTS THE PDP-10 AT HARVARD. THIS SIMPLE ACCESS MECHANISM, THROUGH
THE FILING SYSTEM, ALLOWS STANDARD ARPA PROTOCOLS SUCH AS TELNET AND
FTP TO BE IMPLEMENTED AS SWAPPABLE USER PROGRAMS, RESIDENT ONLY WHEN
NEEDED. FURTHERMORE, A USER MAY WRITE HIS OWN PROGRAMS TO COMMUNICATE
WITH THESE SPECIAL FILES JUST AS THE TELNET PROGRAM DOES. THE SAMPLE
PROGRAM FOUND BELOW DEPICTS THE ESSENTIALS OF NETWORKING FROM UNIX.
```

and concluded (several pages later) with:

```
RELIABILITY

AS OF THIS WRITING, NETWORK UNIX HAS BEEN RUNNING ON A FULL TIME BASIS
FOR ABOUT FOUR WEEKS. DURING THAT PERIOD, THERE WERE BETWEEN THREE AND
FOUR CRASHES A DAY. THIS IS NOT A VALID INDICATOR BECAUSE MANY OF THE
FAILURES WERE DUE TO HARDWARE COMPLICATIONS. MORE RECENTLY THE HARDWARE
HAS BEEN RE-CONFIGURED TO IMPROVE RELIABILITY AND THE CRASH RATE HAS
BEEN REDUCED TO ONE A DAY WITH A DOWN TIME OF 2-3 MINS. THIS IS
EXPECTED TO CONTINUE, BUT THE SAMPLING PERIOD HASNT BEEN LONG ENOUGH
FOR ANY DEPENDABLE ANALYSIS.
```

AVAILABILITY

ALTHOUGH THE UNIX NETWORK SOFTWARE WAS DEVELOPED WITHOUT ARPA SUPPORT, THE CENTER FOR ADVANCED COMPUTATION IS WILLING TO PROVIDE IT GRATIS TO THE PEOPLE OF THE ARPA COMMUNITY.

HOWEVER BELL LABORATORIES MUST BE CONTACTED FOR A LICENSE TO THE BASE SYSTEM ITSELF. BELL'S POLICY IN THE PAST HAS BEEN TO LICENSE THE SYSTEM TO UNIVERSITIES FOR A NOMINAL FEE, $150.00, AND UNFORTUNATELY FOR A COST OF $20,000.00 TO "NONUNIVERSITY" INSTITUTIONS.

OUTLOOK AND FUTURE PLANS

WITH THE ADVENT OF TELNET IN UNIX, CURRENT PLANS ARE TO RUN THE SYSTEM OVER THE NEXT ONE OR TWO MONTHS AND WORK OUT ANY REMAINING BUGS. WHILE THIS IS GOING ON, EXTENSIVE BANDWITH AND LOAD TESTING IS GOING TO TAKE PLACE AND ANY REASONABLE IMPROVEMENTS MADE.

AFTER TELNET HAS PROVED ITSELF RELIABLE, THE OPEN SYSTEM CALL WILL BE EXPANDED TO INCLUDE FURTHER PARAMETERIZATION. THIS PARAMETERIZATION WILL ENCOMPASS CONNECTIONS TO SPECIFIC SOCKETS, SIMPLEX CONNECTIONS BASED ON A SOCKET ALREADY IN USE, AND THE ABILITY TO LISTEN ON A LOCAL SOCKET.

AFTER THOSE EXTENSIONS, NET MAIL, THEN NETWORK FTP AND FINALLY NETWORK RJE WILL BE IMPLEMENTED. ALL WILL RUN AS USER PROGRAMS SO THE KERNEL SYSTEM SIZE WILL NOT INCREASE.

THERE IS ALSO INTEREST IN IMPLEMENTING SOME OF THE PROCEDURE CALL PROTOCOLS BEING DEVELOPED BY THE NATIONAL SOFTWARE WORKS, BUT NO DEFINITE PLANS HAVE BEEN MADE.

The RFC is presented in capital letters, as it was originally released: For many, this will serve as a reminder of the time 20 years ago when many of us worked from teletypewriters and terminals that did not have lower case. What Holmgren, Bunch, and Grossman were doing was putting the net on UNIX, not putting UNIX on the net. The result was not immediate, but it was important: The advent of UNIX brought several other things to the net—a larger audience and new applications.

One of these had, in fact, been demonstrated at the Ballistics Research Lab in Maryland. Mike Muuss had obtained a copy of SEARCH, a multi-user wargame, and modified it for use on a PDP-11/70 running BRL UNIX.

In 1979 the fact that UNIX would run on more than one type of hardware had caught the attention of ARPA. The Agency had become concerned their various contractors were using different hardware and a range of operating systems. While the ARPANET and the new Internet permitted them to communicate and exchange data, there was no possibility of software exchange. ARPA wanted a common base so that there could be more interchange. But it had to be made available at low cost, so that universities would really use it. Kirk McKusick told me that "It was pretty clear that they were going to choose the VAX [the newest line of DEC machines], the question came down to whether VMS or UNIX should be the operating system of choice." It was Bill Joy (then at Berkeley; now a Vice President at Sun Microsystems) who convinced ARPA that UNIX was a better base because it had (at least minimal) portability. It had been ported to the PDP-11 series, the VAX, and to the Interdata 7 and 8. Berkeley's Computer Systems Research Group (CSRG) received a large contract to put performance enhancements into UNIX and get it out rapidly. The release (4BSD, or Fourth Berkeley Software Distribution) was distributable within two months of contract signing.

In September 1979, Mike Muuss extended the prototype BRLNET he had begun developing earlier. It was a 16Mbps LAN, but required homogeneity. The next year, he extended the protocols to deal with heterogeneity; and in late 1980 the BRL team ported the University of Illinois' ARPANET NCP capability to BRL PDP-11 UNIX. It was BRL's PDP-11 TCP/IP that was distributed nationally in 1983, after BRL became a host on the Internet.

In 1979, ARPA went to BBN for improvements in TCP, as well. Rob Gurwitz and Jack Haverty wrote a version, which was given to Berkeley for integration into the next BSD. It was included in 4BSD, but Joy was unhappy with the BBN implementation. He kept on tinkering with it through 1981 and 1982, much to the unhappiness of Duane Adams (the DARPA monitor) and BBN. The result was that rcp, rsh, rlogin, and rwho were all integrated into 4.1aBSD (April 1982). The complete UNIX release with a fully rewritten TCP was released as 4.1cBSD over the winter of 1982–1983 and a major release (4.2BSD) was distributed in September 1983.

Kirk McKusick mentioned to me that 4.2BSD was enormously successful, selling more copies in the first 18 months of availability that all other Berkeley releases combined. By having BBN rewrite the TCP/IP suite for use with UNIX and getting Berkeley to integrate the suite into BSD and distribute it, DARPA was able to instantly reach over 90 percent of North American computer science departments.

There was an interesting synergistic effect here: BSD became popular because it would run on several different machines that were becoming common in universities and other research sites. TCP/IP was integrated into the BSD software, which contained a number of other application programs and utilities that were familiar on single sites. The ability to use familiar tool over the network was a tremendous asset. For example, **cp** on one's own machine copied files; **rcp** copied files from a remote machine to (or from) one's own.

And the success of TCP/IP among academic computer scientists led to its wider use. As Carl-Mitchell and Quarterman pointed out: "Because of the public source of its funding, 4.2BSD was made available at the cost of its distribution and so its use spread quickly." [1993; p. 7]

Solid protocols on a flexible operating system at low cost was an unbeatable combination. OSI never had a chance.

I have several times cited Vint Cerf's adage that the history of the net is the history of its protocols. And certainly for the first decade (say 1969–1979) this was true. But the advent of UNIX, the adoption of the entire suite of TCP/IP, and the widening audience of the network brought with it a demand for services beyond file transfer and telnet. And FTPmail wasn't anywhere near enough.

Chapter 15

UUCP and Usenet

The birth and development of news—another application unheard-of in 1969.

Folks who weren't on the ARPANET in the mid-1970s were anxious to transfer data, too. The question of just how to do this was attacked in 1976 by Mike Lesk at Bell Labs. The result was a program called UUCP, for "UNIX to UNIX Copy." UUCP enabled users to send mail, transfer files, and execute remote commands. Lesk first called it a "scheme for better distribution" (*Mini-System Newsletter*, January 1977); it was referred to as **UUCP** only a month later. UUCP was designed for use over 300 baud lines, and it was finally published in February 1978. It proved to be one of the most important parts of UNIX, because of its wide use. Lesk's invention led to a need for improvements, as the original program just couldn't handle the burden placed upon it by its popularity. The next version of UUCP was written by Lesk and Dave Nowitz (with contributions by Greg Chesson) and appeared in Seventh Edition (October 1978). This version, too, proved inadequate to the tremendous use to which UUCP was being put—more systems, more software, more demands. When Usenet began, UUCP broke. Lesk just hadn't considered what UUCP would be used for. So, in April 1983, Martin Levy sent out a plea for a new UUCP system. It had become clear that a UUCP designed when asynchronous 1200-baud modems were state of the art was inadequate to meet the needs of a growing UNIX network. (Robert T. Morris had revised the code while a summer student at Bell Labs, but this new code wasn't adopted.)

In mid-April 1983 a number of people at AT&T Bell Labs met and the result was the coding of a new version of UUCP by Peter Honeyman (login `honey`), Dave (`dan`) Nowitz, and Brian Redman (`ber`). The result is widely known as HoneyDanBer, or (in System V) BasicNetworkingUtilities 1.

Redman told me how he would phone people to set up UUCP connections and how he began "sending electronic mail on a regular basis," leading to a community. "And that's how NETNEWS came along."

The early history and motivation were described in a 1988 paper by Steve Bellovin and Mark Horton, which has (unfortunately) never been published.

In late 1979, Seventh Edition UNIX had just been installed at the University of North Carolina. Partly as an exercise in learning details of the new system, and partly to fill an administrative need, Bellovin wrote a rudimentary news system. It was written entirely as a UNIX *shell file*—that is, a set of commands—and thus was too slow for general use. In particular, it could not be used to replace the login banner message for administrative announcements. Nevertheless, the primitive version contained some important concepts. Articles could be posted to multiple *newsgroups*; each user could subscribe to as many or as few groups as desired. The UNIX file directory structure was used to implement newsgroups; this helped the otherwise deplorable performance. And the system kept track of the last article read; old articles were not presented again.

Around the same time, Tom Truscott and Bellovin were experimenting with a *uucp* link... between UNC and Duke University. Truscott and Jim Ellis came up with the idea of using *uucp* to distribute news items to other sites. They proposed a network with Duke as the central hub; using their autodialer, they would poll other sites to pick up any inbound news and deliver any outbound news. These sites would then reimburse Duke for its phone charges, and redistribute news items to other sites. It was expected that the primary class of traffic would be UNIX bug reports.

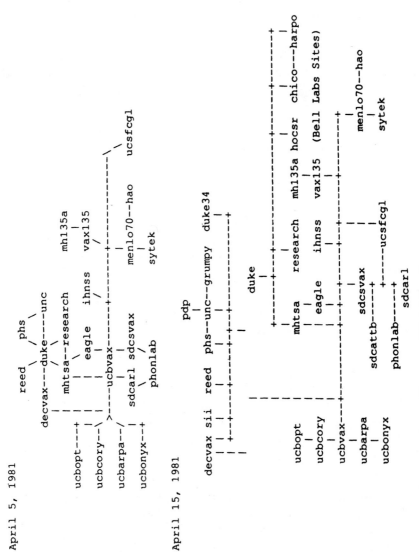

MAP 7   Early USENET Maps (Courtesy of Rick Adams)

Bellovin, Ellis, and Truscott made several assumptions and design decisions:

- The user interface would be modeled on Seventh Edition *Mail;*
- The protocol would be optimized for 1–2 messages per day;
- Local subnets would be possible;
- No changes to the UNIX system components;
- Extensibility was necessary;
- The network would be called **USENET**, patterned upon USENIX, "the new official name for what had been the UNIX Users Group. The hope was that Usenet would some day become the official network of USENIX."

USENET began with two hosts: unc and duke. A third host called phs (also at Duke) was added early in 1980. This set-up was described by Ellis in a pamphlet distributed at the USENIX conference in Boulder, Colorado, at the end of January 1980. An implementation of the A News software (by Steve Daniel) was made available on the "free" distribution tape at the 1980 Summer USENIX conference (in Newark, Delaware). By that time there were 15 sites in the network. But the growth spurt was to come when the University of California joined Usenet. This was the direct responsibility of Armando Stettner and Bill Shannon (of DEC). Stettner told me that someone at the USENIX meeting was complaining about not being able to afford the phone calls to get news to the west coast. So Armando spoke to Bill and they said that if they could get a news feed to decvax (in New Hampshire), they'd pick up the Berkeley phone bill. [Stettner later supplied the first news feeds to Europe, Japan, and Australia, too.]

In under a year, Berkeley (ucbvax) was feeding news to ucbopt, ucbcory, ucbarpa, ucbonyx, sdcarl, sdcsvax, menlo-70, and ucsfcgl, several of which were outside the academic community. Less directly, the High Altitude Observatory hao and Sytek connected through menlo70, for example. The net grew to over 100 sites and 25 articles per day within a year. And this is what caused the system to collapse. Lesk had never contemplated these uses of UUCP; Bellovin, Truscott, and Ellis had never thought in terms of such popularity. (Redman, in New Jersey, put up the news as soon as he could.)

Bellovin had revised his code for USENET, rewriting it in C. This had then been revised by Steve Daniel and then Truscott. The result was A News. In 1981, Mark Horton (a graduate student at UC Berkeley) and Matt Glickman (a high school student) rewrote A News into B news.

Horton continued releasing new versions of the software and maintaining it until 1984 (version 2.10.1). At that point Rick Adams at the Center for Seismic Studies took over coordination and maintenance. He produced version 2.10.2 in 1984. This added the provision for moderated groups (which were inspired by the ARPA mailing lists). Adams told me it was "more like editing a magazine than moderating."

Mark Horton and Karen Summers-Horton constructed the "USENET GEOGRAPHIC MAP" in June 1984. (Map 8)

Late in 1986, version 2.11 of B News was released. This included support for a new naming structure, enhanced batching, and compression. There were a number of further useful modifications to and implementations of *NETNEWS,* by Spencer Thomas, Rick Adams, Ray Essick, Rob Kolstad, and others.

It is worth mentioning the effort of Essick and Kolstad. In 1980–1981, when they were both graduate students at the University of Illinois, they created another distributed news system, called "notes." It was based on the notesfiles that were available on the PLATO system. PLATO was a conferencing system developed at Illinois in the late 1960s. The Control Data Corporation had a commercial version of it, designed for "computer-aided instruction," but it was far too expensive to be successful ($5 million for software plus $6000 per terminal in 1976). notes was announced at the January 1983 USENIX conference (Santa Monica, California), but never achieved wide use and was merged into USENET. "notes would have won," Rick Adams remarked to me, "except for the implementation, which was a bitch to maintain. But the interface was better." Kolstad told me:

> Oh, I think it penetrated fairly high—a few thousand sites (10 percent? 20 percent? At the time, of course). I believe that the

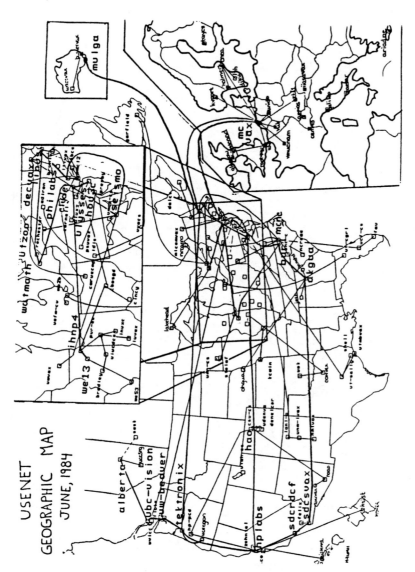

MAP 8   USENET Geographic Map 1984 (Courtesy of Mark Horton)

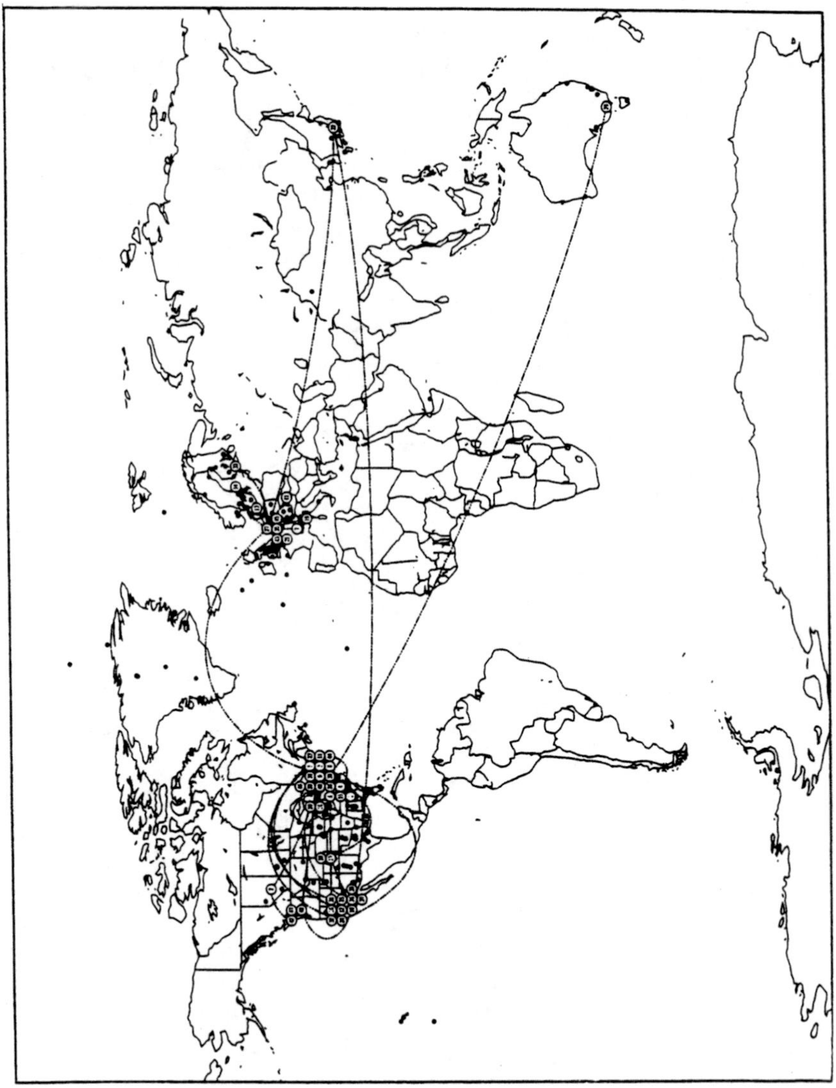

MAP 9   USENET Backbone Map (Courtesy of Brian Reid)

implementation was not its downfall at all—it's easy to maintain. The problem was that it did not interface to B News very well (because of its limit on subject line lengths) and the fact that administrators would flood the net with an entire news feed by accident sometimes.

Len Tower told me "notes would have won easily if it had been first."

There is a current release of B News, 2.11.19 (with article format as in RFC 1036), despite the fact that it has been declared "dead" a number of times. Adams says "it was dead in 1989." This implementation hasn't been updated in many years.

The real cause of the demise was RFC 977 (Brian Kantor and Phil Lapsley, "Network News Transfer Protocol," February 1, 1986). NNTP enabled hosts to exchange news via TCP/IP, rather than UUCP connections over TCP/IP. The protocol grew out of work by Kantor at the University of California in San Diego and Lapsley in Berkeley. NNTP includes support for 4.3BSD, UNIX System V, and for Decnet (running under Ultrix, DEC's version of 4.2BSD). Erik Fair, Steven Grady and Mike Meyer were among the other contributors. The NNTP package was distributed with 4.3BSD, again making it readily accessible to the user community. A glance at the world map that Brian Reid plotted illustrates the spread of news. (Map 9)

In 1987, Henry Spencer and Geoff Collyer of the University of Toronto produced a new alternative, **C News**. This was a rewrite of the lowest levels (those involved with transport between machines, rather than to presentation to the user) to increase processing speed. It was announced at the January 1987 USENIX conference (Washington, DC) and made available that autumn.

There are a number of other news readers and news systems. A few of these are: InterNetNews (INN) by Rich Salz, designed to run on UNIX hosts with a socket interface; ANU-NEWS by Geoff Huston (then at the Australian National University), a complete news system for VMS machines; vnews by Kenneth Almquist (distributed with B News 2.11); rn by Larry Wall (1984); trn, a threaded rn by Wayne Davison; xrn, an X11-based interface by Rick Spickelmier and Ellen Sentovich; and GNUS and Gnews, both GNU Emacs-based readers.

Originally, there were net.general and net.v7bugs, soon followed by net.test. But this was far from enough, and other groups were created. net.jokes was a popular one. The first moderated newsgroup was mod.announce, parallel to net.general. As USENET grew, the major sites transporting news across the country and overseas came to be known as the backbone. This was largely because of a mailing list of site administrators called the "backbone." By 1985, several of the administrators of backbone sites came to see themselves as arbiters or censors of some of the groups or the traffic. Gene Spafford sent out a message stating:

> Greetings,
>
> Following is the text of an invitation to join a short-term mailing list. Individuals already on the list have suggested that I pass along invitations to you so that we might have the benefit of your expertise, experience, and viewpoint:
>
> If you have been following any of the discussion in the net.news groups recently or if you administer a well-placed news site, you are undoubtedly aware that there are a number of nasty problems associated with the current state of the Usenet. We have problems with signal:noise, transmission costs, transmission delays, naming space, etiquette, deciding what groups to carry, when to create and delete groups, etc., etc., etc.
>
> About a year and a half ago, I proposed (in a mailing list and on news) some changes which would involve creating a new name space and then switching the backbone and many sites over to that new namespace. Included would be a forced upgrade to current software, and a new set of *formally stated* policies. The idea was generally well-liked, but people felt it would be too difficult to implement, that many sites would drop off the net, and that many "noisy but fun" newsgroups would go away. Those look less like liabilities all the time....
>
> I do *NOT* think it is a good idea at this time to publish something to the net asking for volunteers. I want to keep the list fairly small and workable, and the net just has too much noise.

It was knowledge of this last that started agitation about a "secret" cabal. In fact, many of the people on the list were openly for a broadening of Usenet's purview, others seeing a reorganization of naming hierarchy as an opportunity for cleansing. In Europe, the reorganization was welcomed, according to Peter Collinson, with no particular reaction to the notion of a "cabal"—though many British and continental sites did not carry the alt groups at first. In November 1985, Spafford wrote:

> Let's consider, for a few moments, the current state of USENET. Backbone sites are dropping newsgroups and discussing ways of automatically limiting volume. There are almost as many different (and often incompatible) versions of news transport software in use as there are newsgroups (and there are far too many of those), and in some groups the space occupied by the control information in each article is nearly two times the contents. A significant fraction of the sites making up the network can't accomodate flexibility in naming, resulting in awkward constraints on newsgroup naming. There is strife and hostility over when and how to create and delete groups, and the sheer volume of postings is drowning sites....
>
> Basically, the USENET is dying. It has a had a long and fruitful life, especially considering how it came about and grew to its present form (not bad for some former shell files, eh?), but its lifetime is limited. Maybe USENET has another year of functionality left. Maybe two at the outside. If you believe the net is still healthy and these are all little problems easily solved, then perhaps this mailing list isn't for you.
>
> What I'm hoping this list will be for, is to discuss what we have all learned from the USENET experience. How can we take the software, transport connections, and sheer human experience and form a better system? What is more, how can we craft a new system so it has some of the best features of the current network, yet keep from growing in such an undisciplined way? In fact, maybe we even need to discuss if we want such a network (Note: I do, or I wouldn't be trying to organize this)....

I don't mean to sound gloomy. This is intended to be a message of hope—of determination to not give up without a fight. Butler Lampson has stated a few times in his papers on OS construction that you should always build a system twice—the first time just to make it work, and the second time to do it right. I think that applies here. I'm keen to try to do it right (and that isn't in any way intended to slight the efforts or work of others that has gone into the current USENET).

A few weeks after the June 1986 USENIX Conference (which was held in Atlanta; he was at Georgia Tech at that time, he has since moved to Purdue), Spafford wrote a long note about renaming, part of which reads (I only cite this to show the level of detail that the "cabal" wished to go to):

Since the moderated groups have been folded into this, you might also try sending the list to the moderators with an explanation and see what they say—sort of going semi-public....

6) comp.peripherals -> comp.hardware comp.text.laser-printers -> comp.hardware.laser-printers comp.terminals -> comp.hardware.terminals ...

11) kill rec.food.veg and fold it in with rec.food

The changes took place in two stages: The unmoderated groups were changed in September 1986, the moderated ones in April 1987. In early 1987 the issue of censorship came to a head when a proposal for a newsgroup (net.rec.drugs) to discuss drugs was rejected. Moreover, another request to have a moderated group called "gourmand" was turned down. The immediate result was that on May 13, 1987, John Gilmore sent out the following:

Newsgroups: alt.drugs

Subject: Test of alt distribution

I have set up alt.drugs and alt.sources and alt.test on hoptoad and will forward them to any of my neighbors who are interested. (Currently, amdcad and mejac.)

Let's get a few more groups together (recipes?) and announce
our existence to the world...

John

Gilmore told me:

In general when faced with obnoxiously centralized control
over something that should be free and/or distributed, I look
for a low overhead way around, that increases freedom in general. Using the USENET software to distribute a new hierarchy, among ONLY the people who chose to get it, was that
way when the USENET 'backbone cabal' decided that drugs
were too controversial a topic to appear in the newsgroup list.
Brian Reid had had a similar experience (the backbone wanted
his newsgroup for recipes to be called "recipes" rather than
"gourmand"—this bit of extraneous editing pissed Brian off.)

Brian Reid was mejac. By Monday, May 25, Gilmore wrote [in
much of what follows I have deleted the names of some addressees, as
I have not obtained their permission]:

I have set up to feed alt to the well.
    I don't know how to conveniently send newgroups to an-
other site without blasting them around the net. Howabout you
add these lines to your sys file?
    alt.drugs 00000 00001 y
    alt.sources 00000 00001 y
    alt.test 00000 00001 y
    alt.gourmand 00000 00001 y
    I am thinking that we should also have an alt.config for
keeping track of where "alt" goes.
    John

The next day he wrote:

On a totally different topic, are you the news or UUCP adminis-
trator for ncoast? Brian Reid, Bandy [Andrew Scott Beals], Gordon
Moffett and I are setting up an "alt" set of newsgroups, e.g.,
"alt.gourmand" for the old mod.recipes, "alt.drugs" for the

banned net.rec.drugs, alt.sources for an unmoderated sources group, etc. We are initially linking up the privately owned and public access UNIX systems, e.g., hoptoad, well, unirot, mejac, as the "backbone" of the alt subnet; of course, any other site that wants them is welcome to 'em. This should limit distribution problems with site management that is afraid of free speech.

So, I'd like to set up a UUCP link to ncoast, and a news link to transfer the "alt" groups. I have PC Pursuit here, so I can call you at least once a night for free (depending how often the dialers are free). If you also have free calling to San Francisco, we could set up a demand link (both sites call whenever they have traffic, after 6PM), otherwise I can poll you.

as well as:

Brian Reid, Bandy, Gordon Moffett, and I are setting up an "alt" set of newsgroups, e.g., "alt.gourmand" for the old mod.recipes, "alt.drugs" for the banned net.rec.drugs, alt.sources for an unmoderated sources group, etc. Depending on your point of view you can see alt as an abbreviation for "alternative," or "altered." We intend for it to be a permanent part of the USENET, free of control by the Backbone Cabal because we are setting up a real continent-wide backbone of our own. Brian has decwrl (and soon decvax) handling it and we have various other links in place here in the Bay Area, and are in the process of setting up links with dasys1 and ncoast now.

And he posted:

Newsgroups: alt.config
    Subject: Current configuration of the "alt" subnet
This message is just to get the ball rolling in alt.config. I've created the newsgroup for discussions and announcements of alt connectivity. This should be easier to handle than a mailing list, since new sites will automatically receive it as the alt distribution expands.

    Currently alt is being handled by these sites, to my knowledge:

    hoptoad, mejac, decwrl, well, amdahl, amdcad

A bozo at amdcad causes them to reject "alt.drugs"; the rest carry the whole subnet.

I have feelers out to unirot [New Jersey], ncoast [Cleveland], and dasys1 [NYC] to set up links from hoptoad. I am encouraging links among privately owned and/or public access machines, to avoid problems like the aforementioned bozo. If we keep connectivity among a set of private machines, we can't be cut off by bureaucrats even if the rest of the sites go away. Of course, if a corporate machine wants an alt feed or wants to feed others, more power to 'em, but let's make sure we don't depend on their generosity or their management's inattention.

The current list of alt newsgroups is:

alt.config	Alternative subnet configuration/connectivity.
alt.drugs	Alternative discussions about drugs, man.
alt.gourmand	Alternative recipes.
alt.sources	Alternative source code, unmoderated.
alt.test	Alternative subnetwork testing.

Feel free to add this to your /usr/lib/news/newsgroups file. At some point I will send out a checkgroups message for alt, which surprisingly enough, works in 2.11; that is, it will just check the alt subnetwork, while leaving the rest alone.

Gilmore's mention of PC Pursuit intrigued me, so I asked him. He responded:

A little-known bit of the history was that our nationwide links were provided over Telenet's flat rate PC Pursuit service for the first year or so; I set up links between my home machine and public-access sites in Chicago, NYC, SoCal, etc, so that alt would have wide distribution. PC Pursuit UUCP data rates were well under 100 cps, but it was flat rate, and our autodialers tended to beat out human dialers for the limited number of modems available. I doubt that this had much effect on PC Pursuit (general load from humans would also have swamped any nationwide flat-rate modem service, and

Telenet apparently wasn't *really* serious about wanting to fill up its timesharing network at night anyway).

In August 1987 the alt groups were:

drwxr-xr-x 2 news	512 Aug 12 05:08 config
drwxr-xr-x 2 news	512 Aug 12 07:30 drugs
drwxrwxr-x 2 news	512 Aug 9 05:22 gourmand
drwxrwxr-x 2 news	512 Aug 3 05:41 sources
drwxrwxr-x 2 news	512 Aug 11 06:41 test

The notion of having an "alternate" hierarchy that was not subject to the formalisms and bureaucracy of USENET caught on rapidly. By early the next year, Bob Page at the University of Lowell was able to post:

Subject: The size of the 'alt' subnet
Date: 24 Feb 88 23:28:03 GMT

About a month ago there was some discussion on alt.config about how big the alt 'network' was. I sent out a sendsys message to find out. Responses have finally stopped coming in. I posted the message on the evening (to me) of February 8, and all the responses were generated (but not delivered to me) by February 16.

Total sites responding: 550

total .uucp sites: 247

total .com sites: 153

total .edu sites: 121

total .org sites: 13

total .gov sites: 6

total other sites: 10 (arpa, bitnet, cdn, csnet, .net, unspecified)

I suppose I could sort & report on the sites geographically, or topologically, but I don't know how much more information it would provide, and I don't have a nice way to to it automatically. (Read: I don't want to do it by hand). However, it is clear that alt does not go very far out of North America, or the sites outside of NA don't respond to sendsys requests.

Reid soon added to the alt. groups:

To end the suspense, I have just created alt.sex That meant that the alt network now carried alt.sex and alt.drugs. It was therefore artistically necessary to create alt.rock-n-roll, which I have also done. I have no idea what sort of traffic it will carry. If the bizzarroids take it over I will rmgroup it or moderate it; otherwise I will let it be.

By February 1990, Spafford posted (with the cooperation of Gilmore and others):

Subject: Alternative Newsgroup Hierarchies (Updated: 16 Feb 1990)
   Summary: describes the following alternate hierarchies: alt, bionet, biz, clarinet, gnu, inet/ddn, pubnet, unix-pc, u3b, vmsnet
   Introduction

   The USENET software allows the support and transport of hierarchies of newsgroups not part of the "traditional" USENET through use of the distribution mechanism. These hierarchies of groups are available to sites wishing to support them and finding a feed. In general, these groups are not carried by the entire network due to their volume, a restricted sphere of interest, or a different set of administrative rules and concerns.

   In general it is a bad idea to forward these newsgroups to your neighbors without asking them first; they should only be received at a site by choice. Not only is this generally-accepted net etiquette, it helps to preserve the freedom to do and say as the posters please in these newsgroups, since the only people who get them are those who asked to get them. This freedom is more restricted in the USENET as a whole, since every mainstream posting and every mainstream newsgroup name must be acceptable to a much wider audience than is present in these hierarchies. Due to the sheer size of the mainstream USENET, extra-long or controversial postings are more likely to cause problems when posted to the USENET; however, these alternative hierarchies exist precisely to support those kinds of postings (if germane to the hierarchy)....

Alt

"alt" is a small collection of newsgroups which are being distributed by a collection of sites that choose to carry them. Many USENET sites are not interested in these groups....

You can join the "alt subnet" by finding a site in your area that carries the groups. Either send mail to the administrators of the sites you connect to, or post something to a local "general" or "wanted" newsgroup for your area. If no sites nearby are getting them, you can get them from uunet.

USENET is now a huge, decentralized association of systems with over 10,000 groups and millions of users. It may be worth seeing how we got to this in 15 years. The earliest of these maps were obtained from Rick Adams; two are from the "mapping project" sponsored by the USENIX Association (Mark Horton and Karen Summers-Horton); most of them are by Brian Reid and reprinted with his permission. (Maps 10–12)

Spafford saw the death of the net looming in 1985; Brad Templeton (the proprietor of ClariNet, the first and largest electronic newspaper service) has repeatedly used "Imminent death..." as a humorous tag-line. In late 1994, Elizabeth Lear-Newman foresaw the same imminent death in an article in *Internet World*. One of the most interesting things about USENET has been its resiliency, partly as a consequence of the inventiveness of its users within the programming community, partly because of the steady increase in communication speed. Gilmore's invention of an alternate network may have been the first, but it is far from the last.

The community of use that Larry Roberts had anticipated had arrived.

The growth of the USENET community can be seen from statistics kept by Rick Adams at UUNET. On October 8, 1984, there were

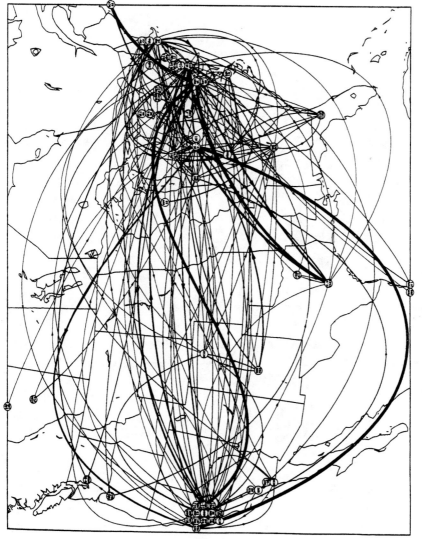

MAP 10   Backbone News Flows (1989) (Courtesy of Brian Reid)

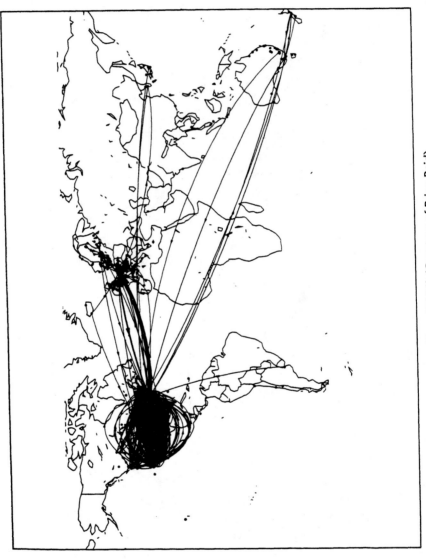

MAP 11   Worldwide Aggregate News Flow (1989) (Courtesy of Brian Reid)

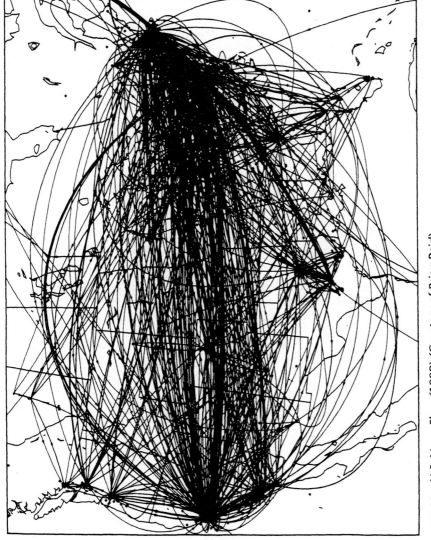

MAP 12   U.S. News Flow (1989) (Courtesy of Brian Reid)

158 groups circulated to 606 sites. A year later, there were 187 groups and 789 sites. In October 1986, it was 221 groups and 1414 sites. Not wanting to make this tedious, let me skip to October 1991, when there were 1,732 groups going to 14,565 sites. A year later this had over doubled to 4,129 groups and 23,253 sites; and in 1993 it was 8,504 groups and 40,972 sites. On September 8, 1994, news went to 58,402 sites; there were 10,696 groups with 1,006,399 articles. The total number of bytes that day was 2,100,318,663! Just let me call to mind the ICCC numbers in October 1972: 43,449 packets per node/day. At 512 bytes/packet that's just over 22 million bytes, about 1 percent of the news alone two decades later.

Bellovin, Ellis, and Truscott were honored at the January 1985 USENIX conference with "Keeper of the Flame" awards.

I have spent so much time on USENET because it was created right at the beginning of the second decade of the ARPANET. And it was news and mail that directly caused the increase in Internet use. These were the applications that began to drive the Internet. It may be worth noting here that while Tomlinson invented email, it was Larry Roberts who appears to have been the first to write an email application ("using a TECO macro," according to Cerf). Roberts was the sole person who foresaw that electronic mail would become crucial to the community.

Diversion 7

Network Working Group   Poorer Richard
Request for Comments: 1216   Almanac Institute
                                                        Prof. Kynikos
                                                Miskatonic University
                                                         1 April 1991

Gigabit Network Economics and Paradigm Shifts

Status of this Memo

This memo proposes a new standard paradigm for the Internet Activities
Board (IAB) standardization track. Distribution of this memo is
unlimited.

1. Introduction

The history of computer communication contains many examples of efforts
to align the capabilities of processors to that of communication media.
Packet switching is the classic case of a careful tradeoff between the
costs of memory, processing, and communications bandwidth.

With all of the attention and publicity focused on gigabit networks,
not much notice has been given to small and largely unfunded research
efforts which are studying innovative approaches for dealing with
technical issues within the constraints of economic science. This memo
defines one such paradigm.

2. Contemporary Network Economics

Recent cost estimates predict a continuing decline in the cost for
processing, memory, and communication. One recent projection put the
decline for $/bit and $/MIP at 99% per decade and put the decline for
$/bps at 90% per decade. Scalable parallel processor designs may
accelerate the cost declines for CPU and memory, but no similar
accelerated decline should be expected in the cost of communications.
Such a decline would imply eventual declines in the cost of 56Kbps
service used for voice, resulting in a negative rate of return for
telecommunications carriers, an unlikely eventuality even if free-
market forces are carried to their logical extreme.

Increases in processing power create additional demand for
communications bandwidth, but do nothing to pay for it. While we will
sell no paradigm before its time, the 9% difference, particularly after
compounding is taken into account, will bankrupt the internet community
unless a paradigm shift takes place.

3. The ULS Paradigm Shift

The ULS paradigm shift breaks the downward spiral by concentrating on end-to-end datagrams and virtual circuit services operating in the .01 uGbps region, namely Ultra Low Speed networking.

However,

"The worlds best technological paradigm shifts are useless unless they (a) are economically viable, (b) have clear applicability, (c) are technically feasible."

—Milton John in "Paradigms Lost"

3.1 Economic Viability

Cost projections indicate that individual ULS circuits can be provided at a cost of <$.03/month due to the unusually high multiplexing that will be possible on Gbit links. The 10 THz bandwidth of existing optical fibers will be able to support on the order of 1 TUser, handling population growth, and even internet growth, for some time. Moreover, if $.03/month is a significant barrier to entry, substantial discounts appear to be economically feasible.

3.2 Clear Applicability

A fundamental principle of networking is that network speed must match the application. We have identified a number of critical applications that are matched to ULS technology. Below we itemize a few of these, but we provide a brief description for only the first; the match for the others should be equally obvious.

- Low priority facsimile: A large percentage of documents and letters are sent via facsimile not because they need sub-minute delivery, but because they carry signatures or graphics. In these cases, a three-hour delivery (comparable to the value reliably achieved on many of today's packet-based email systems) is sufficient. With proper compression, this delivery time can be achieved over a ULSnet.

- Real time data (e.g., tracking glaciers)

- US postal service

- Contracting for research

To be truly viable, ULS networking must scale, and indeed it does.

With some effort, we envision extending the technology to the
extremely-low-speed regime. Applications that scale from the ULS
applications above are:

- Real time data (e.g., gravity wave detectors)
- Italian postal service
- Congressional budget process

3.3 Technical Feasibility

The hardware issues are well in hand. The remaining issues are protocol
related. To examine them, we must extrapolate backward from some well
known networking principles.

"Gigabit networks require new protocols."

The clear inference here is that ULS will require old protocols, so as
we recede into the future, we should expect the following:

ULS will require minimal development. Although we may need research in
storage technology to recover the software from old media such as
decayed magnetic dump tapes, paper tape, and partially recycled card
decks, this effort will be more than offset by the savings.

ULS protocols will be well documented, amenable to verification, and
suitable for MSI implementation in Silicon, or even Germanium or
relays. In particular, the alternating bit protocol [1] is a leading
contender.

"Bad news travel fast."

Therefore, ULS gives preferential treatment to good news. While this
will delay the delivery of bills, notices from timeshare condominiums,
and contest announcements, it will also produce immediate productivity
gains on several mailing lists.

3.4 Problems Requiring Work

ULS is not without problems.

Some other well-known protocol suites are well ahead of ULS in
exploring the desired performance operating point. We note our concern
about the dearth of domestic (U.S.-based) research and development in
this important area. This is particularly disturbing in light of the
level of work now underway in other countries.

Efficiency is a problem:

- All ULS protocols incorporate slow-start.

- Lower data rates mean fewer errors.

- Whereas modern protocols use 32 bit sequence numbers, acknowledgment fields, etc., ULS headers can be quite small (1 bit sequence numbers for the alternating-bit protocol). Thus the header/data ratio shrinks.

The net result is "creeping efficiency" which tends to push us away from the proper ULS operating point. While we have no definitive solution, there are several promising palliatives:

- Forward Error Insertion (FEI)

- Negative window scaling factors

- New protocol layers

- Multiple presentation layers

4. Conclusions

The road to Ultra Low Speed (ULS) technology is long, slow, and easy.

REFERENCES and BIBLIOGRAPHY

[1] Lynch, W. "Reliable full-duplex file transmission over half- duplex telephone lines", CACM, pp. 407–410, June 1968.

Security Considerations

Security issues are not discussed in this memo.

Authors' Addresses

Dr. Poorer Richard
Almanac Institute
Center against Misoneoism
Campo Imperatore, Italy
EMail: none

Prof. Kynikos
Miskatonic University
Arkham, MA.
Email: Kynikos@Cthulu.Miskatonic.EDU

Note: Prof. Kynikos has given me permission to reveal that he is Paul V. Mockapetris of the ISI.—PHS.

* * *

Network Working Group   V. Cerf
Request for Comments: 1217   CSCR
                                                         1 April 1991

        Memo from the Consortium for Slow Commotion Research (CSCR)

Status of this Memo

This RFC is in response to RFC 1216, "Gigabit Network Economics and
Paradigm Shifts." Distribution of this memo is unlimited.

To: Poorer Richard and Professor Kynikos

Subject: ULSNET BAA

From: Vint Cerf/CSCR

Date: 4/1/91

The Consortium for Slow Commotion Research (CSCR) [1] is pleased to
respond to your research program announcement (RFC 1216) on Ultra Low-
Speed Networking (ULSNET). CSCR proposes to carry out a major research
and development program on low-speed, low-efficiency networks over a
period of several eons. Several designs are suggested below for your
consideration.

1. Introduction

Military requirements place a high premium on ultra-robust systems
capable of supporting communication in extremely hostile environments.
A major contributing factor in the survivability of systems is a high
degree of redundancy. CSCR believes that the system designs offered
below exhibit extraordinary redundancy features which should be of
great interest to DARPA and the Department of Defense.

2. Jam-Resistant Land Mobile Communications

This system uses a highly redundant optical communication technique to
achieve ultra-low speed, ultra-robust transmission. The basic unit is
the M1A1 tank. Each tank is labelled with the number 0 or 1 painted
four feet high on the tank turret in yellow, day-glo luminescent paint.
Several detection methods are under consideration:

(a) A tree or sand-dune mounted forward observer (FO) radios to a rear
echelon main frame computer the binary values of tanks moving in a
serial column. The mainframe decodes the binary values and voice-

synthesizes the alphameric ASCII-encoded messages which is then radioed
back to the FO. The FO then dispatches a runner to his unit HQ with the
message. The system design includes two redundant, emergency back-up
forward observers in different trees with a third in reserve in a
foxhole.

(b) Wide-area communication by means of overhead reconnaissance
satellites which detect the binary signals from the M1A1 mobile system
and download this information for processing in special U.S. facilities
in the Washington, D.C. area. A Convection Machine [2] system will be
used to perform a codebook table look-up to decode the binary message.
The decoded message will be relayed by morse-code over a packet meteor
burst communications channel to the appropriate Division headquarters.

(c) An important improvement in the sensitivity of this system can be
obtained by means of a coherent detection strategy. Using long baseline
interferometry, phase differences among the advancing tank column
elements will be used to signal a secondary message to select among a
set of codebooks in the Convection Machine. The phase analysis will be
carried out using Landsat imagery enhanced by suitable processing at
the Jet Propulsion Laboratory. The Landsat images (of the moving tanks)
will be correlated with SPOT Image images to obtain the phase-encoded
information. The resulting data will be faxed to Washington, D.C., for
use in the Convection Machine decoding step. The remainder of this
process is as for (b) above.

(d) It is proposed to use SIMNET to simulate this system.

3. Low Speed Undersea Communication

Using the 16″ guns of the Battleship Missouri, a pulse-code modulated
message will be transmitted via the Pacific Ocean to the Ames Research
Center in California. Using a combination of fixed and towed acoustic
hydrophone arrays, the PCM signal will be detected, recorded, enhanced
and analyzed both at fixed installations and aboard undersea vessels
which have been suitably equipped. An alternative acoustic source is to
use M1A1 main battle tanks firing 150 mm H.E. ordnance. It is proposed
to conduct tests of this method in the Persian Gulf during the summer
of 1991.

4. Jam-Resistant Underwater Communication

The ULS system proposed in (2) above has the weakness that it is
readily jammed by simple depth charge explosions or other sources of
acoustic noise (e.g., Analog Equipment Corporation DUCK-TALK voice
synthesizers linked with 3,000 AMP amplifiers). An alternative is to

make use of the ultimate in jam resistance: neutrino transmission. For all practical purposes, almost nothing (including several light-years of lead) will stop a neutrino. There is, however, a slight cross-section which can be exploited provided that a cubic mile of sea water is available for observing occasional neutrino-chlorine interactions which produce a detectable photon burst. Thus, we have the basis for a highly effective, extremely low speed communication system for communicating with submarines.

There are a few details to be worked out:

(a) the only accelerator available to us to generate neutrino bursts is located at Batavia National Laboratory (BNL).

(b) the BNL facility can only send neutrino bursts in one direction (through the center of the Earth) to a site near Tierra del Fuego, Chile. Consequently, all submarines must be scheduled to pass near Tierra del Fuego on a regular basis to coincide with the PCM neutrino signalling from the BNL source.

(c) the maximum rate of neutrino burst transmission is approximately once every 20 seconds. This high rate can be reduced considerably if the power source for the accelerator is limited to a rate sustainable by discharging a large capacitor which is trickle charged by a 2 square foot solar panel mounted to face north.

5. Options for Further Reducing Effective Throughput

(a) Anti-Huffman Coding. The most frequent symbol is assigned the longest code, with code lengths reducing with symbol probability.

(b) Minimum likelihood decoding. The least likely interpretation of the detected symbol is selected to maximize the probability of decoding error.

(c) Firefly cryptography. A random signal (mason jar full of fireflies) is used to encipher the transmitted signal by optical combining. At the receiving site, another jar of fireflies is used to decipher the message. Since the correlation between the transmitting and receiving firefly jars is essentially nil, the probability of successful decipherment is quite low, yielding a very low effective transmission rate.

(d) Recursive Self-encapsulation. Since it is self-evident that layered communication is a GOOD THING, more layers must be better. It is proposed to recursively encapsulate each of the 7 layers of OSI,

yielding a 49 layer communications model. The redundancy and
retransmission and flow control achieved by this means should produce
an extremely low bandwidth system if, indeed, any information can be
transmitted at all. It is proposed that the top level application layer
utilize ASN.1 encoded in a 32 bit per character set.

(e) Scaling. The initial M1A1 tank basis for the land mobile
communication system can be improved. It is proposed to reduce the
effective data rate further by replacing the tanks with shuttle launch
vehicles. The only slower method of signalling might be the use of cars
on any freeway in the Los Angeles area.

(f) Network Management. It is proposed to adopt the Slow Network
Management Protocol (SNMP) as a standard for ULSNET. All standard
Management Information Base variables will be specified in Serbo-
Croatian and all computations carried-out in reverse-Polish.

(g) Routing. Two alternatives are proposed:

(1) Mashed Potato Routing

(2) Airline Baggage Routing [due to S. Cargo]

The former is a scheme whereby any incoming packets are stored for long
periods of time before forwarding. If space for storage becomes a
problem, packets are compressed by removing bits at random. Packets are
then returned to the sender. In the latter scheme, packets are
mislabelled at the initial switch and randomly labelled as they are
moved through the network. A special check is made before forwarding to
avoid routing to the actual intended destination.

CSCR looks forward to a protracted and fruitless discussion with you on
this subject as soon as we can figure out how to transmit the proposal.

NOTES

[1] The Consortium was formed 3/27/91 and includes David Clark, John
Wroclawski, and Karen Sollins/MIT, Debbie Deutsch/BBN, Bob Braden/ISI,
Vint Cerf/CNRI, and several others whose names have faded into an
Alzheimerian oblivion...

[2] Convection Machine is a trademark of Thoughtless Machines, Inc., a
joint-venture of Hot-Air Associates and Air Heads International using
vaporware from the Neural Network Corporation.

Security Considerations

Security issues are not discussed in this memo.

Chapter 16

The Great Switch

The trauma of January 1, 1983.

There were two powerful reasons to switch from NCP. The first was that the protocol limited the number of hosts to 255. By August 1981, there were 213. The second was inflexibility.

As Padlipsky pointed out, "By 1974 'ARPANET technology' had demonstrated its utility to the point that numerous organizations wanted to attach diverse Host systems to 'ARPA-like nets.' Unfortunately, it had been learned that an ARPA-like NCP was a relatively difficult implementation for operating systems that could not merely adopt (or at worst adapt) NCPs from like operating systems already attached to the original ARPANET." [1985, p. 119] Padlipsky's RFC 647 ("A Proposed Protocol for Connecting Host Computers to ARPA-like Networks via Directly-Connected Front-End Processors," November 12, 1974) was a first stab at this. Cerf and Kahn's TCP was another route.

From 1978 to 1981 an ever-increasing percentage of the hosts on the ARPANET employed the TCP/IP suite. This was especially true of the sites using DEC PDP-11s (as opposed to the IBM and DEC 10 and DEC 20 sites). As the ARPANET gradually became a true Internet, linking local networks in the US and both trans-Atlantic and trans-Pacific networks, heterogeneity began to become burdensome again, especially where addressing and address-space were concerned.

The tremendous increase in electronic mail placed another, different, burden on the system.

On November 1, 1981, Jon Postel issued RFC 801 "NCP/TCP Transition Plan." It said (in part):

Introduction

ARPA-sponsored research on computer networks led to the development of the ARPANET. The installation of the ARPANET began in September 1969, and regular operational use was underway by 1971. The ARPANET has been an operational service for at least 10 years. Even while it has provided a reliable service in support of a variety of computer research activities, it has itself been a subject of continuing research, and has evolved significantly during that time.

In the past several years ARPA has sponsored additional research on computer networks, principally networks based on different underlying communication techniques, in particular, digital packet broadcast radio and satellite networks. Also, in the ARPA community there has been significant work on local networks.

It was clear from the start of this research on other networks that the base host-to-host protocol used in the ARPANET was inadequate for use in these networks. In 1973 work was initiated on a host-to-host protocol for use across all these networks. The result of this long effort is the Internet Protocol (IP) and the Transmission Control Protocol (TCP).

These protocols allow all hosts in the interconnected set of these networks to share a common interprocess communication environment. The collection of interconnected networks is called the ARPA Internet (sometimes called the "Catenet").

The Department of Defense has recently adopted the internet concept and the IP and TCP protocols in particular as DoD wide standards for all DoD packet networks, and will be transitioning to this architecture over the next several years. All new DoD packet networks will be using these protocols exclusively.

The time has come to put these protocols into use in the operational ARPANET, and extend the logical connectivity of the ARPANET hosts to include hosts in other networks participating in the ARPA Internet.

As with all new systems, there will be some aspects which are not as robust and efficient as we would like (just as with the initial ARPANET). But with your help, these problems can be solved and we can move into an environment with significantly broader communication services.

Discussion

The implementation of IP/TCP on several hosts has already been completed, and the use of some services is underway. It is urgent that the implementation of of IP/TCP be begun on all other ARPANET hosts as soon as possible and no later than 1 January 1982 in any case. Any new host connected to the ARPANET should only implement IP/TCP and TCP-based services. Several important implementation issues are discussed in the last section of this memo.

Because all hosts can not be converted to TCP simultaneously, and some will implement only IP/TCP, it will be necessary to provide temporarily for communication between NCP-only hosts and TCP-only hosts. To do this certain hosts which implement both NCP and IP/TCP will be designated as relay hosts. These relay hosts will support Telnet, FTP, and Mail services on both NCP and TCP. These relay services will be provided beginning in November 1981, and will be fully in place in January 1982.

Initially there will be many NCP-only hosts and a few TCP-only hosts, and the load on the relay hosts will be relatively light. As time goes by, and the conversion progresses, there will be more TCP capable hosts, and fewer NCP-only hosts, plus new TCP-only hosts. But, presumably most hosts that are now NCP-only will implement IP/TCP in addition to their NCP and become "dual protocol" hosts. So, while the load on the relay hosts will rise, it will not be a substantial portion of the total traffic.

The next section expands on this plan, and the following section gives some milestones in the transition process. The last section lists the key documents describing the new protocols and services. Appendices present scenarios for use of the relay services.
The General Plan

The goal is to make a complete switch over from the NCP to IP/TCP by 1 January 1983.

It is the task of each host organization to implement IP/TCP for its own hosts. This implementation task must begin by 1 January 1982....

It is not enough to implement the IP/TCP protocols, the principal services must be available on this IP/TCP

base as well. The principal services are: Telnet, File
Transfer, and Mail....

Beyond providing the principal services in the new
environment, there must be provision for interworking
between the new environment and the old environment between now and January 1983....

Postel also promised a number of documents, not least of which
was *Internet Protocol Handbook,* which was to be available in "Jan 82."
This was to be a very different document from the first *Protocol Handbook.* The "Internet Message Protocol" had been revised in RFC 759
(August 1, 1980); the "DoD Standard Internet Protocol," RFC 760 (January 1, 61980) was obsoleted by RFC 777 and then RFC 791; the Telnet
Protocol was revised (RFC 764) as was FTP (RFC 765). Postel then issued a proposed Table of Contents for the Handbook (RFC 766), which
was obsoleted by RFC 774 (October 1, 1980).

Internet Protocol Handbook

Table of Contents

The internet family of protocols is replacing the old ARPANET
protocols. To this end an Internet Protocol Handbook will be prepared
by the Network Information Center. This Handbook is tentatively planned
to be available at the end of 1980. This Internet Protocol Handbook
will closely parallel the old ARPANET Protocol Handbook, and will
primarily be a collection of existing RFCs and IENs....

Overview	
The Catenet Model for Internetworking	IEN-48
Gateway Level	
Internet Protocol	IEN-128 RFC760
Gateway Routing: An Implementation Specification	
	IEN-30
How to Build a Gateway	IEN-109
Gateway Monitoring Protocol	IEN-131
CMCC Performance Measurement Message Formats	
	IEN-157
Host Level	
User Datagram Protocol	RFC768
Transmission Control Protocol	IEN-129 RFC761
Multiplexing Protocol	IEN-90
Application Level	
Time Server Protocol	IEN-142

Name Server Protocol   IEN-116
Trivial File Transfer Protocol   IEN-133
Telnet Protocol   IEN-148 RFC764
File Transfer Protocol   IEN-149 RFC765
Mail Transfer Protocol   RFC772
Internet Message Protocol   IEN-113 RFC759
Appendices
Assigned Numbers   RFC770
Address Mappings   IEN-115
Document File Format Standards   RFC678
Mail Header Format Standards   RFC733

The great switch took place on January 1, 1983. I have spoken to several dozen people who were involved, and they are unanimous in never wanting to repeat such an event.

From December 1982 through February 1983, David Smallberg surveyed Telnet, FTP, and SMTP servers (RFCs 832–843; 845–846). In RFC 847 the previous work was summarized.

This is a summary of the surveys of Telnet, FTP, and Mail (SMTP) servers conducted by David Smallberg in December 1982 and January and February 1983 as reported in RFC 832-843, 845-846. This memo extracts the number of hosts that accepted the connection to their server for each of Telnet, FTP, and SMTP, and compares it to the total host in the Internet (not counting TACs or ECHOS)....

TELNET

RFC	DATE	ACCEPT	TOTAL	PERCENT
832	7 Dec 82	83	315	26
...				
846	22 Feb 83	190	325	56

FTP

RFC	DATE	ACCEPT	TOTAL	PERCENT
832	7 Dec 82	70	315	26
...				
846	22 Feb 83	181	325	56

SMTP

RFC	DATE	ACCEPT	TOTAL	PERCENT
832	7 Dec 82	63	315	20
...				
846	22 Feb 83	178	325	55

The great switch may not have been complete nor regular; but it had been effected. And well over half of the host sites on the Internet were running TCP/IP by Washington's Birthday 1983. It was another revolution.

The reader will have noticed the "User Datagram Protocol" in Postel's Table of Contents. The UDP was described by Postel in RFC 768 (August 28, 1980). Like TCP it depends upon IP, which provides common address space and routing. TCP provides extremely reliable data transmission; UDP transmits discrete data packets without any delivery guarantee. "This protocol provides a procedure for application programs to send messages to other programs with a minimum of protocol mechanism. The protocol is transaction oriented, and delivery and duplicate protection are not guaranteed," the RFC states. TCP guarantees delivery; UDP doesn't. When transmitting (e.g.) graphics or sound, every bit doesn't count, but speed does. When transmitting banking information, accuracy means a great deal. UDP can be used for vision or voice; TCP for data.

At the end of 1969, there were 4 hosts; at the end of 1970, 13; at the time of the ICCC in October 1972 there were 31; two years later there were 49; by the end of 1975, there were 63 IMPs, many of them with multiple hosts. In August 1981 there were 213 hosts; May 1982, 235; August 1983, 562. The explosive growth had begun. TCP could theoretically accomodate a billion hosts—it may still have to.

Chapter 17

More Mail

Switching to sendmail and other flavors.

With the switch in protocols, came a switch in mail service, too. RFC 771 (by Cerf and Postel, September 1, 1980) was the "Mail transition Plan"; RFC 772 (by Sluizer and Postel, same date) was the draft "Mail Transfer Protocol." RFC 771 states:

The principal aim of the mail service transition plan is to provide orderly support for computer mail service during the period of transition from the old ARPANET protocols to the new Internet protocols.

This plan covers only the transition from the current text computer mail in the ARPANET environment to text computer mail in an Internet environment. This plan does not address a second transition from text only mail to multimedia mail.

The goal is to provide equivalent or better service in the new Internet environment as was available in the ARPANET environment. During the interim period, when both protocol environments are in use, the goal is to minimize the impact on users and existing software, yet to permit the maximum mail exchange connectivity....

The Internet protocol environment specifies TCP as the host-to-host transport protocol. The ARPANET protocol environment specifies NCP as the host-to-host transport protocol. Both TCP and NCP provide connection type process-to-process communication. The problem in the transition is to bridge these two different interprocess communication systems.

The objective of this plan is to specify the means by which the ARPANET
computer mail services may be extended into the Internet system without
disruptive changes for the users during the transition....

Cerf and Postel recognized that reading and writing mail was
done using things like "HERMES, MSG, MM, etc." Further they assumed that addresses would be of the form "MAILBOX@HOST." They
allowed for compound names (USC-ISIA, ARPANET-ISIA, SATNET-
NDRE); but the "only restriction is that '@' not appear in either the
'mailbox' or the 'host' strings in the destination address. Their "basic
ground rules" were:

1. ARPANET mailbox names must continue to work correctly.

2. No changes should be required to mail editor software
   which parses message headers to compose replies and the
   like. Specifically, non-ARPANET mailbox designators must
   be accommodated without change to the parsing and
   checking mechanisms of mail processing programs.

3. Automatic forwarding of messages between NCP and TCP
   environments without user (or operator) intervention.

The ARPANET was a relatively small, friendly community. There
was a single file *HOSTS.TXT* that contained all the information necessary for communication among the under 250 hosts—a name-to-ad-
dress mapping for every host. Typically, administrators emailed
changes to the Network Information Center (NIC) at SRI, and periodically ftp-ed the revised and updated HOSTS.TXT file. The NIC updated
HOSTS.TXT twice a week. The change to TCP/IP from NCP meant
many problems, not least those concerning size and volume.

For mail, the real complexities came with the host tables, for
there had to be provisos for "(1) an NCP host with 'old tables,' (2) an
NCP host with 'new tables,' (3) a TCP host, or (4) some other kind of
host. All TCP hosts are assumed to have 'new tables.' 'Old tables' are
those without these flag bits, while 'new tables' do have these flags.
32-bit Internet addresses. (This makes sense for even NCP-only hosts,
since after January 1, 1981 even they must use 96-bit leader format

which requires 24-bit ARPANET physical addresses). Each entry in this table will also have some flag bits."

RFC 772 was rewritten by Sluizer as RFC 780 (May 1981), but it was only 15 months later that Postel issued RFC 821: "Simple Mail Transfer Protocol." SMTP had the objective of transferring mail reliably and efficiently. "SMTP is independent of the particular transmission subsystem and requires only a reliable ordered data stream channel. Obsoletes RFCs 788, 780, 772." So reads the entry in the RFC Index.

In the late 1970s, mailers and readers were a hot item. And there were too many different types. Eric Allman's tale of his invention of *sendmail* is typical.

Eric Schmidt had been working on BerkNet and BerkNet was connected over 9600 baud tty lines—it was a batch system, like UUCP—and that was one of the periods when the relations between Bell and the university seemed to be iffy, so we couldn't get UUCP. Of course we did, fairly quickly. What happens is that industry decides "Oh, we wouldn't want the university to have that because we might lose it"; then the university does it themselves, so industry goes "Oh my God. We wanted ours to be standard, we'd better give it to them." BerkNet was a fine network for its time, but it had little things like the hostnames were single character. We thought the ARPANET was bad for having a limit of 255 hosts this was 26 hosts! C was cory; E was ernie kovacs; I and J were the Ingres 11/70 and VAX, respectively; the Computer Center got A through F, which was UNIX-A through UNIX-F, they thought they were very creative at their naming policies.

So there were lots of people with terminals in their offices and starting to use email and services more. We had this network that supported mail and primitive file copy and even-more primitive remote execution. I really mean primitive, the numbers were about an hour. The pressure that came up was from professors in the department [EECS] who wanted to be on the ARPANET. I think the ARPANET was still on the

11/40 because the interface link wouldn't plug into the 11/70. The result was that we didn't want to give accounts to everyone, but we were forced to. We had to fix things so that ARPANET mail would go out along BerkNet, but not the other way round. You've got to understand, at that time people didn't put headers on their mail, except on the ARPANET, which had RFC 822 [As RFC 822 is 1983, Allman has confused the RFCs here. He most likely meant RFC 733, which was obsoleted by RFC 822.], which wasn't very well enforced.

At that time you had UUCP coming in to ernie kovacs, BerkNet mail within the UC campus, and ARPANET mail going out, each of which used different mail standards. If you wanted to send mail to the ARPANET and to UUCP your only choice was to send it twice. This was, pretty clearly, not a good idea.

I thrashed for a long time, not being able to see what was the right way to fix this. One day I sat down in my living room, I was living on Glen Street, and I said, "OK, this is stupid, I'm going to write down the *ad hoc* code." And as I wrote the *ad hoc* code, it became clear that there were patterns and later that afternoon I figured out what the configuration table should look like. The configuration table for delivermail was compiled in—it looked at characters. It said "Oh, there's an @, it must be the ARPANET; ! it must be UUCP: it must be BerkNet." The idea was that every network had its own magic character.... Anyway, delivermail was shipped on the 4 or the 4.1 tape [it was 4BSD, October 1980]. But it started to become clear that that configuration was inadequate. It was just unwieldy as we got more machines.

So I began working on a revision of delivermail and Bill Joy ragged on me. He said "It's not delivering mail, it just hands it off to another agent." So I changed it to sendmail. So sendmail is really just delivermail version 2 or 3.

It's worth pointing out that during this the ARPANET was undergoing the transition from NCP [Network Control Protocol] to TCP [Transmission Control Protocol]. And that was an extremely painful period, going from mit-xx to mit-xx.ARPA to xx@mit.edu over a couple of years. It didn't take me long to figure out that the easier it was for me to change sendmail, the more likely it would be that I could keep up to date.

Allman wasn't the only person concerned about addressing: SMTP had increased the load; TCP had increased connectivity among the increasing number of networks. In RFC 724 (May 12, 1977), Dave Crocker, J. Vittal, K. Pogran, and J. Henderson proposed a new standard for ARPA network text messages. They revised this six months later in RFC 733. Crocker then updated this in RFC 822 in August 1982—"Standard for the format of ARPA Internet text messages"—the RFC immediately following Postel's on SMTP. From 1986 on, a series of RFCs updated Crocker's work, largely because of the necessity of mapping Internet addressing, MIME (Multipurpose Internet Mail Extensions), and CCITT's X.400 standard.

In November 1983, Paul Mockapetris of the ISI released two RFCs (882 and 883): the first involving a rationale for the "Domain Name System"; the second, a first implementation specification. DNS is a distributed database. The database is structured in the same manner as the UNIX (or MS-DOS) filesystem: an inverted tree. DNS has seven "top-level domains": com (commercial), edu (educational), gov (government), mil (military), net (networking organizations), org (noncommercial organizations), and int (international organizations, like NATO). Later, the ISO two-letter country codes were acknowledged as domain names as well (this is true except for Great Britain, which should be gb, but insists on using uk). Most countries use the three-letter domains, as well (e.g., edu.au for an Australian university or com.sg for a company in Singapore). The British differ here, too, using ac for academic community and co for company. There is also a us top-level domain, as in cnri.reston.va.us, the Corporation for National Research Initiatives in Reston, Virginia.

I should note here that in uk, things were different: Addressing in Britain was the reverse of that in the rest of the world—or at least for members of JANET, the Joint Academic Network. Thus, someone at the Department of Computing at Imperial College in London would be xxx@doc.ic.ac.uk to someone in the U.S., but xxx@uk.ac.ic.doc within the U.K. This led to a number of problems: First of all, addresses originating within the U.K. but bound for destinations outside had to have whatever followed the @ reversed in every address, as did mail destined for the U.K. but originating elsewhere. The U.K. addresses had the smallest entity last, the U.S., etc., had the largest entity last. The styles were referred to as "big-endian" and "little-endian." Among other things, this meant that no computer science entity in the U.K. could use cs in its address, as machines in other countries would interpret this as mail going to Czechoslovakia. Queen Mary College, London, was thus dcs.qmc.ac.uk in the U.S. or uk.qmc.ac.dcs in the U.K. It was very confusing. "Remembering to reverse names was always a problem," Peter Collinson told me. "The commercial world never had to deal with this. It was only those of us who dealt with JANET who had to." (This is "grey book addressing.")

The important thing, however, was that DNS gave to the new protocols a new way of addressing mail and a new coign of advantage for routing it.

In RFC 897 (February 1984), Jon Postel issued a "policy statement on the implementation of the Domain Style Naming System in the Internet." RFC 897 was "an official policy statement of the ICCB [Internet Control and Configuration Board] and the DARPA." The result of this RFC was that on March 14, 1984, "all hosts should start using their domain style names as their official and primary names"; on May 2, 1984, "the use of old style names must be completely phased out"; and that on September 5, 1984, the NIC would "decommission" the old hosts table. It would be the end of a 15-year reign.

Recall that under the Host-Host program there could be 64 hosts. Address space was raised from six bits to eight bits, so that under the NCP there was a maximum of 255 hosts. Under DNS, there could be 127 "Class A" networks, each of which could potentially contain 16,777,214 hosts; 16,384 "Class B" networks, each containing 65,534 hosts; and 2,097,152 "Class C" networks, each containing up to 254 hosts. That's a very large number of possible hosts. By 1992 it was seen to be insufficient.

In January 1986, Craig Partridge summarized all of this in RFC 974, "Mail Routing and the Domain System," which was intended to present "a description of how mail systems on the Internet are expected to route messages based on information from the domain system described in RFCs 882, 883, and 973."

Partridge's explanation was needed, because

Under RFC-882 and RFC-883 certain assumptions about mail
addresses have been changed. Up to now, one could usually
assume that if a message was addressed to a mailbox, for
example, at LOKI.BBN.COM, that one could just open an
SMTP connection to LOKI.BBN.COM and pass the message
along. This system broke down in certain situations, such
as for certain UUCP and CSNET hosts which were not directly attached to the Internet, but these hosts could be
handled as special cases in configuration files (for example, most mailers were set up to automatically forward
mail addressed to a CSNET host to CSNET-RELAY.ARPA).

Under domains, one cannot simply open a connection
to LOKI.BBN.COM, but must instead ask the domain system
where messages to LOKI.BBN.COM are to be delivered. And
the domain system may direct a mailer to deliver messages
to an entirely different host, such as SH.CS.NET. Or, in
a more complicated case, the mailer may learn that it has
a choice of routes to LOKI.BBN.COM.

Effectively, RFC 974 consisted of a set of "guidelines on how
mailers should behave in this more complex world."

But in the meantime, the world was already getting yet more
complex. In July 1984 there had been a meeting at BBN concerning
multimedia mail systems (written up by Harry Forsdick in RFC 910,
August 1984); in December, Elvy and Nedved issued RFC 915 on a
"Network Path Service," which proposed a new service to enable users
to determine "mailbox addresses for hosts that are not part of the
ARPA-Internet but can be reached by one or more relay hosts that
have UNIX to UNIX Copy (UUCP) mail, CSNET mail, MAILNET mail,
BITNET mail, etc."

It was the mid-1980s. With the new protocols, the new mail service and the new non-government networks, the teen-aged ARPANET
was no longer an experiment. It was now a utility, like electricity or
the phone service.

Chapter 18

Bitnet, Fidonet, UUNET

Store-and-forward networks and more on commercialization.

The genuine success of UUCP and USENET was a blow to the tsars of large, centralized, blue Computer Centers, which (of course) didn't run UNIX. What they wanted (and needed) was a different sort of network, one in which news and mail were available, but which didn't involve either remote login or genuine file transfer. Ira Fuchs, then the director of the CUNY Computer Center in Manhattan, came up with the solution in 1981: BITNET ("Because It's Time Network"). The first link was between CUNYVM in Manhattan and YALEVM in New Haven, Connecticut on May 5, 1981. By January 19, 1982, CUNY, Yale, the New Jersey Educational Computer Network, Pennsylvania State University, and Brown University (in Providence, Rhode Island) were linked. Two months later, Cornell, Columbia, and Princeton universities had joined BITNET. Originally, only IBM hosts at university computing centers were linked. BITNET is a "store-and-forward" network and its underlying protocol is NJE (Network Job Entry), which has been implemented on VM (RSCS), MVS (JES/NJE), VMS (JNET), and a few other operating systems. Its structure makes it ideal for mailing lists. (More on IBM's RSCS and VNET in Chapter 19.) Eric S. Raymond (in *The Hacker's Dictionary*, p. 68) calls BITNET "Everybody's least favorite part of the network..." and goes on to state "The BITNET hosts are a collection of IBM dinosaurs and VAXen...that communicate using 80-character EBCDIC card images...[and] tend to mangle the headers and text of third-party traffic...with annoying regularity."

In actuality, though BITNET users can be considered part of the Matrix, they are not really users of the basic Internet applications. BITNET has a highly sophisticated mailing-list maintainer and an archive server. But it did not have remote login (telnet), and only acquired this facility among VM hosts in 1988. Nor does it have general file transfer. In 1990, BITNET joined with CSNet to form The Corporation for Research and Educational Networking (CREN); the principal constituents of CREN are the BITNET/CSnet hosts; NetNorth in Canada; and EARN in Europe; though there are a number of Japanese sites. Over the past few years, many former BITNET hosts have dropped BITNET and linked to the Internet. But in 1992, CREN had 550 members and affiliates in the US and the logical network consisted of "almost 3,500 mini- and mainframe computers in about 1400 organizations spanning 47 countries" [*BITNET Overview,* Jan. 13, 1992]. A year later, Jim Conklin's "The Future of CREN and BITNET" said:

> CREN and its Cooperating Networks worldwide provide NJE connectivity to some 1,400 educational and research organizations, largely in higher education, in 48 countries. The future, however, lies with the more powerful Internet Protocol and rapidly evolving services built on that protocol. CREN has been actively encouraging its members to install Internet-compatible mail software. It is beginning to seek mechanisms by which it may facilitate low-cost Internet connectivity for CREN members, perhaps through agreements with organizations whose primary purpose is that of supplying connectivity services.

According to the BITEARN (the European BITNET-technology network), there were 3,477 hosts world-wide in July 1992 (for more on EARN, see Chapter 20). Though of historical importance in connecting the many large IBM-based academic computer centers to the Matrix, it is hard to see BITNET as being a major force in the future. (In fact, *Matrix News* in July 1993 reported "BITNET is dying"; and in October 1994 documented this in an article called "The Rise and Fall of BITNET.")

FidoNet is a cooperative network of PCs and compatibles running MS-DOS. It was formed in 1983 and runs on the Fido protocol, which

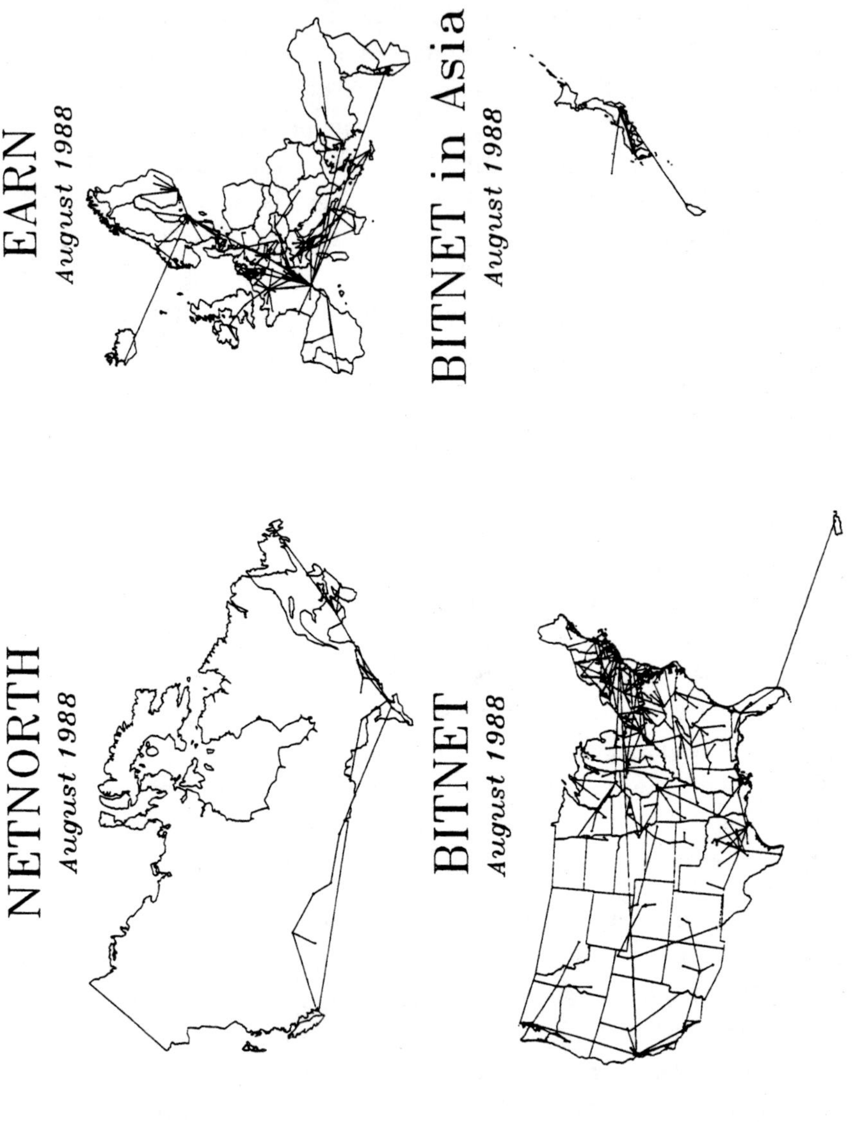

EARN
August 1988

BITNET in Asia
August 1988

NETNORTH
August 1988

BITNET
August 1988

MAP 13   BITNET Map (Courtesy of Rick Adams)

is similar to UUCP, and employs XModem and ZModem. The protocol was developed by Tom Jennings. There are a number of mailers and types of bulletin board software. While most sites are in North America, there are connections to Europe, Indonesia, and South Africa. There were 16,303 FidoNet hosts in 1992. In 1993, there was still growth, though not explosive.

Remember USENET? In late 1980, it had 50 sites. By 1983, there were ten times as many. There were 2500 two years later; and by mid-1987, there were 6500. At that time, there were about 12,000 articles every fortnight being posted. Several proposals were made concerning centralization and distribution. At the summer 1984 USENIX Conference in Salt Lake City, Lauren Weinstein suggested a system for "broadcasting Netnews and Network Mail via Satellite." The broadcast was to be via the "vertical blanking interval" of a cable TV system. The USENIX Association invested in the project and, with the help of Lou Katz (founding president of USENIX), Weinstein installed a UUCP site, "stargate," on December 3, 1984, at the uplink facilities of Southern Satellite Systems in Georgia. Stargate was a Fortune 32:16 system with a 30Mbyte disk. The transmissions appeared "as a portion of the vertical interval on...WTBS." Katz wrote about the project in the December 1984 ;login: and Weinstein described the actual installation at the USENIX conference in Dallas in January 1985.

At its meeting in Denver (January 1986), the USENIX Board expressed unhappiness at Stargate's "lack of direction and purpose." At its next meeting (Napa, California, March 1986), Katz reported that Weinstein had not produced any sort of plan. The USENIX Board then published a call for "UUCP and/or USENET Proposals" in the May/June ;login: and at the Board meeting in Atlanta in June, asked John Quarterman and Wally Wedel to analyze a written proposal from Weinstein and Mark Horton. Wedel's analysis (presented in October) showed the plan to be unworkable.

In the meantime, Rick Adams had written to Debbie Scherrer (then Vice President of USENIX) with a plan for a centralized site, which would be accessed via Tymnet by subscribers; in email on December 6, 1985, Scherrer expressed interest in exploring this. Adams was at the October 1986 Board meeting and asked whether another proposal would be entertained. There was a generally positive response. A plan was forthcoming in January 1987, and a revision was presented to the Board in New Orleans in March. It was approved with enthusiasm and I was appointed to spend up to $35,000 for a brief experimental period. UUNET was born. It was the first organization to sell UUCP and USENET access.

Set up in May, UUNET had 50 customers by June 1987. At the outset, UUNET had the (unprecedented) support of DARPA, not only where the use of hardware and staff were concerned, but also to test the feasibility of mail forwarding between ARPANET and non-ARPANET sites. UUNET was subsequently spun off as a non-profit communications service offering UUCP mail and USENET news to other networks; it then became a for-profit corporation, offering a variety of connections and services under the name AlterNet. UUNET soon paid its debt to USENIX. With several thousand customers in 1994, it has shown itself a worthwhile investment. I will return to UUNET later.

Diversion 8

Network Working Group   C. Partridge
Request for Comments: 1313   BBN
                                                        1 April 1992

                Today's Programming for KRFC AM 1313
                         Internet Talk Radio

Status of this Memo

This memo provides information for the Internet community. It does not
specify an Internet standard. Distribution of this memo is unlimited.

Welcome!

Hi and welcome to KRFC Internet Talk Radio, your place on the AM dial
for lively talk and just-breaking news on internetworking. Sponsored by
the Internet Society, KRFC serves the San Francisco Bay Area. For those
of you outside the Bay Area, copies of program transcripts can be
anonymously FTPed from archives.krfc.com the day after the program, or
you can listen in via vat.

Here's today's programming for today, Wednesday, 1 April 1992.

Hacker's Hour with Phil Karn (Midnight)

Phil's special guest today is Dr. David Mills, who will explain the
special problems of correcting for the Doppler effect when trying to
properly synchronize the new WWV receiver chip in your PC while flying
on the Concorde.

Nighttime News (1AM)

Award winning Nighttime News gives you a full hour on those key facts
you need to know before going to bed. Be sure to catch our network
outage report with Elise Gerich. (Elise's report is sponsored by ANS.)

Late At Night With Ole (2 AM)

Call in your favorite Internetwork questions to Ole Jacobsen and his
guests. Tonite's featured guests are John Moy, prime author of OSPF,
and Milo Medin who will talk about how OSPF is great, but you really
need to test it on 1822 networks to understand why.

Marty in the Morning (6 AM)

Join the irrepressable Marty for five hours of eye-opening talk and
commentary. Hear the latest on the commercial state of data networking
in the US and who is at fault for limiting its growth. Special guest
Kent England plans to drop by the studio today—listen in for the
flames!

Education Report (11 AM)

Gordon Cook solicits advice from Prof. David Farber on good ways to
develop a research career. (In the likely event that Prof. Farber is
unavailable at the last minute, Prof. Farber has arranged for Prof.
David Sincoskie to take his place).

Lunch with Lynch (11:30 AM)

Dan Lynch is on vacation this week and Vint Cerf is taking his place.
Today Vint has lunch with Mitch Kapor of the EFF, MacArthur genius
Richard Stallman, and Gen. Norman Schwartzkopf. Don't miss Vint's
suggestions for wines to go with today's business lunch! [Lunch with
Lynch is sponsored by Interop. Wines are provided by the vineyards in
return for promotional considerations].

News (1 PM)

Join Joyce and Jon as they report on the key networking news of the
day. Don't miss their update on the latest address and port assignments
and tips on upcoming RFCs!

Two by Four Time (2 PM)

Today Marshall Rose will take out his two-by-four and apply it to Phill
Gross for violating the Internet Standard Meeting Rules at the last
IETF and starting a session before 9 AM. Additional victims to be
announced. Today's show will be available as a book from Prentice Hall
by next Tuesday.

Mike at the Mike (4 PM)

Listen in to the Marina's favorite local DJ. Hear why They never listen
and Never will! How come The Book's publishers don't seem to be able to
add and why ATM is Another Technical Mistake. Then join MAP at 7:45 for
a wee bit of this week's preferred single malt.

The Protocol Police (8 PM)

Liven up your evening with the protocol police. Join our intrepid team
of Stev Knowles and Mike St. Johns as they debug various TCP/IP
implementations from the comfort of Mike's hot tub using Stev's water-
proof portable PC. Last week they caught Peter Honeyman hijacking an
NFS implementation. This week they're joined by Yakov Rehkter with his
new Roto-Router tool, designed to catch routing anomalies. Who will our
team nab this week?

Family Hour (10 PM)

As part of this week's special series on children and networking, Bob
Morris and Jerry Estrin talk about how much you should teach your young
children about networking.

Securely Speaking (11 PM)

Come eavesdrop as Steve Kent and Steve Crocker give you this week's
latest security news (if they're allowed to talk about it). And
remember, just after 11 o'clock Steve and Steve will be reading this
week's encrypted message. If you're the first caller to call in with
the right DES key to decrypt the message, you'll win $1,000 and an all
expenses paid trip to Ft. Meade! (U.S. nationals only please).

Security Considerations

Security issues are discussed in the above section.

Part 4

TIME LINE—Part IV (1982–1989)

1982   EUnet (European UNIX Network) begun at the April EUUG meeting in Paris.

1983   All hosts and networks communicating with the ARPANET are required to use TCP/IP instead of the previous NCP protocols.

ARPANET splits into two networks: MILNET, which later became the Defense Data Network (DDN), and ARPANET, the research backbone of the ARPA Internet.

EARN, the European Academic and Research Network, is established.

NSF forms an office that can do networking, with the intention of connecting national supercomputer centers.

JANET is established in the U.K., from the former SERCnet.

JUNET, the Japan UNIX Network, established by Jun Murai and others.

1985   Following the decision breaking up AT&T, companies begin laying fiber optic cable as a basis for fast data links.

1985   NSF funds the first five national supercomputer centers, which are intended to interconnect with a national NSFNET backbone.

1986   Craig Partridge invents MX (Mail Exchanger) records, which permit hosts on non-IP networks such as CSNet and UUCP, and later BITNET and FidoNet, to have domain addresses.

Original NSFNET backbone implemented.

NNTP (Network News Transfer Protocol) specified by Brian Kantor and Phil Lapsley.

DFN (German Research Network) established.

CNRI is founded.

1987   UUNET, the first organization to sell UUCP and USENET access, begins.

NSF agrees to allow Merit, Inc. to manage the NSFNET backbone, in cooperation with MCI and IBM.

First Interop conference is held.

1989   The ARPANET is shut down.

Chapter 19

Proprietary Nets

Largely concerning IBM's VNET.

While I have concentrated on the ARPANET and its developments, in order to recognize the realities we will have to look at what was going on outside of the ARPA and NATO circle. IBM's SNA had been a motivator of a good deal of network activity. But it was network activity that focused upon store-and-forward and on homogeneity, rather than heterogeneity. This was not the "evil nature of Big Blue," as one networker suggested to me; it was rather the feeling that by setting up good communications among its own products, the corporation would sell more of those products.

IBM's internal networks grew out of the NJE (Network Job Entry) protocol suite in 1972 and the Remote Spooling Communication Subsystem (RSCS), which began in 1974 (the earliest mention I know of is in IBM's September 10, 1974, announcement of VM/370 Release 2). NJE was used for mail transfer; that same year, RSCS was apparently written as a private communication tool by Ed Hendricks in Cambridge, Massachusetts, and Tim Hartmann in Poughkeepsie, New York, who were working on a joint project. Hendricks' focus was on transferring data. He was the originator of the store-and-forward design still used in BITNET and EARN as well as thinking through a layered architecture with interfaces between various parts of the networking system. In 1972 another IBM project had begun development of a spool-based network. It was this that became the HASP multi-leaving tool and the functional concepts were used in the internal IBM network under the prescient name "SUN" (Subsystem Unified Network). This SUN-interface was refined and NJE was "developed to the new interface, and support was upgraded in all participating systems" [Hendricks and Hartmann 1979]. General availability of VM/370 in January 1975 led to increased use of RSCS. By April 16, 1975, there were 22 VM systems on the IBM (internal) network, three of them in the U.K.

This network is usually called VNET, though IBM for a time called it the "Corporate Job Network." VNET, in turn, became "the archetype for Pass-Through," as described by Mendelsohn, Linehan, and Anzick (1983). Pass-Through (from 1978 on) was seen as complementary to RSCS/VNET, providing "a complementary interactive networking function." It was Pass-Through that "opened a migration path into a more sophisticated, comprehensive SNA [Systems Network Architecture] network." The VM/Pass-Through Program Product was released in January 1980.

In ARPANET terms, Pass-Through was a virtual-circuit network with static routing. Each node had a look-up table with next-hop information for "each possible destination." No node had the complete network map. A major shortcoming was the fact that the tables were maintained manually and had to be "hand-checked for consistency."

VNET was a popular and interesting endeavor. Nodes 1000 (Copenhagen) and 1001 (Iceland) were linked in June 1983. By the end of 1986, there were 2,297 hosts. (At the same time, there were 5,089 Internet hosts.)

Other proprietary networking systems worth mentioning are the Xerox Internet, using XNS (Xerox Network Services) protocols, which has been influential in work on remote procedure calls and external data formats; and DNA, Digital Network Architecture, and the DEC-NET protocols, which are used in DEC's EASYnet, have had influence through their work on congestion control (and DECNET's interoperability with OSI).

VNET Network April 16, 1975

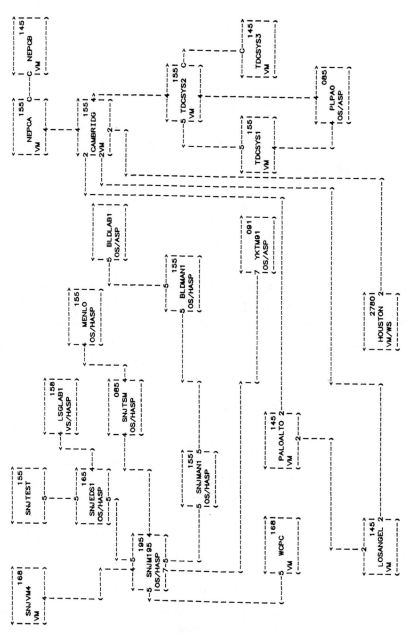

MAP 14   VNET Map (Courtesy of Peter Capek)

Chapter 20

Europe and Asia in the 1980s

The birth of UKnet, EUnet, JUNET, etc.

With the great switchover to TCP/IP, the ARPANET became the Internet. But much was going on in Europe and in Asia. In fact, as ARPA's experiment became a teenager (the UCLA node turned 13 on September 2, 1982), it began to enter a growth spurt and achieve international popularity.

UKnet and EUnet

As I remarked earlier, Armando Stettner was responsible for netnews getting to Europe. His machine, decvax, eventually became the source of news trans-Atlantically and trans-Pacifically. His connection to Europe was to the Mathematical Center in Amsterdam, to mcvax. This was a UUCP connection. Teus Hagen and his colleagues in Amsterdam then fed the news to, among others, Peter Collinson at the University of Kent in Canterbury. Collinson told me that in 1980–81, Hagen had asked, "We've got a feed, do you want one?" "But we couldn't dial out, so they called us," Collinson said. "Martin Levy, who had been a student at UKC, was in the U.S. and he brought over an American modem. And he began sending us news from the U.S. So we could now dial out as both a news feed and to send mail to Europe—it may have even been an X.25 connection. The summer that Martin left that job, the news feed died and we switched full time to X.25, until I could get to EUUG and convince them to give UKC a grant for £5000."

Peter Houlder, formerly of UKC, now with EUnet GB, told me that 1979 was the year that U.K. institutions first made email connections. Neither Peter Collinson nor Peter Houlder kept track of the UKnet sites until Collinson began billing in 1985. At that time, there were 22 billable sites on the net:

acorn	Acorn, now Olivetti
csbstan	St. Andrews University
edai	Edinburgh University AI Department
edcaad	Edinburgh University Computer-Aided Design Department
flame	University of Warwick
glasgow	Glasgow University
hwcee	Heriot Watt University
icdoc	Imperial College London
idec	ICL Information Technology Services
inset	The Instruction Set, now Hoskyns
ist	IST
kcl-cs	Kings College London
logitek	Logitek
paisley	University of Paisley
qmw-dcs	Queen Mary College London
qtlon	Quantime
root44	Root Computers, now Unisoft
spider	Spider Systems
stl	STL—then became STC
tivax	Turing Institute
ucl-cs	University College London
ulcs	University of Leeds

Houlder told me, "the only reference I can still find to actual sites we linked earlier than that is in a paper dated October 1983, which shows that in the the previous nine months we had grown from 30 to 78 email/news links. I don't know how many were email only and how many were news."

UKnet "never ran OSI," Houlder said. "It did run UUCP over X.25 to Amsterdam and UUCP combined with coloured book software on U.K. links. The coloured book software was OSIish in that the various colours of the protocol roughly related to levels in the 7-layer model but the name ordering was, of course, reversed." The coloured books are the volumes issued by JANET: Orange—Cambridge Ring 82; Pink—Ethernet; Grey—JNT Mail Protocol; etc. It is the grey book which specifies Britain's famed backward addressing scheme.

At the April 1982 meeting of the European Unix systems User Group in Paris, Hagen, Collinson, and Keld Simonsen from Denmark sat down and set up a system of UUCP connections—EUnet. Piet Beertema was involved as hardware implementor and network engineer and Daniel Karrenberg, as IP initiator. (Even then the UNIX community was inclined towards TCP/IP.)

Teus Hagen told me: "Originally, I designed a cost calculation algorithm for the international PTT costs. First, I separated email and news (the only data types transported). For email, the European initiator or European recipient paid for the the trans-Atlantic cost, based on amount of data transported on total transport of email and news data sent on the phone line. All news was sent to Holland: so that was the transport cost for the Atlantic line. For each recipient backbone site in Europe the amount of extracted data was calculated and that gave a cost calculation factor for the backbone site for the news data costs. The backbone site paid for the rental or phone line to Holland (we used star topology), and did the same calculation for its end sites, based on the amount of news data the end site received and the costs it entailed on the route from the U.S.A. to it.

"Thus, if the news article was posted in a country and distributed within Europe, the poster paid for the upload costs to Holland, and the receiver its distribution share from Holland to his site. So for every message a poster (Email or News) would pay within Europe or abroad, and the recipient would have to pay the costs involved in order to get the data on a transport-cost-based way. Later an extra amount of money was included in the costs to pay the manpower at CWI [the successor to MC], machine, and travel costs for all backbone manager meetings. Clearly this schema was very different from the usual schema used by the PTTs in which the originator pays."

Keld Simonsen pointed out to me that DKnet was "the first to pay Amsterdam in the beginning of 1983 for our services via mcvax. It was the computer science institute (DIKU) of University of Copenhagen which executed the agreement, and there were commercial customers from the beginning, including NCR Software Engineering in Copenhagen." So, by 1983 both Denmark and the UK had mixed commercial, academic, and research/government hosts in the neworks.

Jaap Akkerhuis told me about the first line between MC and Washington—also to **seismo**. In the summer of 1986 he and Beertema were "running out of X.25 bandwidth. So I literally calculated on the back of an envelope that we could make up the leasing cost in a year, which was very lucky because our budget cycle in Amsterdam was one year. So Piet went and convinced our Director. We leased a line from the Dutch PTT and Rick Adams sent us a modem. All of a sudden, a week before we were to begin, the PTT asked us what we were going to connect our line to. 'You need to cover the second half of the ocean,' they said. So the price instantly doubled. But we convinced AT&T to lease us a 9600 baud SLIP connection. And we were up in October 1986. But after a month we were cut off. I called the PTT and they said that their part was fine, I would have to talk to AT&T. I phoned them and they said 'We cut you off because you didn't pay.' I told them we had received no bill. It turned out they had sent the bill surface mail. They reconnected, and a month later they cut us off again. We still hadn't gotten the first bill. All in all, we were cut off and reconnected three times that year. I finally located a supervisor who arranged to have our bills sent by air."

Beertema confirmed Akkerhuis' tale: "Not only did we find it hard to get AT&T to mail our bill by air, at one point I had them send it to seismo, and they then sent it on by air mail. I still have one of the invoices, addressed 'CENTRUM VOOR WISKUNDE / C/O CTR FOR SEISMIC STUDIES...' and dated '22 July 1988.' The line was installed in

July 1986. It was upgraded to 64kbps in 1989, though we had ordered the upgrade in August 1988."

Japan

Jun Murai and his colleagues were not behind their North American and European colleagues. JUNET—Japanese Universities and Research Net—was begun in 1984, when NTT still controlled all communications within Japan, though it was well-known that telecommunications would be decontrolled in April 1985. As Carl Malamud tells the story, "All the senior researchers had been debating how to take advantage of deregulation to put in networks. Meetings were held to debate the subtleties of various OSI architectures. To Jun, this was a waste of time. As he puts it, 'I was young and that was boring.'

"He took two modems, scammed a phone line from university administrators..., and started running UUCP transfers. That was the start of JUNET. While the establishment continued to attend OSI meetings, JUNET continued to grow." (The main OSI project in Japan was Sigma, eventually cancelled by MITI.)

Links were set up to mcvax and to seismo in Washington. In 1986, there was a domestic IP network. By 1988, JUNET connected over 2,000 computers in 200 organizations via dial-up lines using UUCP, leased lines with TCP/IP and X.25, and IP/X.25 for international connections. In 1989, Murai and Torben Nielsen established a link to Hawaii. Larry Landweber helped hook Japan to CSNET. More recently, the WIDE Project took over operation of the Japanese IP backbone. It supplies a range of internet services and connects to a number of Japanese (regional) and international networks.

The ISO-OSI protocols were never used by JUNET, as far as I have been able to ascertain.

EARN

I earlier mentioned EARN as the European version of BITNET. EARN (European Academic Research Network) was, indeed, formed in 1983 on the BITNET model. IBM funded the transatlantic phone links between them until 1987, at the same time the corporation (I have been reliably told) invested over $15 million to support EARN.

EARN is administratively a French organization, but it currently links a thousand hosts in Europe, North Africa and India. Many EARN hosts are IBM VM or DEC VAX VMS machines. However, because of real deficiencies in the NJE protocols, EARN began migration to ISO-OSI protocols in 1988, the migration being coordinated by RARE.

RARE

RARE (Reseaux Associes pour la Recherche Europeenne) is an association of European networks, with its headquarters in the Netherlands. It is not a network. There have been on-going plans for coordination among EUnet, EARN, and HEPnet (High Energy Physics network) for five years. The basic problem at the original meeting in 1987 was the same one that still exists today: RARE has decided that the networks should run ISO-OSI protocols. There is, indeed, a conversion plan, but the extant networks don't fit this model: most of them are TCP/IP networks and don't use OSI. The problem is not intractible, as can be seen from RFC 1616 (May 1994) by the RARE Task Force on X.400 (1988l).

RFC 1616 "shows that both X.400 (1988) and RFC 822 / MIME / PEM will be developed and used within the European R&D community." It concludes "that X.400 (1988) will be the preferred protocol for inter organizational connection for European industry and government and parts of the European R&D community. RFC 822 / MIME / PEM will be the preferred protocol suite for inter-organisational connection for the Internet community and, as products are already widely available, it is the preferred protocol for parts of the European R&D community." Just how this will be done is unclear, especially as even this taskforce admits that "RFC 822 (and MIME) based services will be around for a long time to come."

In 1994, EARN merged with RARE to become Terena.

Thus, EUnet began in 1982, JANET and EARN in 1983, and JUNET in 1984.

Chapter 21

MILNET, CSNET, NSFNET

The breakup of the ARPANET.

Effective on January 1, 1983, the Defense Communications Agency (DCA) mandated the shift of the ARPANET hosts to TCP/IP. It also split ARPANET into ARPANET and MILNET, the TCP/IP successor to AUTODIN II. The internetwork thus created was called DDN (Defence Data Network). Other components of DDN were DISNET (Defense Integrated Secure Network) and WINCS (World Wide Military Command and Control System Intercomputer Network Communication Subsystem).

MILNET

MILNET actually split from the ARPANET in October 1983. It was a worldwide network that, in many ways, duplicated the ARPANET routes until ARPANET was retired and NSFNET became the "other" backbone for the Internet.

The maps show the spread of MILNET in Europe and in Asia in July 1986 and in the US in October 1986. The sites marked "TAC" are Terminal Access Controller nodes, which provided only client access to MILNET.

CSNET

In 1979, Lawrence Landweber, then chair of Computer Science at the University of Wisconsin, initiated discussion concerning a computer

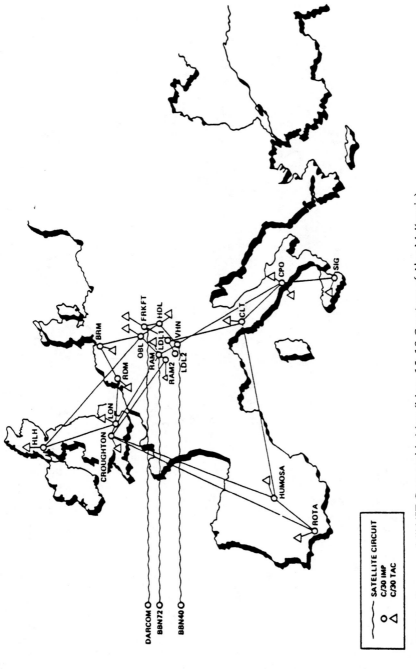

MAP 15   European MILNET Geographic Map (Maps 15–18 Courtesy of Alex McKenzie)

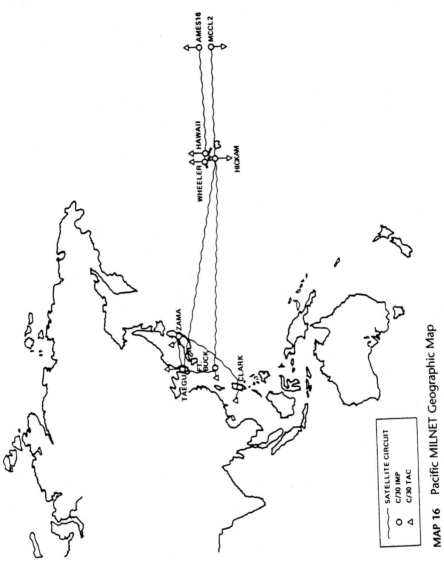

MAP 16   Pacific MILNET Geographic Map

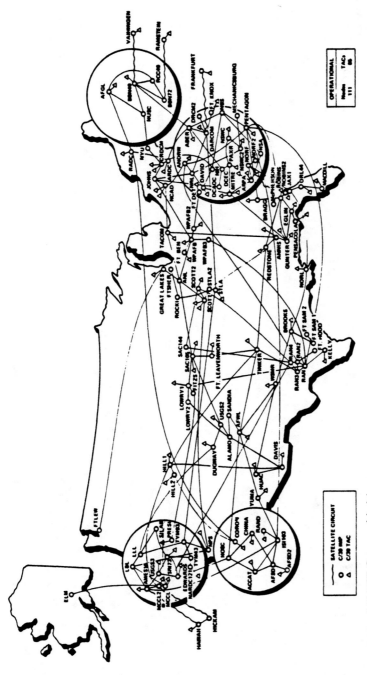

MAP 17   MILNET Geographic Map

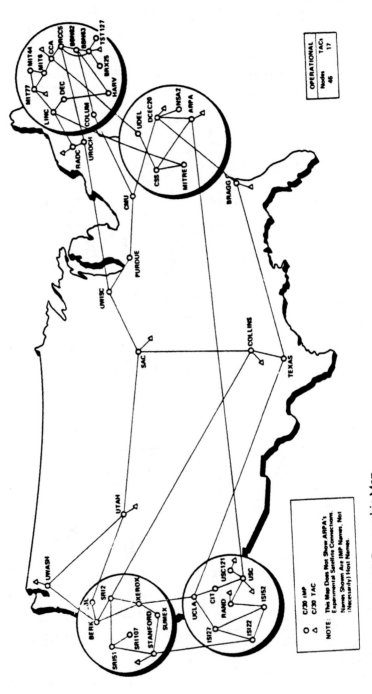

MAP 18   ARPANET Geographic Map

network for departmental research. A proposal was made to NSF in late 1979, but deferred. Subsequently, a planning group met in May 1980 and a revised proposal submitted in October 1980. In January 1981 CSNET was set up to provide access to computer science and engineering researchers. Over the years the restrictions on access have been relaxed and now the concept of just who is doing research includes corporate sites as well as academic and government ones. While CSNET is largely North American, it possessed good links to the Pacific Rim and to Europe.

Interestingly, CSNET provided different services over different links. Part of this (PhoneNet) was store-and-forward; another part (X25Net) ran TCP/IP on top of the X.25 protocols.

CSNET was administered by the Coordination and Information Center at BBN, under the oversight of the National Center for Atmospheric Research. In late 1988, the boards of CSNET and BITNET independently voted to merge into a single organization, CREN (as related in Chapter 18).

NSFNET

In 1984, the National Science Foundation set up an Office of Advanced Scientific Computing. OASC went to work by initiating two programs: One to set up a set of supercomputing centers, the other to connect these centers in a way that would provide for national access to them and (eventually) become a national academic network.

In 1985, NSF funded the John von Neumann Supercomputer Center at Princeton, the San Diego Supercomputing Center at UCSD, the National Center for Supercomputing Applications at the University of Illinois, the Theory Center at Cornell, and the Pittsburgh Supercomputing Center, jointly managed by Carnegie-Mellon University, Westinghouse and the University of Pittsburgh.

The initial work on NSFNET was done by Illinois and a Network Operations Center was managed by Cornell. Backbones for NSFNET were LSI 11/73 gateway systems with 512Kbytes of memory. The operating system plus application programs was called Fuzzball [D. Mills, 1988], and was primarily a packet switch/gateway. The backbone was reengineered by a consortium consisting of Merit Computer Network

(University of Michigan), MCI and IBM over the winter and spring of 1988. The links were upgraded to T1 by MCI. The next plan was to transform these into T3 capability. Advanced Network & Services (ANS) was created in September 1990 by the consortium to provide a dedicated network during the upgrade process.

ANS

The NSFNET backbone was T1, pushing the 1988 limit for speed and routing. But the traffic was such that the NSF asked Merit to upgrade the backbone to T3. Rather than attempting to upgrade the existing backbone, Merit proposed providing the service over a shared, privatized network owned and operated by the new company, ANS. In May 1991, ANS formed a for-profit taxable subsidiary, ANS CO+RE Systems, Inc., providing T3 services for commercial entities. But this was not without problems.

The handing over of the infrastructure of NSFNET to a commercial entity made some of the other commercial network suppliers a bit queasy: After all, the NSFNET, built with taxpayer's funds, would now be in competition (as ANS) with private entities, and ANS had agreed with MERIT (in November 1992) to "monitor commercial traffic" on the backbone to ensure that commercial users weren't eating into the bandwidth promised to NSF research and education clients. (I will not go into detail here, but refer the interested and concerned reader to Gordon Cook's reports. It is interesting to note that ANS was bought up by AOL in late 1994.)

In mid-1993, the Corporation for Regional and Enterprise Networking (CoREN) announced that it had formed an alliance with MCI to provide Internet access. As CoREN was an alliance of eight regional providers (BARRNet, CICNet, MidNet, NEARNET, NorthWestNet, NYSERNet, SURAnet, and Westnet) this meant that there would now be parallel interconnections regionally, rather than mere linkages to the NSFNET. This means, as Quarterman has pointed out, that "the Internet, for routing purposes, is becoming more and more a mesh, rather than a hierarchy." Let's glance at two of the regionals.

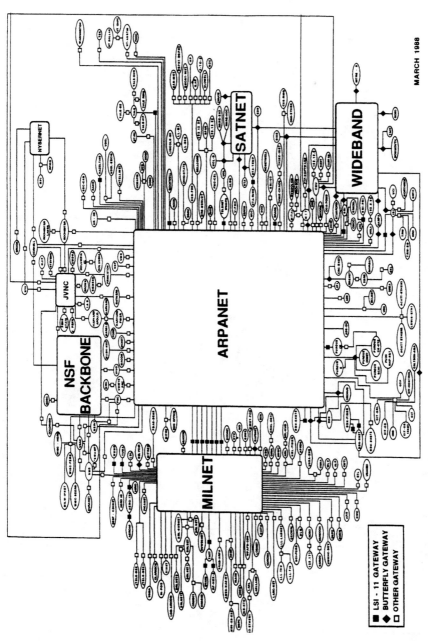

FIGURE 21.1   Rick Adams' "ARPANET ON A CHIP" (Courtesy of Rick Adams)

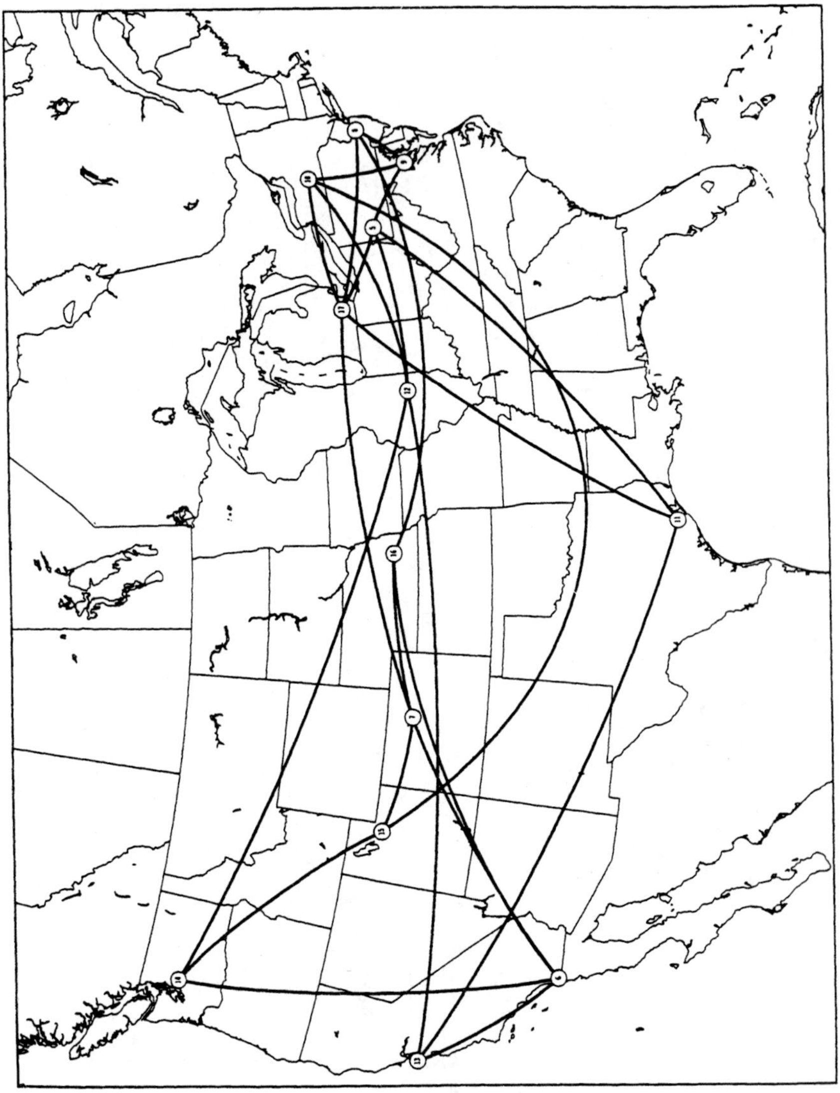

MAP 19   NSFNET Map (Courtesy of Alex McKenzie)

Subordinate Nets

The structure of NSFNET is such that a very large number of "mid-level networks" are attached to it. As I don't want to belabor the point, let me use NYSERNet (New York State Educational and Research Network) as an example.

Organized in 1985, NYSERNet supplies dial-up services, dedicated connection services, mail, ftp, Telnet, and news to individuals and organizations on a membership-fee basis. It connects to NSFNET through the Cornell Theory Center. It has about 200 affiliate sites.

NEARNET (New England Academic and Research Network) is another instance of a mid-level net. NEARNET, which is administered by BBN, became operational in 1989, when it was connected to ARPANET. This connection was phased out in favor of an NSFNET connection.

NEARNET was created by Boston University, Harvard University, and the Massachusetts Institute of Technology (MIT) in 1989 to support the research and academic communities, to strengthen the regional competitiveness of New England, and to meet a growing need for fast, reliable information exchange.

NEARNET grew very rapidly, from fewer than 10 members in the Boston area in 1989 to over 300 members throughout the six New England states today.

In June 1988, James Bruce, vice president for Information Systems at MIT; Stephen Hall, director of the Office of Information Technology at Harvard; and John Porter, Vice Provost for Information Technology at Boston University, began discussing the idea of linking their three campus computer networks together. They were approached by Mark Pullen of DARPA, who requested that the new network they were designing include Internet access for several local research and development sites that were losing their ARPANET access because of the decommission of the ARPANET. These companies included BBN, DEC, Encore, Lincoln Laboratory, MITRE, and Thinking Machines. The result is that BBN has operated NEARNET since its inception.

In June 1994, BBN signed a letter of intent to acquire the Bay Area Regional Research Network (BARRNet) from Stanford University, thereby spanning the US from Boston to San Francisco.

I am not going to enumerate networks beyond this, Frey and Adams (Fourth edition, 1994) list over 200 functioning nets (from AARNet—the Australian Academic and Research Network—to XLINK—the Karlsruhe Extended LAN) in countries ranging from Argentina to Zimbabwe. Quarterman has noted that there are sites connected to the Matrix from north of the Arctic Circle (in Greenland) to Antarctica. I will, however, glance at use and applications later.

Chapter 22

Organization and Reorganization

The ARPANET is reborn from its fragments.

The growth of the ARPANET/Internet meant that there was also an increase in the number of individuals involved. After the first decade, it was no longer that small group of folks it had been in 1968–69.

In 1979, ARPA convened an informal committee to guide the technical evolution of the protocol suite. This group was called the Internet Configuration Control Board (ICCB) and was established by Vint Cerf (at that time ARPA program manager for the effort). David C. Clark of the Laboratory for Computer Science at MIT was named chairman of the committee.

In RFC 1160, Cerf described the history and the organization of the committee.

In January, 1983, the Defense Communications Agency, then responsible for the operation of the ARPANET, declared the TCP/IP protocol suite to be standard for the ARPANET and all systems on the network converted from the earlier Network Control Program (NCP) to TCP/IP. Late that year, the ICCB was reorganized by Dr. Barry Leiner, Cerf's successor at DARPA, around a series of task forces considering different technical aspects of internetting. The re-organized group was named the Internet Activities Board [IAB].

As the Internet expanded, it drew support from U.S. Government organizations including DARPA, the National Science Foundation (NSF),

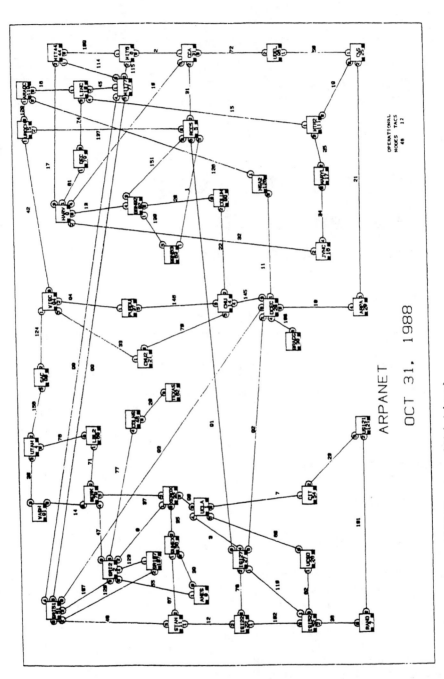

OPERATIONAL
NODES   TACS
48   12

ARPANET

OCT 31, 1988

MAP 20   ARPANET in 1988 (Courtesy of Rick Adams)

the Department of Energy (DOE) and the National Aeronautics and Space
Administration (NASA). Key managers in these organizations, responsible
for computer networking research and development, formed an informal
Federal Research Internet Coordinating Committee (FRICC) to coordinate
U.S. Government support for and development and use of the Internet
system. The FRICC sponsored most of the U.S. research on internetting,
including support for the Internet Activities Board and its subsidiary
organizations.

In the summer of 1989 the IAB was reorganized. Within the IETF
and supervisory to the various working groups was the Internet Engineering Steering Group (IESG). But let's return to Cerf's narrative.

In 1990, the FRICC was reorganized as part of a larger initiative
sponsored by the networking subcommittee of the Federal Coordinating
Committee on Science, Engineering and Technology (FCCSET). The
reorganization created the Federal Networking Council (FNC) and its
Working Groups. The membership of the FNC included all the former FRICC
members and many other U.S. Government representatives. The first
chairman of the FNC is Dr. Charles Brownstein of the National Science
Foundation. The FNC is the Federal Government's body for coordinating
the agencies that support the Internet. It provides liaison to the
Office of Science and Technology Policy (headed by the President's
Science Advisor) which is responsible for setting science and
technology policy affecting the Internet. It endorses and employs the
existing planning and operational activities of the community-based
bodies that have grown up to manage the Internet in the United States.
The FNC plans to involve user and supplier communities through creation
of an external advisory board and will coordinate Internet activities
with other Federal initiatives ranging from the Human Genome and Global
Change programs to educational applications. The FNC has also
participated in planning for the creation of a National Research and
Education Network in the United States.

At the international level, a Coordinating Committee for
Intercontinental Research Networks (CCIRN) has been formed which
includes the U.S. FNC and its counterparts in North America and Europe.
Co-chaired by the executive directors of the FNC and the European
Association of Research Networks (RARE), the CCIRN provides a forum for
cooperative planning among the principal North American and European
research networking bodies.

Internet Activities Board

The Internet Activities Board (IAB) is the coordinating committee for
Internet design, engineering and management. The Internet is a

collection of over two thousand of packet switched networks located principally in the U.S., but also in many other parts of the world, all interlinked and operating using the protocols of the TCP/IP protocol suite. The IAB is an independent committee of researchers and professionals with a technical interest in the health and evolution of the Internet system. Membership changes with time to adjust to the current realities of the research interests of the participants, the needs of the Internet system and the concerns of constituent members of the Internet.

IAB members are deeply committed to making the Internet function effectively and evolve to meet a large scale, high speed future. New members are appointed by the chairman of the IAB, with the advice and consent of the remaining members. The chairman serves a term of two years and is elected by the members of the IAB. The IAB focuses on the TCP/IP protocol suite, and extensions to the Internet system to support multiple protocol suites.

The IAB has two principal subsidiary task forces:

1) Internet Engineering Task Force (IETF)

2) Internet Research Task Force (IRTF)...

All decisions of the IAB are made public. The principal vehicle by which IAB decisions are propagated to the parties interested in the Internet and its TCP/IP protocol suite is the Request for Comment (RFC) note series....

The IAB performs the following functions:

1) Sets Internet Standards,

2) Manages the RFC publication process,

3) Reviews the operation of the IETF and IRTF,

4) Performs strategic planning for the Internet, identifying long-range problems and opportunities,

5) Acts as an international technical policy liaison and representative for the Internet community, and

6) Resolves technical issues which cannot be treated within the IETF or IRTF frameworks....

The Internet Engineering Task Force

The Internet has grown to encompass a large number of widely
geographically dispersed networks in academic and research communities.
It now provides an infrastructure for a broad community with various
interests. Moreover, the family of Internet protocols and system
components has moved from experimental to commercial development. To
help coordinate the operation, management and evolution of the
Internet, the IAB established the Internet Engineering Task Force
(IETF)....

The IAB has delegated to the IESG [Internet Engineering Steering Group]
the general responsibility for making the Internet work and for the
resolution of all short- and mid-range protocol and architectural
issues required to make the Internet function effectively.

The charter of the IETF includes:

1) Responsibility for specifying the short and mid-term Internet
   protocols and architecture and recommending standards for IAB
   approval.

2) Provision of a forum for the exchange of information within the
   Internet community.

3) Identification of pressing and relevant short- to mid-range
   operational and technical problem areas and convening of Working
   Groups to explore solutions.

The Internet Engineering Task Force is a large open community of
network designers, operators, vendors, and researchers concerned with
the Internet and the Internet protocol suite. It is organized around a
set of eight technical areas, each managed by a technical area
director. In addition to the IETF Chairman, the area directors make up
the IESG membership....

At present, the eight technical areas and chairs are:

1) Applications   - Russ Hobby/UC-Davis
2) Host and User Services - Craig Partridge/BBN
3) Internet Services   - Noel Chiappa/Consultant
4) Routing   - Robert Hinden/BBN
5) Network Management   - David Crocker/DEC
6) OSI Integration   - Ross Callon/DEC and Robert Hagens/UWisc.
7) Operations   - Phill Gross/CNRI (Acting)
8) Security   - Steve Crocker/TIS

At the very outset, according to Doug Comer, the "chairman of the IAB had the title *Internet Architect....*"

As might be expected, the IAB, the IETF, and the IESG have changed considerably over the past five years. Not least was Cerf's handing the chair's gavel to Lyman Chapin, then at Data General, now with BBN.

Lyman Chapin graduated from Cornell University in 1973 with a B.A. in Mathematics, and spent the next two years writing COBOL applications for Systems & Programs (NZ) Ltd. in Lower Hutt, New Zealand. After a year travelling in Australia and Asia, he joined the newly-formed Networking group at Data General Corporation (DG) in 1977. At DG, he was responsible for the development of software for distributed resource management (operating-system embedded RPC), distributed database management, X.25-based local- and wide-area networks, and OSI-based transport, internetwork, and routing functions for DG's open-system products. In 1987, he formed the Distributed Systems Architecture group and was responsible for the development of DG's Distributed Application Architecture (DAA) and for the specification of the directory and management services of DAA. He moved to Bolt Beranek and Newman in 1990 as the Chief Network Architect in BBN's Communications Division, where he serves as a consultant to the Systems Architecture group and the coordinator for BBN's open system standards activities. He has been the chairman of ANSI-accredited task group X3S3.3, responsible for Network and Transport layer standards, since 1982; chairman of the ACM Special Interest Group on Data Communications (SIGCOMM) since July 1991; and chairman of the IAB (till December 1993), of which he has been a member since 1989.

"I started out in 1977 working with X.25 networks and began working on OSI in 1979—first the architecture (the OSI Reference Model), and then the transport, internetwork, and routing protocol specifications," he has said. "It didn't take long to recognize the basic irony of OSI standards development: there we were, solemnly anointing international standards for networking, and every time we needed to send electronic mail or exchange files, we were using the TCP/IP-based Internet! I've been looking for ways to overcome this anomaly ever since; to inject as much of the proven TCP/IP technology into OSI as possible, and to introduce OSI into an ever more pervasive and worldwide Internet. You know," he went on, "the Europeans have a natural tendency toward uniformity. They insisted on pushing the system to a single way of doing 'x'. We never actually got to look at OSI realistically. Its point wasn't to actually build a monolithic standard...But you just can't write specs in a vacuum. OSI just lacked an experimental infrastructure."

In July 1991 the Center for National Research Initiatives, with Bob Kahn as its President and Vint Cerf as its Vice President, together with EDUCOM and the IAB, announced the establishment of the Internet Society. Cerf became the first president of ISOC in 1992. The IAB and ISOC then decided that the IAB should come within ISOC's responsibility. Quarterman and Wilhelm have diagrammed the relationship among these bodies as shown in Figure 22.1.

Kahn had left his post at the IPTO in October 1985 to found CNRI. He was joined by Keith Uncapher, a veteran of USC's ISI, and—in early 1986—by Vint Cerf, who had spent 1982–86 with MCI. Starting with a half-million dollars each from DEC and Xerox, Kahn's vision was to lead the nation's information infrastructure. Nearly a decade ago, CNRI was planning the information highway recently discovered by politicians. "The situation is similar to the very early post-war period when the lack of an interstate highway system constrained the growth of the auto and housing industries," Kahn told the *Washington Business Journal* in 1986. "We have a communications infrastructure (the telephone system) but not an information infrastructure," Cerf added. From its formation, CNRI was involved in research on the design of the infrastructure which could "improve the country's long-range scientific and engineering productivity." The establishment of ISOC was a step along that path.

But with the establishment of CSNET and NSFNET and the split-off of MILNET (MINET—the Military Intelligence Network—in Europe), ARPANET was gone. Networks no longer depended upon IMPs; TCP/IP had taken over from NCP; neither protocols nor applications were actively developed on it. The Internet had arrived.

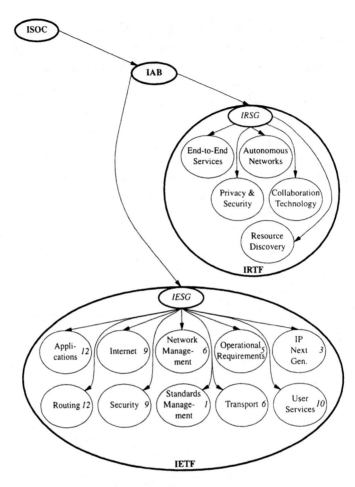

FIGURE 22.1 IAB Diagram (From Quarterman and Wilhelm, *UNIX, POSIX, and Open Systems: The Open Standards Puzzle* (p. 43, 44), © 1993 by Addison-Wesley Publishing Company, Inc.; reprinted with permission of the publisher)

Diversion 9

Requiem for the ARPANET
by
Vint Cerf

Like distant islands sundered by the sea,
We had no sense of one community.
We lived and worked apart and rarely knew
that others searched with us for knowledge, too.

Distant ARPA spurred us in our quest
and for our part we worked and put to test
new thoughts and theories of computing art;
we deemed it science not, but made a start.

Each time a new machine was built and sold,
we'd add it to our list of needs and told
our source of funds "Alas! Our knowledge loom will
halt 'til it's in our computer room!"

Even ARPA with its vast resources
could not buy us all new teams of horses
every year with which to run the race
Not even ARPA could keep up that pace!

But, could these new resources not be shared?
Let links be built; machines and men be paired!
Let distance be no barrier! They set
that goal: design and build the ARPANET!

And so it was in nineteen sixty-nine,
a net arose of BBN design.
No circuit switches these, nor net complete
but something new: a packet switching fleet.

The first node occupied UCLA
where protocols and measurements would play
a major role in shaping how the net
would rise to meet the challenges unmet.

The second node, the NIC, was soon installed.
The Network Info Center, it was called.
Hosts and users, services were touted;
to the NIC was network knowledge routed.

Nodes three and four soon joined the other two:
UCSB and UTAH came on cue.
To monitor it all around the clock
at BBN, they built and ran the NOC.

The protocol was built for host-to-host
communcation. Running coast-to-coast,
below the TELNET and the FTP,
we called this protocol the NCP.

The big surprise for most of us, although
some said they guessed, was another protocol used more than all the rest to shuttle
mail in content flaming or most subtle.

When we convened the first I Triple C,
the ARPANET was shown for all to see.
A watershed in packet switching art,
this demo played an overwhelming part.

Within three years the net had grown so large
we had to ask that DCA take charge
to operate a system guaranteed
for R&D and military need.

Exploring other packet switching modes,
we built the first spread spectrum mobile nodes.
The Packet Radio, the mobile net,
worked on the ground and even in a jet.

Deployed at SAC and Eighteenth Airborne Corps,
the Packet Radio unlocked the door
to what we now know as the Internet.
The driver for it all was PRNET.

The Packet Satellite, another new
technique, was added to the new milieu.
And then to shed more light upon the dark,
there came the Ethernet from Xerox PARC.

To these we added yet another thing
from MIT: a local token ring.
We saw the local net techniques compound
until the list could easily confound.

The Internet foundation thus was laid.
Its protocols from many sources made.
And through it all the ARPANET grew more;
It was, for Internet, the central core.

The hardware of the net was changing, too.
The Honeywell was first, and then the SUE,
which forms the heart of Pluribus today
though where this platform sits one cannot say.

The next big change was called the MBB.
It emulated Honeywell, you see,
so one by one they modified each node,
by means of closely written microcode.

Now known as 30 prefixed with a C,
these nodes are everywhere from A to Z.
The European MINET too was full
of nodes like these from Mons to Istanbul.

The second Autodin was long desired
but once accepted instantly expired.
Then to the rescue rode the ARPANET!
And soon the MILNET by its side was set.

By Nineteen-Eighty DoD opined
its data networks soon must be aligned
with Internetwork protocols, to wit:
by Eighty-Three the TCP was IT!

Soon every host that sat on ARPANET
became a gateway to a local net.
By Eighty-Six new long haul nets appeared
as ARPANET its second decade neared.

THE NSFNET and its entourage
began a stately national dressage
and soon was galloping at T1 speed
outdistancing its aging peer indeed.

And so, at last, we knew its course had run,
our faithful servant, ARPANET, was done.
It was the first, and being first, was best,
but now we lay it down to ever rest.

```
Now pause with me a moment, shed some tears.
For auld lang syne, for love, for years and years
of faithful service, duly done, I weep.
Lay down thy packet, now, O friend, and sleep.
```

Copyright © 1989 Vinton G. Cerf; reprinted with permission. This poem previously appeared in Tracy LaQuey, ed., *Users' Directory of Computer Networks* (Bedford, Massachusetts: Digital Press, 1990); and in *CONNEXIONS: The Interoperability Report.*

Chapter 23

Growth

The Internet develops into the Matrix.

With the daily newspapers filled with estimates of the numbers of "users" of the Internet, let me take a few moments to both contemplate how to estimate the number of users and to actually record the numbers.

Perhaps it is not so strange to realize that there are wildly variant opinions as to what it might mean to be "on the Internet." It is not like the telephone where, if you have a number, that's it. The stringent end of the definition holds that if you cannot use the basic tools (here defined as **ftp** and **telnet**), you are not on the Internet (John Quarterman may be the best example of this view). The liberal end, typified by Lyman Chapin, would hold that if you can send and receive mail and have access to news and bulletin boards, you are on the net—but maybe not on the "Internet."

In *Matrix News* for October 1994, Quarterman wrote "The core Internet consists of computers that are reachable with ICMP ECHO (ping) and at least some of the basic TCP/IP application services, such as FTP, the File Transfer Protocol." Thus, to him, the millions of users who are connected via store-and-forward networks like BITNET are not part of the Internet, nor are those who subscribe to America On Line or Compuserve, though they are part of the Matrix. To Chapin, all these individuals are net users. My personal feeling is that the Information Highway of the CNRI is there, even if you choose to bicycle on it rather than speed along in a sports car.

ARPANET Hosts

In the early years, the numbers of hosts and the estimates of users were quite straightforward. The number of hosts was ascertainable by just counting the entries in the host table. In January 1992, Mark Lottor put together RFC 1296, which enumerates the number of hosts from August 1981 to January 1992. Although the Domain Name System was introduced in 1984, it was not fully implemented until 1988.

Recall the Host-Host Program permitted 63 hosts, the NCP permitted 255 and the IP permits many millions, especially in its current (IPv4) version. ($2^6 - 1 = 63$; $2^8 - 1 = 255$.) The earliest numbers (derived from the BBN Reports) are easy:

Date	Hosts
12/69	4
01/71	13
04/72	23
01/73	35
10/74	49
01/76	63

In October 1975, BBN had modified the Network Control Center's program so that it would be able to handle more than 63 IMPs. In January 1976 they made it possible for there to be more than 63 IMPs on the net and more than four hosts on an IMP. This brought the possible number of hosts to 255. Over the next decade, which included the shift to TCP/IP and then to DNS, the numbers reported by Lottor are:

Date	Hosts	Host Table
08/81	213	#152
05/82	235	#166
08/83	562	#300
10/84	1,024	#392
10/85	1,961	#485
02/86	2,308	#515

The great switch occurred on January 1, 1983. It was none too soon. The 562 hosts of August 1983 just wouldn't have been feasible under the older protocols and the older scheme. But yet more growth was at hand.

Date	Hosts
11/86	5,089
12/87	28,174
07/88	33,000
10/88	56,000
01/89	80,000
07/89	130,000
10/89	159,000
10/90	313,000
01/91	376,000
07/91	535,000
10/91	617,000
01/92	727,000

In doing a user-calculation, it is important to recognize that many hosts have more than one IP address and that most IP addresses have more than one user. Lottor's figures for numbers of IP addresses for January 1, 1992 are (only first 10 entries are shown):

Addresses	Hosts
1	715143
2	9015
3	1027
4	556
5	314
6	213
7	100

8	85
9	58
10	71

How many?

Just what the median number of users per IP address is has been repeatedly estimated. The highest number I have seen is 10—promulgated by the Internet Society (which is the number that *TIME* and *Newsweek* used in early 1994 to get to their "over 30 million" Internet users). A more sensible range, used by Craig Partridge, is 5-10. At the end of 1994, Quarterman (on the basis of polling a number of site administrators) lowered the number to 3.5. This would mean that as of 1992, there were about 2.6 million users.

More recent pollings of hosts have shown that the number has doubled each year since Lottor's RFC, to about 1.5 million in 1993 and 3.1 million in 1994. Again, the 3.1 million is the figure that the news weeklies multiplied by ten to get their "over 30 million." If we use the more conservative figure, we would get about 11 million users in 1994, plus the several million "second-class citizens" who are on BITNET or subscribe to the various on-line services.

In the December 1994 *Matrix News*, Quarterman published a preliminary report on a demographic survey. The calculations (which have a confidence interval of 38%) yielded:

1. 7.8 million users of the core Internet; that is, of computers that can provide interactive services such as TELNET (remote login), FTP (file transfer); or WWW (hypertext).

2. 13.5 million users of the consumer Internet; that is, of computers that can access interactive services supplied by the core Internet. The consumer Internet includes the core Internet. If you can use FTP to ftp.ripe.net or use Mosaic or Lynx to reach http://www.ripe.net, you are a user of the consumer Internet. We derived this total by taking the figure of 12 million projected from the survey responses and

adding to it 1.5 million users of large commercial centralized systems such as America Online (AOL) and BIX that
permit their users true Internet access. We did not add in
users of systems such as CompuServe or Prodigy that do not
yet permit their users more than electronic mail access....

"Electronic mail is the most widespread service on every computer network, including the Internet, but mail alone does not consti-
tute Internet access. Other distributed networks, such as UUCP and
FidoNet, can also send mail, as can centralized systems such as CompuServe. We did ask how many users could send mail from inside to
outside the organization's domain, and from the responses we can estimate 16 million users of the Matrix affiliated with the organizations
we polled. However, that is not all Matrix users, since we only asked
organizations that are connected to the Internet. Since we also know
of about 8 million who use centralized systems such as CompuServe,
PCVAN, and Prodigy, and as many as 3.5 million on distributed networks such as UUCP, FidoNet, and BITNET, we could estimate 27.5
million users of electronic mail in the worldwide Matrix of such networks."

My guesstimate is that as of the end of 1994, something like 18
million people have genuine Internet access (they are able to use both
telnet and **ftp**) and another five to seven million have the ability to
send and receive mail and participate in bulletin boards. Refraining
from the class distinction I discussed at the outset of this chapter, this
means that there are about 25 million users of the Matrix, close to
Quarterman's number. This is not yet 30 million, but if the doubling
were to continue, there would be over 500 million users worldwide in
the year 2000. (In an interview with Katie Hafner in September 1994,
Cerf said there would be 300 million users by 2000; two months later,
he had raised the number to 400 million. At neither time was it clear
whether he meant the Internet or the Matrix. Quarterman has pointed
out that if one plots the population growth curve against the Internet's, they cross by 2010, at which time we might have more addresses
than people on the planet. As with many such projections, this was intended to be tongue-in-cheek.)

Domains

Let me use one more set of Lottor's figures: hosts per top-level domain. That is, in an address, which .xxx occur the most frequently? On New Year's Day 1992, the top 10 were

243020	edu	[educational institution]
181361	com	[commercial business]
46463	gov	[government]
31622	au	[Australia]
31016	de	[Germany]
27492	mil	[military]
27052	ca	[Canada]
19117	org	[organization]
18984	uk	[United Kingdom]
18473	se	[Sweden]

I would assume that over the past few years .com has overtaken and passed .edu, largely because businesses have discovered the value of communicating electronically and there has been no notable increase in the number of educational institutions. If we extrapolate from the proportions to the numbers of hosts, there are most likely around 300,000 educational institutions and nearly a million businesses on the Matrix at the end of 1994. I will return to the commercialization of the net in Chapter 25.

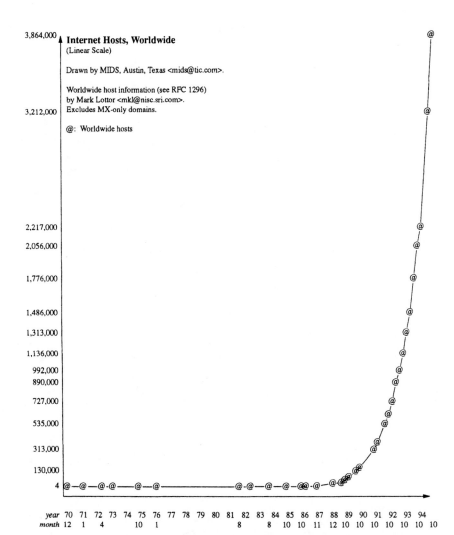

FIGURE 23.1   Quarterman's Internet Growth graph (Courtesy of John Quarterman, Copyright © 1995 MIDS, Austin, Texas <mids@tic.com>; reprinted with permission)

Part 5

TIME LINE—Part V (1988–1994)

1988   NSFNET T1 (1.544Mbps) backbone operational.

U.S. National Bureau of Standards (NBS) publishes GOSIP (Government OSI Profile).

1989   Berlin Wall falls.

CSNET merges with BITNET under the name CREN (Corporation for Research and Education Networking).

RIPE (Reseaux IP Europeens) established as a coordinating body for IP networks in Europe.

1990   The World (world.std.com) becomes first site to offer full commercial Internet dial-up access to the general public but is restricted to roughly half the net by NSF's AUP. (In August 1992, The World will obtain the first official permission from NSF to route its Internet dial-up access to NSFnet and thus the entire Internet.)

ANS (Advanced Network and Services, Inc.) founded by Merit, MCI, and IBM.

NSFNET T3 (45Mbps) backbone implementation begun.

ARPANET decomissioned.

1990   The archie indexer of anonymous FTP archives invented at McGill University by Alan Emtage and Peter Deutsch.

WAIS (Wide Area Information Servers) invented by Brewster Kahle, backed by Thinking Machines, Inc., and others.

1991   Hosts on the Internet in Europe increase by a factor of four, despite governmental pressures to use OSI.

EUnet decides to commercialize (incorporates in 1992).

U.S. National Institute of Standards and Technology (NIST, formerly NBS) publishes GOSIP Version 2.

Alternet, PSINet, and CERFnet form the Commercial Internet Exchange (CIX), transferring traffic among their customers without any government funded intermediary.

In the U.S., Senator Al Gore (Tennessee) proposes and Congress approves the High Performance Computing Act (HPCA) of 1991, providing initial funding for a National Research and Education Network (NREN).

Gopher invented at the University of Minnesota by Paul Lindner and Mark P. McCahill.

Mike Schwartz of the University of Colorado at Boulder invents netfind and the term 'resource discovery' to refer to it and to archie, WAIS, Gopher, and WWW.

The Internet Society (ISOC) founded.

1992   OSI is clearly dead, although X.400 (mail) and X.500 (directory) services live on.

World Wide Web (WWW) invented by Tim Berners-Lee and others at CERN (European Nuclear Research Center).

NSFNET T3 (45Mbps) backbone implementation completed.

EBONE deployed in Europe as a transcontinental IP backbone; this was done as a cooperative venture without significant initial government backing or funding.

1993 DARPA becomes ARPA again.

A consortium of industry figures proposes a National Information Infrastructure (NII), emphasizing voice and video.

ANS joins CIX.

PSINet and AlterNet deploy T3 backbones.

Delphi becomes the first of the large systems to join the Internet.

IIJ begins commercial IP access in Japan (gains international connectivity in 1994).

1994 America Online (AOL) connects to the Internet.

MCI offers IP service.

AOL purchases ANS.

In a (final?) FIPS, NIST buries OSI.

Chapter 24

Applications

Searching the Matrix: Tools for finding what you want.

I have noted that in the first decade of the net, progress was driven by the protocols. But once TCP/IP and DNS had come into full force, new applications grew to supplement the basic tools of **ftp**, **telnet**, **mail**, and **news**. As computing became ever more ubiquitous and disk storage became cheaper, more archives and more data were accessible electronically.

The tools came into being because among the millions of hosts on the net are many millions of files containing useful information. Furthermore, the millions of new users of the Matrix—unlike the originators of the ARPANET, Internet, or BITNET—weren't interested in the network. They were (and are) interested in using it. The problem became one of locating and achieving painless access to the information. Peter Deutsch described this as "the way we use it [the Internet] and the way we think about it."

As Deutsch saw it, from 1990 on "there has been a number of changes in the way we perceive and make use of the net. Of course, the number of users continues to climb at a dizzying pace and the sheer volume of traffic continues to climb along with the population, but there's more to it than that.... The Internet is no longer just an interesting experimental testbed.... The net is now a daily tool for hundreds of thousands of people who couldn't tell an IP packet from a burst of tty line noise." [1992: 375] (In a normal week, I access bibliographic material at

MIT, Harvard, and Berkeley; I glance at the weather forecast; I tap the earthquake data at the U.S. Geologic Service; etc. And I do this from home.)

archie

Work on finding files across the Internet began in 1990 at McGill University in Montreal. Alan Emtage, Deutsch, and Bill Heelan developed **archie** (from "archive") as a search tool and made it available in 1991. (Emtage and Deutsch have since formed a company, Bunyip Information Services, which licenses the **archie** server system. Version 3.0 appeared in fall 1992.)

archie is basically an extension of **ftp**—the old file transfer protocol—so that **ftp** organizes files and searches for named objects by "anonymous" **ftp**. Anonymous **ftp** permits anyone to retrieve a file, but it isn't very effective at spreading information widely, because potential file-users have no way of searching for particular files. **archie** attempts to find all the sites on the Internet that provide for anonymous **ftp**, extracts a list of files from each of these sites, and builds a global index to the information obtained. Users can then search this index for desired data.

Gopher

Gopher, developed at the University of Minnesota, whose "team" mascot is the "Golden Gopher," is another extension to **ftp**. The focus in **Gopher** was not on cataloging, as in **archie**, but on making storage and retrieval easy. **Gopher** creates a Gopher server on any machine on which it is installed. And that Gopher server becomes a storage and retrieval site. According to Win Treese's "Internet Index," Gopher traffic grew 1076% in 1993 and 197% in 1994.

Veronica and Jughead

archie is not only the name of a tool; it is also the name of a famous cartoon character. It was not long before Steven Foster and Fred Barrie at the University of Nevada at Reno created an **archie**-like tool for

Gopher. They called their tool **Veronica**—Very Easy Rodent-Oriented Net-wide Index to Computerized Archives. First made available in November 1992, **Veronica** has rapidly become a valuable search tool.

Once reverse-engineering of a cartoon character's name for a tool was established, it did not take long for Rhett Jones ("Jonzy") of the University of Utah to invent **Jughead**—Jonzy's Universal Gopher Hierarchy Excavation and Display—in 1993. As Paul Gilster has put it: "**Veronica** expands **Gopher** by allowing you to consolidate your information gathering in gopherspace; **Jughead** moves in the opposite direction. Its concept is to allow you to search gopherspace, but in a user-delimited fashion."

archie, **Gopher**, **Veronica**, and **Jughead** all execute surface searches: the results are lists of the titles of files. We have no idea what the information in those files is. And as many files bear the same name, yet contain very different things, our searches result in much that is unnecessary.

WWW and Mosaic

World Wide Web was developed by Tim Berners-Lee at CERN. It is a descendant of the hypertext model initiated by Doug Engelbart 20 years ago and implemented over the past decade. Thus, here one can think of a document as an amalgam of multimedia objects, rather than a linear text. In this collection of objects, each item has pointers to other relevant objects. The user can thus browse hyperspace by following this network—web—of pointers, without any concern as to where the things being searched are actually stored. **Mosaic** is the most popular user interface to **WWW**. Created at the National Center for Supercomputing Applications at the University of Illinois by Marc Andreessen and Eric Bina, **Mosaic** is now under development by several dozen programmers. **Mosaic** highlights areas of the screen in color, enabling the point-and-click mouse technology (another Engelbart invention) to activate hypertext links.

Mosaic integrates graphics, text, and sound into "pages" of information. These graphical, textual and auditory sources can be pulled in from all over the Internet—a local file, an Australian picture, an Israeli audio file.

WAIS

WAIS (Wide Area Information Service), invented by Brewster Kahle at Thinking Machines, is a very different approach to searching for information. In **WWW**, the user follows Web pointers in searching for information. **WAIS** uses a Connection Machine, a highly parallel supercomputer, to enable search queries to be made directly of the server. While **WWW** enables users to browse cyberspace, **WAIS** has a computer do the browsing for the user.

Treese reported growth of WWW traffic in 1993 at 443,931% and 1713% in 1994.

Search and browsing tools are interesting and useful. But they are far from being the end now that the general populace has discovered the utility of the Matrix.

In 1992, Nathaniel Borenstein and N. Freed of Bellcore (RFC 1341) came forward with a method for sending multimedia messages across the Internet—it was called MIME. Prior to this, sending binary files like WordPerfect documents, graphics, or voice was impossible, unless they were first converted to ascii format. MIME was not a mailer; it was a standard way for exchanging multimedia mail messages that was backward compatible with SMTP (RFC 822). MIME has been expanded repeatedly in the past three years, most recently in RFC 1652 (for 8-bit extensions) and RFC 1641 (Unicode). Multimedia mail is now reality—barely a decade after Harry Forsdick's meeting in 1984.

Diversion 10

Network Working Group
Request for Comments: 1438

L. Chapin
BBN
C. Huitema
INRIA
1 April 1993

Internet Engineering Task Force
Statements Of Boredom (SOBs)

Status of this Memo

Discussion

The current IETF process has two types of RFCs: standards track documents and other RFCs (e.g., informational, experimental, FYIs). The intent of the standards track documents is clear, and culminates in an official Internet Standard. Informational RFCs can be published on a less formal basis, subject to the reasonable constraints of the RFC Editor. Informational RFCs are not subject to peer review and carry no significance whatsoever within the IETF process.

The IETF currently has no mechanism or means of publishing documents that express its deep concern about something important, but otherwise contain absolutely no useful information whatsoever. This document creates a new subseries of RFCs, entitled, IETF Statements Of Boredom (SOBs). The SOB process is similar to that of the normal standards track. The SOB is submitted to the IAB, the IRSG, the IESG, the SOB Editor (Morpheus), and the Academie Francais for review, analysis, reproduction in triplicate, translation into ASN.1, and distribution to Internet insomniacs. However, once everyone has approved the document by falling asleep over it, the process ends and the document is discarded. The resulting vacuum is viewed as having the technical approval of the IETF, but it is not, and cannot become, an official Internet Standard.

References

[1] Internet Activities Board, "The Internet Standards Process", RFC 1310, IAB, March 1992.

[2] Postel, J., Editor, "IAB OFFICIAL PROTOCOL STANDARDS", RFC 1410, IAB, March 1993.

Security Considerations

Security issues are not discussed in this memo, but then again, no
other issues of any importance are discussed in this memo either.

Chapter 25

Commerce and Security

Businesses discover the Internet and just how easily computers can be accessed.

Karl Marx wrote that the only kind of history was economic history. In the case of the Matrix this is demonstrably true. Though packet networking began as a government-sponsored project (and even if we include CYCLADES and the work at the NPL, the efforts were government sponsored), the tale of PCI and Telenet demonstrates how early the commercial possibilities of the Matrix were recognized. Over the past decade, with TCP/IP and DNS in place and the extension of the networks into both homes and places of business, the extension of the Matrix into the workplace has been rapid and pervasive.

By 1985 there were enough TCP/IP vendors for Dan Lynch to organize and run INTEROP, an enormous trade show, and for both he and Ole Jacobsen to begin publication of *ConneXions*, a monthly newsletter, the initial publication of which was instigated by ARPA. Originally a semiannual event, INTEROP has waxed along with the Matrix. In 1994, for example, it held four major events: two in the U.S., one in France, and one in Japan. The May NetWorld+Interop 94 (held in Las Vegas) drew 90,000 people; the July event (in Tokyo) drew over 30,000 according to the report in *Matrix News* (August 1994). Over the years, because it has drawn large numbers of programmers, vendors, and users together, INTEROP (in its various manifestations) has had a great influence on the commercialization of the Matrix.

The Matrix offers competitive advantage to businesses using it, just as the telephone did over a century ago. Resnick and Taylor [1994] have put these advantages under six headings: "electronic mail, access to research, tracking competitors, inexpensive remote collaboration, enhanced customer service, and low-cost marketing and advertising."

The value of mail is obvious: Being able to communicate in real time with other users—colleagues, customers, vendors—anywhere in the world is most likely the most frequent reason for companies to "get on the Net."

Research in a commercial sense is not limited to data in a laboratory sense: on-line access to census data aids marketers and planners; on-line access to the weather reports and forecasts aids on the one hand the shipping industry, on another the relief and emergency services; with the availability of corporate and financial reports from the Securities and Exchange Commission, the text of U.S. Supreme Court decisions, UN information (e.g., world health statistics), as well as the texts of White House press briefings, the Matrix user has a wealth of information available on which to base her business decisions.

Competitive information is freely available on many bulletin boards and in newsgroups which reveal comments about your products (and those of your competitors) in public forums. New product announcements and customer service are also accessible.

Collaboration was one of the foundation stones for the ARPANET. The increased speed and ubiquity of the Net has made this ever-more-useful. As was seen with the story of IBM's VNET, development within and outside the TCP paradigm has been going on for two decades.

With between 20 and 30 million users worldwide, the Matrix is clearly an enormous marketplace. As many of those users are affluent, marketing and advertising to them is a productive method of utilizing bandwith. Offering a free sample of one's wares has proven useful to some vendors. But vendors must be careful: This is a marketplace wherein the customer can strike back, as the damage to Canter and Siegel, the Arizona law firm that blanketed the news groups only to become a pariah, has shown.

The Internaut may ask about the "Acceptable Use Policy" at this point. The response is that there is none. When the NSFnet was set up a decade ago, the National Science Foundation promulgated a set of rules for its backbone. In part, these read:

> NSFNet Backbone services are provided to support open research and education in and among U.S. research and instructional institutions, plus research arms of for-profit firms when engaged in open scholarly communication and research. Use for other purposes is prohibited.

The U.S. Department of Energy and NASA have adopted similar AUPs. But outside of this portion of the Internet, there is none. And for the greatest part of the Matrix, none exists either. As the U.S. government withdraws further from funding the Internet (see next chapter), there will be increasingly less control over what is and what is not posted to the users at large.

However, as the Matrix is largely chaotic and user-driven, I fully expect that unscrupulous marketers will flood it periodically with virtual "junk mail." It will be up to the users to control this. As Eric McKinney pointed out in *Matrix News* for October 1994, not only is there no "ban" on advertising on the Internet, there isn't even a "mutual agreement against" advertising in general.

Customer service is more than merely supplying answers to request. Right now, customer support relays technical advice, makes software available, monitors and relays customer compliments (and gripes), and provides the user with information about new products. The result of doing this via a leased line Internet hookup is cost-effective for companies of nearly any size.

Services

Once there was an Internet and a Matrix, several entrepreneurs realized that there were many services that users were willing to pay for. Among these services are news (in the strict sense), which Brad Templeton began supplying as ClariNet in 1989. It now supplies parts of an electronic newspaper in several hundred groups, modeled on the Usenet software, to over 80,000 subscribers. Other suppliers (e.g., Dialog, Mead Data Central) enable subscribers to access the *Official Airline Guide*, legal data (Lexis), business and financial data (Nexis). The amount of information available from the Library of Congress, the White House, and other public sources is gigantic. Let me emphasize that this is not a purely North American phenomenon: You can get, for example, the trading data of the Vienna Stock Exchange, interactively.

Suppliers

The preceding was about doing business *on* the Matrix and obtaining information by using it. The bigger money-maker is supplying hardware and software so that people can access the Matrix. I am not going to go into either the hardware end (the supplying of modems, routers, etc.) nor the software, insofar as kermit, Red Ryder, and commercial products like Internet Anywhere are concerned. As the early attempts of PCI and the more recent one of UUNET have been mentioned earlier, let me briefly mention network access suppliers.

BYTE magazine began the BYTE Information Exchange (BIX) in 1985, using the CoSy (Conferencing System) software from the University of Guelph. By November 1988 it had over 22,000 subscribers. It was subsequently bought up by the company which runs the Delphi service.

The Delphi Internet Services Corporation runs DELPHI, which has members throughout the United States and in over 50 countries. DELPHI offers electronic mail, telex, FAX, public message forums, and real-time conferencing. DELPHI also offers a wide range of financial information designed for businesses or personal investors. Stock and commodity quotes for over 9000 stocks are delayed 15 minutes. Finally, DELPHI was the first of the "big three" services to offer full Internet access, including gopher, mail, Usenet, telnet, and ftp. Previously, AlterNet, PSINet, and smaller suppliers like The World had done so.

CompuServe provides many services, though not "genuine" Internet connections. Of the three largest providers (the others are AOL and Prodigy), CompuServe is the oldest. It had over 2,000,000 subscribers in 1994. It is run by the financial services company H&R Block, and has the richest array of business, professional, and consumer information of the group. It has an extremely low basic fee and individual charges for nearly a thousand possible services (some have a surcharge as high as $22.80 per hour, according to *The New York Times* of November 29, 1994). It charges recipients for Internet mail ($0.15 per message) and also limits mail length to 100,000 characters, making it difficult (to be personal) for me to send the bits for this book to several interested parties who have CompuServe accounts. CompuServe has "aging plumbing and cracks in the wall" [*New York Times*], but says it is upgrading its software.

GEnie is the General Electric Network for Information Exchange, a U.S. conferencing service. GEnie users must pay a surcharge to receive non-GEnie mail; if you write to GEnie users who have not paid the surcharge, they will not receive your mail.

America Online (AOL) had over 1.25 million subscribers at the end of 1994, despite the fact that it did not provide true Internet access. The irony in this for those subscribers is that AOL is the owner of ANS. AOL does have an extremely slick user interface as well as an active mail gateway, so one can mail AOL subscribers.

The largest of these commercial suppliers of mail and bulletin-board-services is Prodigy, which was set up as a subsidiary by IBM and Sears. Unlike several other suppliers, Prodigy appears to have stalled. The service (at the end of 1994) did have the ability to write and read Internet mail online. Previously, Prodigy members wishing to "do Internet mail" had to use a separate mail manager.

This is certainly not true for MCI, which started out as a service for CB truckers, moved over a bit into telephony when AT&T was broken up, and began a service called MCI Mail, a commercial electronic mail system. In late 1994, however, MCI announced an "internetMCI" service which would serve as an interactive shopping mall.

Finally, there are now a very large number of independent service providers like The World in Brookline, Massachusetts, Netcom with about three dozen sites, Zilker in Austin, Texas, or The Well in Sausalito, California, as well as "free" connection providers. The World, perpetrated by Barry Shein, appears to have been the very first site to offer commercial Internet dial-up service. At first, The World was restricted in its ambit by the NSF's AUP. However, after a year, Shein received permission to use the NSF backbone.

I mentioned the founding and growth of UUNET earlier. Originally a not-for-profit, UUNET became a for-profit, UUNET Technologies, Inc., and began an IP service, AlterNet. AlterNet began by offering T1 (1.5Mbps) services, but in 1993 introduced 10Mbps service to 10 major cities. While the service is not "cheap," it is certainly economical for businesses.

It is clear that business use of the Matrix has only just begun. But there are several things to keep in mind. First is the fact that over fifty years after the beginnings of television, home shopping still requires the viewer to call an 800 number; second is the fact that the very first image projected by Philo T. Farnsworth on his "orthicon" in 1927 was a dollar sign.

Security

The problem introduced by the dollar sign is that information is valuable. And there are many who attempt to gain access to private information.

The ARPANET was never designed to be a truly secure system. But early on some of the problems were recognized (see Metcalfe's RFC 602; Diversion 3). But the incidents of meddlesome crackers and of the Internet worm made both governmental and commercial users nervous. Over the years, there have been documents concerning questions of security among the RFCs (1108, 1244, 1281, 1352, 1446, 1455, 1457, 1472, 1507-1509, and 1535), culminating in RFC 1636 (June 1994).

RFC 1636 is the report on the IAB Workshop on Security, which was held February 8–10, 1994. About 30 experts attended. The RFC runs over 50 pages, but is summarized by the following:

```
the objectives of this workshop were (1) to explore the
interconnections between security and the rest of the Internet
architecture, and (2) to develop recommendations for the Internet
community on future directions with respect to security. These
objectives arose from a conviction in the IAB that the two most
important problem areas for the Internet architecture are scaling and
security. While the scaling problems have led to a flood of activities
```

on IPng [see next chapter], there has been less effort devoted to
security.

Although some came to the workshop eager to discuss short-term security
issues in the Internet, the workshop program was designed to focus more
on long-term issues and broad principles. Thus, the meeting began with
the following ground rule: valid topics of discussion should involve
both security and at least one from the list: (a) routing (unicast and
multicast), (b) mobility, and (c) realtime service....

Almost everyone agrees that the Internet needs more and better
security. However, that may mean different things to different people.
Four top-level requirements for Internet security were identified: end-
to-end security, end-system security, secure QOS, and secure network
infrastructure....

One requirement is to support confidentiality, authentication and
integrity for end-to-end communications. These security services are
best provided on an end-to-end basis, in order to minimize the number
of network components that users must trust. Here the "end" may be the
end system itself, or a proxy (e.g., a firewall) acting on behalf of an
end system....

Good security administration is labor-intensive, and therefore
organizations often find it difficult to maintain the security of a
large number of internal machines. To protect their machines from
outside subversion, organizations often erect an outer security wall or
"perimeter." Machines inside the perimeter communicate with the rest of
the Internet only through a small set of carefully managed machines
called "firewalls." Firewalls may operate at the application layer, in
which case they are application relays, or at the IP layer, in which
case they are firewall routers.

The Conclusions of the Workshop included:

As a practical matter, security must be added to the Internet
incrementally. For example, a scheme that requires, as a precondition
for any improvement, changes to application code, the DNS, routers and
firewalls all at once will be very hard to deploy. One of the reasons
the workshop explored schemes that are local to the IP layer is that we
surmise that they might be easier to deploy in practice.

There are two competing observations that must shape planning for
Internet security. One is the well known expression: "the best is the

enemy of the good." The other is the observation that the attacks are getting better.

I feel that it is important to note that inviolable security (of any kind) may be unattainable. The doors on our residences and their bolts and locks are merely impediments to a determined break in. Similarly, encryption, passwords, and firewalls are obstacles we place in the path of the determined cybercriminal. Luckily, there are few of these.

Chapter 26

NREN and NII

The U.S. government's vision of our information future.

In 1988 the Computer Science and Technology Board of the National Research Council issued a report, *Toward a National Research Network*, which looked at technology needs, interactions between commercial providers and those supported by the government, and the implications of the broadening user community. Since then, the growth in commercialization, the attention to educational use, the announced withdrawal of the NSF from funding the backbone, and several architectural issues have been added to the menu.

In 1994, the White House issued a variety of statements enunciating the Clinton-Gore vision of a national information infrastructure (there were two press releases and a speech by Vice President Al Gore on January 11 and an "Administration White Paper on Communications Reforms" on January 27, to start the year off). Some of the points that seemed to be extractable from these were:

1. Encourage private investment.
2. Provide for and protect competition.
3. Provide open access to the network.
4. Avoid creating a society of "haves" and "have nots."
5. Encourage flexible government action.
6. Protect privacy and copyright.

7. Ensure that the U.S. remains a leader.

8. Provide for interoperability.

9. Create new jobs, new companies, new products, etc.

10. Improve delivery of health care.

11. Lower prices.

12. Create diversity of choice.

13. Spur economic growth.

14. Democratize information.

15. Provide long-distance learning opportunities.

16. Link citizens to their government.

Oh, yes. "By the year 2000."

The NRENAISSANCE Committee of the NRC, which was chaired by Len Kleinrock, put its vision in a more precise fashion:

> *Full integration of communications and information infrastructure...is supported by the committee, which believes that integration should be an explicit goal if the networks of today are to evolve to a general information infrastructure serving society with a broad range of services.* The committee, in developing its vision of a future NII, has been strongly influenced by the Internet's openness, a characteristic that has been key to its unprecedented success. It therefore characterizes its vision in terms of an Open Data Network (ODN).
>
> A national information infrastructure should be capable of carrying information services of all kinds, from suppliers of all kinds, across network service providers of all kinds, in a seamless accessible fashion. The long-range goal is to provide the capability of universal access to universal service, but one that goes beyond a lowest-common-denominator approach. [p. 34]

The NII is clearly an extension of NREN: the National Research and Education Network, itself a direct outgrowth of the ARPANET/Internet. In 1991, Al Gore, then Senator from Tennessee, proposed the High Performance Computing Act, which was supported by President

George Bush and enacted by Congress (PL102-194). After Gore became Vice President, he and President Bill Clinton began using the federal budget process to expand the HPCC program to include the NII, in the form of an Information Infrastructure Technology and Applications component, with a program to advance options to schools, hospitals and libraries. The Clinton-Gore administration also included an NII category in its budget proposals.

The NREN program had emerged in the Bush administration as the launch of the HPCC. Within NREN, many federal agencies (NSF, ARPA, the Department of Energy, and NASA) set up or expanded their networks, interconnecting them so that they became part of the Internet.

Transition and Addresses

The NSF/ANS switch is but a part of the transition that the Internet will undergo in 1995. As noted earlier, CoREN has contracted with MCI to provide 45Mbps transport among the CoREN regionals. These regionals have set up a Joint Technical Committee, co-chaired by Scott Bradner of Harvard (who is also the chair of the NEARNET Technical Committee) and Phill Gross of MCI.

But there are other complications that this transition will bring about. Remember that IPv4/DNS allowed for about four billion hosts on 16.7 million networks. Surely that's enough? No. In August 1990 during the Vancouver IETF meeting, Frank Solensky, Phill Gross and Sue Hares projected that the current rate of assignment would exhaust the Class B space by March 1994. The obvious remedy of assigning multiple Class C addresses in place of Class B addresses introduced the additional problem of expanding the size of the routing tables in the backbone routers. Even with this, it was revealed at the July 1994 Toronto meeting of the IETF that, using the current allocation statistics, the Internet would exhaust the IPv4 address space between 2005 and 2011.

The result was the formation of an "IPng" task force. Recommendations from that task force were released in October 1994 for discussion at the December 1994 IETF meeting. The basic goal is to have something in place before 2000, so that the time limit will not be pushed. Unfortunately, as Bradner and Mankin put it in their recommendation, "Some people pointed out that this type of projection makes an assumption of no paradigm shifts in IP usage. If someone were to develop a new 'killer application' (for example cable-TV set top boxes), the resultant rise in the demand for IP addresses could make this an over-estimate of the time available."

Mike O'Dell remarked to me that the recommendation "allows for 2^{128} addresses. That's more than the estimated total number of molecules in the universe."

Diversion 11

Network Working Group   W. Shakespeare
Request for Comments: 1605   Globe Communications
Category: Informational   1 April 1994

SONET to Sonnet Translation

Status of this Memo

Abstract

Because Synchronous Optical Network (SONET) transmits data in frames of
bytes, it is fairly easy to envision ways to compress SONET frames to
yield higher bandwidth over a given fiber optic link. This memo
describes a particular method, SONET Over Novel English Translation
(SONNET).

Protocol Overview

In brief, SONNET is a method for compressing 810-byte (9 lines by 90
bytes) SONET OC-1 frames into approximately 400-byte (fourteen line
decasyllabic) English sonnets. This compression scheme yields a roughly
50% average compression, and thus SONNET compression speeds are
designated OCh-#, where 'h' indicates 50% (one half) compression and
the # is the speed of the uncompressed link. The acronym is pronounced
"owch."

Mapping of the 2**704 possible SONET payloads is achieved by matching
each possible payload pattern with its equivalent Cerf catalog number
(see [1], which lists a vast number of sonnets in English, many of
which are truly terrible but suffice for the purposes of this memo).

Basic Transmission Rules

The basic transmission rules are quite simple. The basic SONET OC-1
frame is replaced with the corresponding sonnet at the transmission end
converted back from the sonnet to SONET at the receiving end. Thus, for
example, SONET frame 12 is transmitted as:

When do I count the clock that tells the time
And see the brave day sunk in hideous night;
When I behold the violet past prime,
And sable curls,...

For rates higher than OC-1, the OC-1 frames may either come interleaved or concatenated into larger frames. Under SONNET conversion rules, interleaved frames have their corresponding sonnet representations interleaved. Thus SONET frames 33, 29 and 138 in an OC-3 frame would be converted to the sequence:

Full many a glorious morning have I seen
When, in disgrace with fortune and men's eyes,
When my loves swears that she is made of truth
Flatter the mountain-tops with sovereign eye
I all alone beweep my outcast state,
I do believe her, though I know she lies
Kissing with golden face...

while in an OC-3c frame, the individual OC-1 frames concatenated, one after another, viz.:

Full many a glorious morning have I seen Flatter the mountain-tops with sovereign eye Kissing with golden face...

When, in disgrace with fortune and men's eyes, I all alone beweep my outcast state,...

When my loves swears that she is made of truth I do believe her, though I know she lies...

(This example, perhaps, makes clear why data communications experts consider concatenated SONET more efficient and esthetically pleasing).

Timing Issues

It is critical in this translation scheme to maintain consistent timing within a frame. If SONET frames or converted sonnets shift in time, the SONET pointers, or worse, poetic meter, may suffer.

References

[1] Cerf, B., "A Catalog of All Published English Sonnets to 1950," Random House, 1953. (Now out of print.)

Security Considerations

Security issues are not discussed in this memo.

[The author of this RFC was Craig Partridge.]

Network Working Group   J. Onions
Request for Comments: 1606   Nexor Ltd.
Category: Informational   1 April 1994

A Historical Perspective On The Usage Of IP Version 9

Status of this Memo

This memo provides information for the Internet community. This memo
does not specify an Internet standard of any kind. Distribution of this
memo is unlimited.

Abstract

This paper reviews the usages of the old IP version protocol. It
considers some of its successes and its failures.

Introduction

The take-up of the network protocol TCP/IPv9 has been phenomenal over
the last few years. Gone are the days when there were just a few
million hosts, and the network was understood. As the IP version 9
protocol comes to the end of its useful life, once again due to address
space exhaustion, we look back at some of the success of the protocol.

Routing

The up to 42 deep hierarchy of routing levels built into IPv9 must have
been one of the key features for its wide deployment. The ability to
assign a whole network, or group of networks to an electronic component
must be seen as one of the reasons for its takeup. The use of the
Compact Disk Hologram units is typical of the usage. They typically
have a level 37 network number assigned to each logical part, and a
level 36 network number assigned to the whole device. This allows the
CDH management protocol to control the unit as a whole, and the high-
street vendor to do remote diagnostics on discreet elements of the
device. This still allows sub-chip routing to be done using the 38th
level addressing to download new nanocode. As yet, no requirement has
been found for levels 40-42, with level 39 still being used for
experimental interrogation of atomic structure of components where
required.

Allocation

The vast number space of the IPv9 protocol has also allowed allocation
to be done in a straight forward manner. Typically, most high street

commercial internet providers issue a range of 1 billion addresses to
each house. The addresses are then dynamically partitioned into subnet
hierarchies allowing groups of a million addresses to be allocated for
each discreet unit (e.g., room/floor etc.) The allocation of sub groups
then to controllers such as light switches, mains sockets and similar
is then done from each pool.

The allocation process is again done in a hierarchical zoned way, with
each major application requesting a block of addresses from its
controller. In this way the light bulb requests an address block from
the light switch, the light switch in turn from the electrical system
which in turn requests one from the room/floor controller. This has
been found to be successful due to the enormous range of addresses
available, and contention for the address space being without problems
typically.

Whilst there are still many addresses unallocated the available space
has been sharply decreased. The discovery of intelligent life on other
solar systems with the parallel discovery of a faster-than- light
transport stack is the main cause. This enables real time communication
with them, and has made the allocation of world-size address spaces
necessary, at the level 3 routing hierarchy. There is still only 1
global (spatial) level 2 galaxy wide network required for this galaxy,
although the establishment of permanent space stations in deep space
may start to exhaust this. This allows level 1 to be used for inter-
galaxy routing. The most pressing problem now is the case of parallel
universes. Of course there is the danger of assuming that there is no
higher extrapolation than parallel universes...

Up to now, the hacking into, and setting of holo-recorder devices to
the wrong channel from remote galaxies, has not been confirmed, and
appears to be attributable to finger problem with the remote control
whilst travelling home from the office.

Applications

The introduction of body monitors as IPv9 addresseable units injected
into the blood stream has been rated as inconclusive. Whilst being able
to have devices lodged in the heart, kidneys, brain, etc., sending out
SNMPv9 trap messages at critical events has been a useful monitoring
tool for doctors, the use of the blood stream as both a delivery and a
communication highway, has been problematic. The crosstalk between the
signals moving through the blood stream and the close proximity of
nerves has meant that patients suffering multiple events at once, can
go into violent spasm. This, coupled with early problems with
broadcasts storms tending to make patients blood boil, have led to a

rethink on this whole procedure. Also, the requirement to wear the silly satellite dish hat has led to feelings of embarrassment except in California, where it is now the latest trend.

The usage of IPv9 addresseable consumer packaging has been a topic of hot debate. The marketing people see it as a godsend, being able to get feedback on how products are actually used. Similarly, the recycling is much improved by use of directed broadcast, "All those packages composed of cardboard respond please." Consumers are not so keen on this seeing it as an invasion of privacy. The introduction of the handy-dandy directed stack zapper (which is also rumoured to be IPv9 aware) sending directed broadcasts on the local food package net effectively resetting the network mask to all 1's has made this an area of choice.

The advent of the IPv9 magazine was universally approved of. Being able to ask a magazine where its contents page was being the most useful of the features. However combined with the networked newspaper/magazine rack, the ability to find out where you left the magazine with the article that was concerned with something about usage of lawn mowers in outer space is obvious. The ability to download reading habits automatically into the house controller and therefore alert the reader of articles of similar ilk is seen as marginal. Alleged querying of this information to discover "deviant" behaviour in persons within political office by members of contending parties is suspected.

Sneakernet, as pioneered by shoe specialists skholl is seen to be a failure. The market was just not ready for shoes that could forward detailed analysis of foot odour to manufacturers...

Manufacture

Of course, cost is one of the issues that was not considered when IPv9 was designed. It took a leap of imagination to believe that one day anything that wished to be could be IPv9 addresseable. It was assumed that IPv9 protocol machines would drop in price as with general chip technology. Few people would have forseen the advance in genetic manipulation that allowed viruses to be instructed to build nano-technology IPv9 protocol machines by the billion for the price or a grain of sugar. Or similarly, the nano-robots that could insert and wire these in place.

The recent research in quark-quark transistors, shows some promise and may allow specially built atoms to be used as switches. The manufacture of these will be so expensive (maybe up to 10cent an IPv9 stack) as to be prohibitive except for the most highly demanding niches.

Conclusions

Those who do not study history, are doomed to repeat it.

Security Considerations

Security issues are not discussed in this memo.

Chapter 27

The Future

The message in the bottle.

One of the most sobering thoughts about the Matrix arises from something Lyman Chapin remarked to me when I asked him to look into a metaphorical crystal ball: "It doesn't matter what we extrapolate," he said. "It'll be too little. It won't feature the central thing that becomes important. Those were smart guys in 1969, but they never thought of mail or news—and twenty years later, those were the principal uses of bandwidth. A few years ago, I had never imagined a MUD [multi-user dungeon]. We thought that six bits, then eight bits, then 16 bits would be enough address space. I have no idea what will come up next year, much less in 2000."

One of the "smart guys" from 1969, Vint Cerf, said (on September 10, 1994) that he thought there would be 300 million users of the Matrix by 2000. By November 21, he had upped that to 400 million.

In 1979 MIT Press published *The Computer Age: A Twenty-Year View*. Of the 20 authorities whose essays fill nearly 500 pages, only J.C.R. Licklider talks about the growing importance of the net and of the computer as a communications tool. And only Marvin Denicoff, who was then in charge of relations between the Office of Naval Research and ARPA, mentions the ARPA network—but with some doubts as to its future.

I asked Len Kleinrock whether he had forseen the 1994 Matrix in 1968–69: "Frankly, the extent and reach and impact of this networking technology has surpassed my wildest expectations. No way did we anticipate so much penetration in so many walks of life. We knew we had created something very, very special, but our vision was not clear enough to see what has finally transpired."

I then asked Paul Gilster, who has written several books on the use of the Matrix, about his vision. He responded:

> The Internet is clearly moving into the realm of multimedia, and we can envision a broad-bandwidth network of the future providing audio and video at much greater speeds than today. But the truly exciting thing about the coming broadband network is that it will make it possible to do the things the Internet only gives us glimpses of today. I can already search the Library of Congress catalog, for example; widening the data pipe will someday make it possible to choose a particular item and read it on-line. Michael Hart, the founder of Project Gutenberg, dreams of an Encyclopedia Galactica, housing the corpus of human knowledge. We're a long way from that vision, but digitizing information for transmission over the Internet and its successors is the great project of our time. It is not so different from the work of the medieval scholastics who preserved our science and literature by patiently, character by character, creating the illuminated manuscripts of monastic libraries. Theirs was a task of preservation, and if we proceed wisely, our digital future will likewise preserve and spread our culture even as it pushes us into a new world of educational possibilities.

Gilster's analogy is a good one, for every large library in the world is confronted by the problem of storing and preserving the millions of objects on paper it possesses. And while the ravages of time on paper are slower than the pyre of the Library of Alexandria, time is an even more relentless scourge. Digitizing the materials and making them available on-line will preserve the old materials, if only because the moisture, oils, and acids of human skin will no longer be deposited upon them.

But whatever happens will take money.

A quarter century ago, the first BBN contract was for a quarter of a million dollars. The cost of the NSF backbone was many millions. With ANS (AOL) taking this over, and the U.S. government terminating its funding, where will the funds come from?

Hal Varian and Jeffrey MacKie-Mason have written several articles and reports on the economics of the Internet. They point out that because of connectivity and the thousands of linked networks, it is difficult to estimate just what the Internet costs. But we do know that in 1993 NSF paid Merit $11.5 million to run the backbone. About 80% of that went for the routers and the leasing of fiber-optic lines. Another 7% went for the NOC (Network Operations Center). If 60% of the 25 million users are in the U.S. (15 million), then the NSF was paying under a dollar per year per user to run the backbone.

But this was a mere 10% of the cost of the backbone. And the NSF backbone had become but one of many transcontinental U.S. backbones.

A 1994 CNN/*USA Today* poll showed that individuals were willing to pay $5/month to "ride the information superhighway." My current connectivity costs several times that; gigabit connectivity would cost much more. If we actually paid for high-efficiency services, my guess is that true costs would run to several times the basic telephone bill. This, in turn, would cause a great change in the Clinton-Gore policy of not having information haves and have nots. Yet who will foot the bills to put gigabit terminals in public libraries?

The problems of growth and connectivity are not confined to the U.S. EUnet became a for-profit corporation recently, and the European Community has agreed that in 1998 national telecoms markets will be open to competition. This will be a tremendous shock to the government-protected monopolies of France, Germany, Italy, etc. (Britain has already privatized its telecom.) I foresee great problems in Europe, as DGXIII, the EU directorate for telecommunications, is heavily bureaucratized, with most of its large staff stemming from the national monopolies themselves. *The Economist* has noted that "The telecoms world is in the throes of a revolution. What a waste if, by the time Europeans noticed that reform means more than setting deadlines, their chance to join had already passed." [December 3, 1994]

On the commercial front, the MCI venture I mentioned earlier will be the first major step. MCI calls its "new venue for electronic commerce and interactive marketing on the Internet" *marketplaceMCI*. The MCI announcement continues: "Located on the World Wide Web (an advanced navigation system that organizes its Internet-related contents by subject matter), marketplaceMCI is a turnkey 'shopping mall' that enables businesses and information delivery providers to establish and implement business-to-business and business-to-consumer electronic commerce."

In line with this, it is important to note that in his January 1995 "State of the Art" report in *Telecommunications*, Lyman Chapin remarked that WWW "has spread so rapidly that in August, 1994, the amount of Web traffic on the principal Internet backbones exceeded the amount of electronic mail traffic—1.3 terabytes on the NSFnet backbone alone, accounting for 8% of all traffic.... From 500 sites a year ago, the Web has grown to over 5,000 sites today, and the growth rate is accelerating."

After discussing several other topics, Chapin takes up the new IP (IPv6 or IPng):

> The depletion of the Internet address space and corresponding expansion of Internet routing tables are well-publicized consequences of the Internet's recent explosive growth. The Internet Engineering Task Force (IETF) dealt with these issues in 1994 by developing and approving the specification of a replacement for the current Internet Protocol (IP), which...expands the size of the Internet address space from 4 bytes to 16 bytes, and includes a number of other features intended to provide better IP-level support for route aggregation, automatic host configuration, security, and the identification of "flows" for differential quality-of-service selection.
>
> Although IPv6 is intended to be a straightforward fix for the Internet's most pressing problems of scale, it is still the subject of considerable debate within the IETF and the industry at large concerning some of its most fundamental characteristics, and is not likely to displace the current IP in the near future. For at least the next four or five years, the Internet will

be based on today's TCP/IP, with incremental enhancements and improved algorithms (particularly in the case of TCP) to deal with the expansion of the Internet and the expected increase in backbone speeds into the gigabit per second range....

In the meantime, of course, just outside the conference rooms in which these agency, working group, task force, and other meetings are taking place, the actual Internet is growing and diversifying faster than even "State of the Art" commentators can predict. It seems obvious that whatever the Global Information Infrastructure (the more politically correct extension of the NII concept to include the world outside of North America) looks like when it arrives, it will be here as tomorrow's actual Internet long before policy-makers have agreed on what it "should" be.

When I spoke to Chapin about IPng he smiled: "I will confidentially assert that 128 bits is way too small. I have no notion of what's around the corner."

I don't either. But I have to raise my hat to Vannevar Bush and J.C.R. Licklider, whose crystal balls were more limpid than mine.

Recalling that rate-of-change is a second derivative function, I invite readers to contemplate the growth of the ARPANET from 0 to 4 hosts in three months in 1969 to 9 six months later, to 15 in April 1971, to 37 two years later, and to 49 in October 1974—five years after IMP #2 was installed at SRI. By that time, the 6-bit addresses were being pushed. In January 1976, the ARPANET hit 63 hosts and 8-bit addresses were in use. A decade later, there were 2,308 hosts (February 1986). Five years later, there were 376,000 hosts (January 1991) and a year later over 720,000. Mark Lottor's figures for October 1994 are 3,864,000 hosts and over 56,000 domains. I find the numbers staggering.

Who knows, perhaps Cerf's estimate of 400 million users in the year 2000 is "way too small," too.

Appendix

The Past and Future History

At the dinner celebrating the 25th Anniversary of the ARPANET, which BBN sponsored (September 10, 1994), Leonard Kleinrock, now Poet Laureate of the Matrix, read a revision of his "The Big Bang!" He has kindly permitted me to print it here. I also thank Vint Cerf for his version of the history, which appeared as RFC 1607, April Fool's Day, 1994.

THE BIG BANG! (or the birth of the ARPANET)
by
Leonard Kleinrock

It was back in '67 that the clan agreed to meet.
The gangsters and the planners were a breed damned hard to beat.
The goal we set was honest and the need was clear to all:
Connect those big old mainframes and the minis, lest they fall.

The spec was set quite rigid: it must work without a hitch.
It should stand a single failure with an unattended switch.
We decided UCLA would be first node on the net
As the best researchers out there, we would be the perfect bet.

I suspect you might be asking "What means FIRST node on the net?"
Well frankly, it meant trouble, 'specially since no specs were set.
For you see the interface between the nascent IMP and HOST
Was a confidential secret from us folks on the West coast.

BBN had promised that the IMP was running late.
We welcomed any slippage in the deadly scheduled date.
But one day after Labor Day, it was plopped down at our gate!
Those dirty rotten scoundrels sent the damned thing out air freight!

As I recall that Tuesday, it makes me want to cry.
Everybody's brother came to blame the other guy!
Folks were there from ARPA, BBN and Honeywell.
UCLA and ATT and all were scared as hell.

We cautiously connected and the bits began to flow.
The pieces really functioned - just why I still don't know.
Messages were moving pretty well by Wednesday morn.
All the rest is history - packet switching had been born!


```
Network Working Group                                      V. Cerf
Request for Comments: 1607                          Internet Society
Category: Informational                                 1 April 1994


                    A VIEW FROM THE 21ST CENTURY


Status of this Memo

This memo provides information for the Internet community. This memo
does not specify an Internet standard of any kind. Distribution of this
memo is unlimited.


A NOTE TO THE READER

The letters below were discovered in September 1993 in a reverse time-
capsule apparently sent from 2023. The author of this paper cannot
vouch for the accuracy of the letter contents, but spectral and
radiation analysis are consistent with origin later than 2020. It is
not known what, if any, effect will arise if readers take actions based
on the future history contained in these documents. I trust you will be
particularly careful with our collective futures!


THE LETTERS

To: "Jonathan Bradel" <jbradel@astro.luna.edu>
CC: "Therese Troisema" <ttroisema@inria.fr>
From: "David Kenter" <dkenter@xob.isea.mr>
Date: September 8, 2023 08:47.01 MT
Subject: Hello from the Exobiology Lab!
```

Hi Jonathan!

I just wanted to let you know that I have settled in my new offices at the Exobiology Lab at the Interplanetary Space Exploration Agency's base here on Mars. The trip out was uneventful and did let me get through an awful lot of reading in preparation for my three year term here. There is an excellent library of material here at the lab and reasonable communications back home, thanks to the CommRing satellites that were put up last year here. The transfer rates are only a few terabits per second, but this is usually adequate for the most part.

We've been doing some simulation work to test various theories of bio-history on Mars and I have attached the output of one of the more interesting runs. The results are best viewed with a model VR-95HR/OS headset with the peripheral glove adapter. I would recommend finding an outdoor location if you activate the olfactory simulator since some of the outputs are pretty rank! You'll notice that atmospheric outgassing seriously interfered with any potential complex life form development.

We tried a few runs to see what would happen if an atmospheric confinement/replenishment system had been in place, but the results are too speculative to be more than entertaining at this point. There has been some serious discussion of terra-forming options, but the economics are still very unclear, as are the time-frames for realizing any useful results.

I have also been trying out some new exercises to recover from the effects of the long trip out. I've attached a sample neuroscan clip which will give you some feeling for the kinds of gymnastics that are possible in this gravity field. My timing is still pretty lousy, but I hope it will improve with practice.

I'd appreciate it very much if you could track down the latest NanoConstructor ToolKit from MIT. I have need of some lab gear which isn't available here and which would be a lot easier to fabricate with the tool kit. The version I have is NTK-R5 (2020) and I know there has been a lot added since then.

Therese,

I wanted you to see the simulation runs, too. You may be able to coax better results from the EXAFLOP array at CERN, if you still have an account there. We're still limping along with the 50 PFLOP system that Danny Hillis donated to the agency a few years back.

The attached HD video clip shows the greenhouse efforts here to grow
grapes from the cuttings that were brought out five years ago. We're
still a long ways from '82 Beaucastel!

Gotta get ready for a sampling trip to Olympus Mons, so will send this
off for now.

Warmest regards,

David

* * *

To: "David Kenter" <dkenter@xob.isea.mr>
CC: "Therese Troisema" <ttroisema@inria.fr>
From: "Jonathan Bradel" <jbradel@astro.luna.edu>
Date: September 10, 2023 12:30:14 LT
Subject: Re: Hello from the Exobiology Lab!

David,

Many thanks for your note and all its news and interesting data!
Melanie and I are glad to know you are settled now and back at work.
We've been making heavy use of the new darkside reflector telescope
and, thanks to the new petabit fiber links that were introduced last
year, we have very effective controls from Luna City. We've been able
to run some really interesting synthetic aperture observations by
linking the results from the darkside array and the Earth- orbiting
telescopes, giving us an effective diameter of about 200,000 miles. I
can hardly wait to see what we can make of some of the most distant
Quasars with this set-up.

We had quite a scare last month when Melanie complained of a recurring
vertigo. None of the usual treatments seemed to help so a molecular-
level brain bioscan was done. An unexpectedly high level of localized
neuro-transmitter synthesis was discovered but has now been corrected
by auto-gene therapy.

As you requested, I have attached the latest NanoConstructor ToolKit
from MIT. This version integrates the Knowbot control subsystem which
allows the NanoSystem to be fully linked to the Internet for control,
data sharing and inter-system communication. By the way, the Internet
Society has negotiated a nice discount for nano- fab services if you
need something more elaborate than the ISEA folks have available at
XOB. I could put the NanoSystem on the Solex Mars/Luna run and have it
to you pretty quickly.

Keep in touch!

Jon and Melanie

* * *

To: "David Kenter" <dkenter@xob.isea.mr>
CC: "Jonathan Bradel" <jbradel@astro.luna.edu>
CC: "Troisema" <rm1023@geosync.hyatt.com>
From: "Therese Troisema" <ttroisema@inria.fr>
Date: September 10, 2023 12:30:14 UT
Subject: Re: Hello from the Exobiology Lab!

Bon Jour, David!

I am writing to you from the Hyatt Geosync where your email was
forwarded to me from INRIA. Louis and I are here vacationing for two
weeks. I have some time available and will set up a simulation run on
my EXAFLOP account. They have the VR-95HR/OS headsets here for
entertainment purposes, but they will work fine for examining the
results of the simulation.

I have been taking time to do some research on the development of the
Interplanetary Internet and have found some rather interesting results.
I guess this counts as a kind of paleo-networking effort, since some of
the early days reach back to the 1960s. It's hard to believe that
anyone even knew what a computer network was back then!

Did you know that the original work on Internet was intended for
military network use? One would never guess it from the current state
of affairs, but a lot of the original packet switching work on ARPANET
was done under the sponsorship of something called the Advanced
Research Projects Agency of the US Department of Defense back in 1968.
During the 1970s, a number of packet networks were built by ARPA and
others (including work by the predecessor to INRIA, IRIA, which
developed a packet network called CIGALE on which the CYCLADES network
operating system was built). There was also work done by the French PTT
on an experimental system called RCP that later became a commercial
system called TRANSPAC. Some seminal work was done in the mid-late
1960s in England at the National Physical Laboratory on a single node
switch that apparently served as the first local area network! It's
very hard to believe that this all happened over 50 years ago.

A radio-based network was developed in the same 1960s/early 1970s time
period called ALOHANET which featured use of a randomly-shared radio
channel. This idea was later realized on a coaxial cable at XEROX PARC

and called Ethernet. By 1978, the Internet research effort had produced 4 versions of a set of protocols called "TCP/IP" (Transmission Control Protocol/Internet Protocol"). These were used in conjunction with devices called gateways, back then, but which became known as "routers." The gateways connected packet networks to each other. The combination of gateways and TCP/IP software was implemented on a lot of different operating systems, especially something called UNIX. There was enough confidence in the resulting implementations that all the computers on the ARPANET and any networks linked to the ARPANET by gateways were required to switch over to use TCP/IP at the beginning of 1983. For many historians, 1983 marks the start of global Internet growth although it had its origins in the research effort started at Stanford University in 1973, ten years earlier.

I am going to read more about this and, if you are interested, I can report on what happened after 1983.

I will leave any simulation results from the EXAFLOP runs in the private access directory in the CERN TERAFLEX archive. It will be accessible using the JIT-ticket I have attached, protected with your public key.

Au revoir, mon ami, Therese

* * *

To: "Troisema" <rm1023@geosync.hyatt.com>
CC: "Jonathan Bradel" <jbradel@astro.luna.edu>
CC: "Therese Troisema" <ttroisema@inria.fr>
From: "David Kenter" <dkenter@xob.isea.mr>
Date: September 10, 2023 17:26:35 MT
Subject: Internet History

Dear Therese,

I am so glad you have had a chance to take a short vacation; you and Louis work too hard! I changed the subject line to reflect the new thread this discussion seems to be leading in. It sounds as if the whole system started pretty small. How did it ever get to the size it is now?

David

* * *

To: "David Kenter" <dkenter@xob.isea.mr>
CC: "Therese Troisema" <ttroisema@inria.fr>
CC: "Troisema" <rm1023@geosync.hyatt.com>
From: "Jonathan Bradel" <jbradel@astro.luna.edu>
Date: September 11, 2023 09:45:26 LT
Subject: Re: Internet History

Hello everyone! I have been following the discussion with great
interest. I seem to remember that there was an effort to connect what
people thought were "super computers" back in the mid-1980's and that
had something to do with the way in which the system evolved. Therese,
did your research tell you anything about that?

Jon

* * *

To: "Jonathan Bradel" <jbradel@astro.luna.edu>
CC: "David Kenter" <dkenter@xob.isea.mr>
CC: "Troisema" <rm1023@geosync.hyatt.com>
From: "Therese Troisema" <ttroisema@inria.fr>
Date: September 12, 2023 16:05:02 UT
Subject: Re: Internet History

Jon,

Yes, the US National Science Foundation (NSF) set up 5 super computer
centers around the US and also provided some seed funding for what they
called "intermediate level" packet networks which were, in turn,
connected to a national backbone network they called "NSFNET." The
intermediate level nets connected the user community networks (mostly
in research labs and universities at that time) to the backbone to
which the super computer sites were linked. According to my notes, NSF
planned to reduce funding for the various networking activities over
time on the presumption that they could become self-sustaining. Many of
the intermediate level networks sought to create a larger market by
turning to industry, which NSF permitted. There was a rapid growth in
the equipment market during the last half of the 1980s, for routers
(the new name for gateways), work stations, network servers, and local
area networks. The penetration of the equipment market led to a new
market in commercial Internet services. Some of the intermediate
networks became commercial services, joining others that were created
to meet a growing demand for Internet access.

By mid-1993, the system had grown to include over 15,000 networks,
world-wide, and over 2 million computers. They must have thought this
was a pretty big system, back then. Actually, it was, at the time, the
largest collection of networks and computers ever interconnected.

Looking back from our perspective, though, this sounds like a very modest beginning, doesn't it? Nobody knew, at the time, just how many users there were, but the system was doubling annually and that attracted a lot of attention in many different quarters.

There was an interesting report produced by the US National Academy of Science about something they called "Collaboratories" which was intended to convey the idea that people and computers could carry out various kinds of collaborative work if they had the right kinds of networks to link their computer systems and the right kinds of applications to deal with distributed applications. Of course, we take that sort of thing for granted now, but it was new and often complicated 30 years ago.

I am going to try to find out how they dealt with the problem of explosive growth.

Louis and I will be leaving shortly for a three-day excursion to the new vari-grav habitat but I will let you know what I find out about the 1990s period in Internet history when we get back.

Therese

* * *

To: "Troisema" <rm1023@geosync.hyatt.com>
CC: "David Kenter" <dkenter@xob.isea.mr>
CC: "Therese Troisema" <ttroisema@inria.fr>
From: "Jonathan Bradel" <jbradel@astro.luna.edu>
Date: September 13, 2023 10:34:05 LT
Subject: Re: Internet History

Therese,

I sent a few Knowbot programs out looking for Internet background and found an interesting archive at the Postel Historical Institute in Pacific Palisades, California. These folks have an incredible collection of old documents, some of them actually still on paper, dating as far back as 1962! This stuff gets addicting after a while.

Postel apparently edited a series of reports called "Request for Comments" or "RFC" for short. These seem to be one of the principal means by which the technology of the Internet has been documented, and also, as nearly as I can tell, a lot of its culture. The Institute also has a phenomenal archive of electronic mail going back to about 1970 (do you believe it? Email from over 50 years ago!). I don't have time to set up a really good automatic analysis of the contents, but I did leave a couple of Knowbots running to find things related to growth, scaling, and increased capacity of the Internet.

It turns out that the technical committee called the Internet Engineering Task Force was very pre-occupied in the 1991-1994 period with the whole problem of accommodating exponential growth in the size of the Internet. They had a bunch of different options for re- placing the then-existing IP layer with something that could support a larger address space. There were a lot of arguments about how soon they would run out of addresses and a lot of uncertainty about how much functionality to add on while solving the primary growth problem. Some folks thought the scaling problem was so critical that it should take priority while others thought there was still some time and that new functionality would help motivate the massive effort needed to replace the then-current version 4 IP.

As it happens, they were able to achieve multiple objectives, as we now know. They found a way to increase the space for identifying logical end-points in the system as well increasing the address space needed to identify physical end-points. That gave them a hook on which to base the mobile, dynamic addressing capability that we now rely on so heavily in the Internet. According to the notes I have seen, they were also experimenting with new kinds of applications that required different kinds of service than the usual "best efforts" they were able to obtain from the conventional router systems.

I found an absolutely hilarious "packet video clip" in one of the archives. It's a black-and-white, 6 frame per second shot of some guy taking off his coat, shirt and tie at one of the engineering committee meetings. His T-shirt says "IP on everything" which must have been some kind of slogan for Internet expansion back then. Right at the end, some big bearded guy comes up and stuffs some paper money in the other guy's waistband. Apparently, there are quite a few other archives of the early packet video squirreled away at the PHI. I can't believe how primitive all this stuff looks. I have attached a sample for you to enjoy. They didn't have TDV back then, so you can't move the point of view around the room or anything. You just have to watch the figures move jerkily across the screen.

You can dig into this stuff if you send a Knowbot program to concierge@phi.pacpal.ca.us. This Postel character must have never thrown anything away!!

Jon

* * *

To: "Jonathan Bradel" <jbradel@astro.luna.edu>
CC: "David Kenter" <dkenter@xob.isea.mr>
CC: "Troisema" <rm1023@geosync.hyatt.com>
From: "Therese Troisema" <ttroisema@inria.fr>
Date: September 15, 2023 07:55:45 UT
Subject: Re: Internet History

Jon,

thanks for the pointer. I pulled up a lot of very useful material from
PHI. You're right, they did manage to solve a lot of problems at once
with the new IP. Once they got the bugs out of the prototype
implementations, it spread very quickly from the transit service
companies outward towards all the host computers in the system. I also
discovered that they were doing research on primitive gigabit-per-
second networks at that same general time. They had been relying on
unbelievably slow transmission systems around 100 megabits-per-second
and below. Can you imagine how long it would take to send a typical 3DV
image at those glacial speeds?

According to the notes I found, a lot of the wide-area system was moved
over to operate on top of something they called Asynchronous Transfer
Mode Cell Switching or ATM for short. Towards the end of the decade,
they managed to get end to end transfer rates on the order of a
gigabyte per second which was fairly respectable, given the technology
they had at the time. Of course, the telecommunications business had
been turned totally upside down in the process of getting to that
point.

It used to be the case that broadcast and cable television, telephone
and publishing were different businesses. In some countries, television
and telephone were monopolies operated by the government or operated in
the private sector with government regulation. That started changing
drastically as the 1990s unfolded, especially in the United States
where telephone companies bought cable companies, publishers owned
various communication companies and it got to be very hard to figure
out just what kind of company it was that should or could be regulated.
There grew up an amazing number of competing ways to deliver
information in digital form. The same company might offer a variety of
information and communication services.

With regard to the Internet, it was possible to reach it through mobile
digital radio, satellite, conventional wire line access (quaintly
called "dial-up") using Integrated Services Digital Networking,
specially-designed modems, special data services on television cable,
and new fiber-based services that eventually made it even into

residential settings. All the bulletin board systems got connected to
the Internet and surprised everyone, including themselves, when the
linkage created a new kind of publishing environment in which authors
took direct responsibility for making their work accessible.

Interestingly, this didn't do away either with the need for traditional
publishers, who filter and evaluate material prior to publication, nor
for a continuing interest in paper and CD-ROM. As display technology
got better and more portable, though, paper became much more of a
specialty item. Most documents were published on-line or on high-
density digital storage media. The basic publishing process retained a
heavy emphasis on editorial selection, but the mechanics shifted
largely in the direction of the author - with help from experts in
layout and accessibility. Of course, it helped to have a universal
reference numbering plan which allowed authors to register documents in
permanent archives. References could be made to these from any other
on-line context and the documents retrieved readily, possibly at some
cost for copying rights.

By the end of the decade, "multimedia" was no longer a buzz-word but a
normal way of preparing and presenting information. One unexpected
angle: multimedia had been thought to be confined to presentation in
visual and audible forms for human consumption, but it turned out that
including computers as senders and recipients of these messages allowed
them to use the digital email medium as an enabling technology for
deferred, inter-computer interaction.

Just based on what I have been reading, one of the toughest technical
problems was finding good standards to represent all these different
modalities. Copyright questions, which had been thought to be what they
called "show-stoppers," turned out to be susceptible to largely-
established case law. Abusing access to digital information was impeded
in large degree by wrapping publications in software shields, but in
the end, abuses were still possible and abusers were prosecuted.

On the policy side, there was a strong need to apply cryptography for
authentication and for privacy. This was a big struggle for many
governments, including ours here in France, where there are very strong
views and laws on this subject, but ultimately, the need for
commonality on a global basis outweighed many of the considerations
that inhibited the use of this valuable technology.

Well, that takes us up to about 20 years ago, which still seems a far
cry from our current state of technology. With over a billion computers
in the system and most of the populations of information-intensive
countries fully linked, some of the more technically-astute back at the

turn of the millennium may have had some inkling of what was in store
for the next two decades.

Therese

* * *

To: "Therese Troisema" <ttroisema@inria.fr>
CC: "Jonathan Bradel" <jbradel@astro.luna.edu>
From: "David Kenter" <dkenter@xob.isea.mr>
Date: September 17, 2023 06:43:13 MT
Subject: Re: Internet History

Therese and Jon,

This is really fascinating! I found some more material, thanks to the
Internet Society, which summarizes the technical developments over the
last 20 years. Apparently one of the key events was the development of
all-optical transmission, switching and computing in a cost-effective
way. For a long time, this technology involved rather bulky equipment -
some of the early 3DV clips from 2000- 2005 showed rooms full of gear
required to steer beams around. A very interesting combination of fiber
optics and three-dimensional electro-optical integrated circuits
collapsed a lot of this to sizes more like what we are accustomed to
today. Using pico- and femto-molecular fabrication methods, it has been
possible to build very compact, extremely high speed computing and
communication devices.

I guess those guys at Xerox PARC who imagined that there might be
hundreds of millions of computers in the world, hundreds or even
thousands of them for each person, would be pleased to see how clear
their vision was. The only really bad thing, as I see it, is that those
guys who were trying to figure out how to deal with Internet expansion
really blew it when they picked a measly 64 bit address space. I hear
we are running really tight again. I wonder why they didn't have enough
sense just to allocate at least 1024 bits to make sure we'd have enough
room for the obvious applications we can see we want, now?

David

* * *

Final Comments

The letters end here, so we are left to speculate about many of the
loose ends not tied up in this informal exchange. Obviously, our

current struggles ultimately will be resolved and a very different, information-intensive world will evolve from the present. There are a great many policy, technical and economic questions that remain to be answered to guide our progress towards the environment described in part in these messages. It will be an interesting two or three decades ahead!

Security Considerations

Security issues are not discussed in this memo.

References and Further Readings

This is not intended to be either an academic list of sources nor a reading list. It is a list of books and other sources the interested reader might wish to look into. Much of this book's contents is in the words of the participants. My thanks to them is expressed in the Preface.

There are three major sources for other material: the RFCs themselves, the BBN reports, and the history of the IPTO by the staff of the Charles Babbage Institute. I am told that this last is to be published by the Johns Hopkins University Press. Most of the RFCs are available electronically from a variety of sites around the world. I have found most in internic.ret, directory **rfc**.

I recommend Steve Crocker's narrative in RFC 1000 and Larry Roberts' paper at the January 1986 ACM Conference on the History of Personal Workstations most highly. The latter is in: Adele Goldberg, editor, *A History of Personal Workstations* (ACM Press – Addison-Wesley, 1988). The very best short history of the net is Dan Lynch's in Lynch and Rose, editors, *Internet System Handbook* (Addison-Wesley, 1993). The personal history of Vint Cerf is in Bernard Adoba's *Online User's Encyclopedia* (Addison-Wesley, 1993). Many of the historically important papers are collected in Craig Partridge, editor, *Innovations in Networking* (ARTECH House, 1988).

Chapter 1

George Stibitz' story, in his own words, may be found in N. Metropolis, J. Howlett, and G.-C. Rota, editors, *A History of Computing in the*

Twentieth Century (Academic Press, 1980); James M. Nyce and Paul Kahn have put together a really good volume of work by and honoring Bush: *From Memex to Hypertext: Vannevar Bush and the Mind's Machine* (Academic Press, 1991)—among other things, it contains Engelbart's letter; two of Licklider's papers and a brief note by Bob Taylor are available as *In Memoriam: J.C.R. Licklider 1915–1990*, Technical Report 61 of the Systems Research Center, Digital Equipment Corporation (Palo Alto, CA, August 7, 1990); there is also a fine paper by Licklider in the Goldberg volume. The summary of the Baran et al. papers appeared in IEEE *Transactions on Communication Systems* CS–12, 1 (March 1964) 1–9.

Chapter 2

The definition is from Martin H. Weik, *Communication Standard Dictionary* (Van Nostrand Reinhold, 1983). An excellent introduction to the concepts is Mischa Schwartz, *Telecommunications Networks* (Addison-Wesley, 1987). Len Kleinrock's two-volume *Queueing Systems* (John Wiley, 1975–76) is difficult but worthwhile.

Chapter 3

The Babbage Institute's history and the proceedings of the 1967 ACM *Symposium on Operating Systems Principles* are the best places to read further, as the BBN *Completion Report* has never been "published," nor has Shapiro's "Study..." I have seen a copy of Kennedy's telegram. It is not a tall tale.

Chapter 4

The only reliable reference is 1822 itself, in any of its instantiations.

Chapter 5

The best introductions to the software are two articles by Dave Walden and Alex McKenzie: "The Evolution of Host-Host Protocol Technology," IEEE *Computer* (September 1979), 29–38; and "ARPANET, the Defense Data Network, and Internet," in Fritz E. Froelich et al., eds., *Encyclopedia of Telecommunications* (Marcel Dekker, 1991) I.341–376. Though, as I have remarked, he is acerbic and opinionated, Michael A. Padlipsky's *The Elements of Networking Style* (Prentice-Hall, 1985) remains the most readable critique of the OSI model. Vint Cerf's outline of the "Core Protocols" in Lynch and Rose (1993) is superb.

Chapter 6

The sources here are the RFCs and the BBN *Reports* themselves and comments made to me. Larry Roberts' remarks were made at the 1986 ACM Conference and are printed in Adele Goldberg's volume.

Chapter 7

Larry Roberts described ALOHA in "Extension of Packet Communication Technology to a Hand Held Personal Terminal," *AFIPS Conference Proceedings* 40 (1972) 295–298, with an amplification in *AFIPS* 44 (1975) 217–251. Ethernet is described by Metcalfe and Boggs in "Distributed Packet Switching for Computer Networks" *CACM* 19 (July 1976) 395–404.

Chapter 8

A good place to survey the European nets is John S. Quarterman's *The Matrix* (Digital Press, 1990). I understand that an updated edition is in the works. Davies and Barber, *Communication Networks for Computers* (John Wiley, 1973) and Davies et al., *Computer Networks and their Protocols* (Wiley, 1979) are excellent. Pouzin edited a volume *The Cyclades Computer Network* (North-Holland, 1982), which is very hard to locate.

Chapter 9

Recent books on mail include Quarterman and Carl-Mitchell's *E-Mail Companion* (Addison-Wesley, 1994) and Marshall Rose's *The Internet Message* (Prentice Hall, 1993). On a nuts-and-bolts level, Brian Costales et al.'s *sendmail* (O'Reilly & Associates, 1993) is recommended.

Chapter 10

The Kahn and Cerf paper of 1974 is still the best: "A Protocol for Packet Network Interconnection," *IEEE Transactions on Communications*, COM-22, 5, pp. 637–648.

Chapter 11

As noted, the PCI tale derives from a paper and an interview (with Ralph Alter) posted by Simson Garfinkel in **com-priv** in January 1993. I trust that the material will be published eventually.

Chapter 12

Cerf's piece in Lynch and Rose and Padlipsky are the best work here.

Chapter 13

On OSI, Fred Halsall's *Data Communications, Computer Networks and Open Systems* (Third edition, Addison-Wesley, 1992) is a detailed exposition. On TCP, the four volumes of Douglas Comer and David Stevens, *Internetworking with TCP/IP* (Prentice Hall, 1987–1994) and the two by Richard Stevens, *TCP/IP Illustrated* (Addison-Wesley, 1993–1995) are both splendid expositions.

Chapter 14

See Peter H. Salus, *A Quarter Century of UNIX* (Addison-Wesley, 1994), for more detail on the origin and development of the operating system.

Chapter 15

As the Bellovin and Horton paper has never been published, greater detail on UUCP can be found in my *Quarter Century of UNIX*. Most of the correspondence on reorganization came from a file kept by John Gilmore. Brad Templeton supplied me with a chronology file he has kept.

Chapter 16

The RFCs and personal communications are the sources.

Chapter 17

The Domain Name System and the Berkeley Internet Name Domain implementation are well-covered in Paul Albitz and Cricket Liu's *DNS and BIND* (O'Reilly & Associates, 1992). Otherwise, see the references in Chapter 9.

Chapter 18

Matrix News, ;login:, and the various USENIX Association Conference Proceedings are the main sources. I am indebted to Rick Adams, the founder of UUNET, for the data on Usenet and UUNET.

Chapter 19

This chapter could not have been written without the active aid of Peter Capek, of IBM's Research Division, who was for many years the publisher of the IBM (internal) VM Newsletter. He supplied me with vast sheaves of IBM reports and maps and pointed me to the articles cited: E.C. Hendricks and T.C. Hartmann, "Evolution of a virtual machine subsystem," *IBM Systems Journal* 18.1 (1979) 111–142; and Noah Mendelsohn, Mark H. Linehan and William J. Anzick, "Reflections on VM/Pass-Through: A facility for interactive networking," *IBM Systems Journal* 22.1/2 (1983) 63–79. Thanks, too, to Jack Kulas, of IBM Austin, who relayed data to me via Capek.

Chapter 20

Again, Quarterman's *The Matrix* gives the outline; the various interviewees have supplied the "meat."

Chapter 21

The sources for the privatization of the NSFNET appear in issues 10 and 11 of the *COOK report on Internet -> NREN* (January 1, 1993), summarized in *Matrix News* 3.1 (January 1993). CoREN's announcement is in *Matrix News* 3.9 (September 1993).

I am indebted to Rebecca Wetzel of BBN for the information on NEARNET. Information on a vast number of networks is available in

Donnalyn Frey and Rick Adams, *!%@:: A Directory of Electronic Mail Addressing and Networks* (Fourth edition, O'Reilly & Associates, 1994).

Chapter 22

RFC 1160 ("The Internet Activities Board") by Vint Cerf, RFC 1602 ("The Internet Standards Process") by Lyman Chapin, and RFC 1718 ("The Tao of IETF") by Gary Scott Malkin are the best sources for IAB/IETF information. A good overview of the IAB can be found in John S. Quarterman and Susanne Wilhelm, *UNIX, POSIX, and Open Systems* (Addison-Wesley, 1993).

Chapter 23

Marc Lottor's data and the articles in *Matrix News* are the sole reliable sources for numbers: newspapers, magazines, and television reports waver between silly and nonsensical.

Chapter 24

The Fall 1992 issue of *Computing Systems* (volume 5, number 4), guest-edited by Peter Deutsch, was devoted to Internet resource discovery. On a more everyday level, Paul Gilster's *Finding it on the Internet* (John Wiley & Sons, 1994) is an excellent resource.

Chapter 25

There are more books on business and the Matrix than I care to think about. One of the better ones is Rosalind Resnick and Dave Taylor, *The Internet Business Guide* (Sams Publishing, 1994). William Stallings' *Network and Internetwork Security* (Prentice Hall, 1994) and Steve Bellovin and Bill Cheswick's *Firewalls and Internet Security* (Addison-Wesley, 1994) cover the Internet security field very well. Those interested in break-ins should read Clifford Stoll, *The Cuckoo's Egg* (Doubleday, 1989) and Katie Hafner and John Markoff, *Cyberpunk* (Simon & Schuster, 1991).

Chapters 26 and 27

For those interested in what's on and beyond the horizon, there are several books on FDDI and ATM. There are also the proceedings of the USENIX Association's workshops on Mobile Computing (Cambridge, Massachusetts, 1993) and High-Speed Networking (Oakland, California, 1994). The IPng draft by Scott Bradner and A. Mankin of October 1994 is **draft-ipng-recommendation-01.txt**. The report of the NRE-NAISSANCE Committee of the National Research Board, chaired by Len Kleinrock, is the best resource for the current state and future prospects of "The Internet and Beyond": *Realizing the Information Future* (National Academy Press, 1994).

Index

Note: This Index is in ASCII order. The Foreword, Preface, Appendix, and Further Readings are not included in this Index. By and large, items within cited RFCs are not included, either.

— *P.H.S.*

Unix and Open Systems Series

Series Editors
John S. Quarterman
Marshall Kirk McKusick

Network Management: *A Practical Perspective*	Allan Leinwand, Karen Fang
UNIX, POSIX, and Open Systems: *The Open Standards Puzzle*	John S. Quarterman, Susanne Wilhelm
Practical Internetworking *with TCP/IP and UNIX*	Smoot Carl-Mitchell, John S. Quarterman
Programming under Mach	Joseph Boykin, David Kirschen, Alan Langerman, Susan LoVerso

The Internet Connection:
  System Connectivity
  and Configuration
	John S. Quarterman, Smoot Carl-Mitchell

A Quarter Century of UNIX	Peter H. Salus
Casting the Net: *From ARPANET to* *Internet and Beyond*	Peter H. Salus